Cloud Foundry for Developers

Deploy, manage, and orchestrate cloud-native applications with ease

Rick Farmer
Rahul Jain
David Wu

BIRMINGHAM - MUMBAI

Cloud Foundry for Developers

First published: November 2017

Production reference: 1271117

Published by Packt Publishing Ltd.
Livery Place
35 Livery Street
Birmingham
B3 2PB, UK.

ISBN 978-1-78839-144-3

www.packtpub.com

Credits

Authors
Rick Farmer
Rahul Jain
David Wu

Reviewer
Sean Keery

Commissioning Editor
Gebin George

Acquisition Editor
Shrilekha Inani

Content Development Editor
Devika Battike

Technical Editor
Prachi Sawant

Copy Editor
Safis Editing

Project Coordinator
Judie Jose

Proofreader
Safis Editing

Indexer
Francy Puthiry

Graphics
Tania Dutta

Production Coordinator
Aparna Bhagat

About the Authors

Rick Farmer is one of the founders and a leader of the Pivotal Cloud Foundry Solutions enterprise consulting and delivery team at Pivotal. Over the last two decades, he established a track record of navigating complex organizational technology and services to deliver breathtaking results for mission-critical initiatives at over 70 of the world's most recognizable companies and government entities. Many of the engagements he has anchored have won various personal and project awards. Rick unlocks innovation and business value using Cloud Foundry to inject enterprise agility into even the most challenging environments by aligning digital transformation, technical and business opportunities. He enjoys speaking at conferences on subjects ranging from Cloud Foundry to Data Science to Digital Transformation to Agility in the Enterprise. Since 1997, Rick has surfed tropical events hitting the Texas Gulf Coast. He has a data science visualization project inducted into the Visualization Hall of Fame at the Harvard School of Engineering and Applied Sciences. He can be followed on Twitter @rick_farmer.

Rahul Jain is one of the founding members of the Pivotal Cloud Foundry Solutions delivery and architecture team at Pivotal. He has worked in the field of technology for over a decade, developing security products and applications. During his day job, he leverages best practices to help solve technical and business challenges for organizations using the Cloud Foundry platform. He enjoys researching and blogging on technology-related topics that are difficult to solve. During his free time, he contributes to the community by creating open source tools to manage the Cloud Foundry platform. Rahul holds a bachelor's degree in electrical and electronics engineering from University Visvesvaraya College of Engineering. He can be followed on Twitter @rahulkj.

David Wu has been developing software for over 17 years and has in-depth software and embedded device engineering experience in financial, photographic, medical, science and technology, and cinematic/broadcast industries, from the perspective of both enterprise and product development and for various operating systems such as Windows, MacOS, and Linux. A number of these applications and products have been highly praised, internationally recognized and have won prestigious awards. Wu holds a first class honors in the bachelors of computer science at Monash University and a Ph.D. in computer engineering at RMIT, Australia. In addition to software development, he is also an expert in image processing, compression, video analytics, and forensic imaging. He currently serves as an Advisory Solutions Architect at Pivotal, an agent of change helping transform organizations with Cloud Foundry and build better software. He can be followed on Twitter `@_Doc_Dave_`.

Acknowledgements

Faith Indigo Farmer for hands-on writing and collaboration during the initial stages of outlining this book in enormous detail, and for help with early chapter drafts.

Sean Keery for lending us his deep and thoughtful Cloud Foundry expertise in the form of chapter-by-chapter guidance and technical reviews that shaped the end product in numerous ways.

Haydon Ryan for his invaluable discussions, insights, and advice that helped shape the content of the book through the vast lens of his Cloud Foundry experience.

Scott Frederick for the Spring Music test app that has become the de facto Hello World! for every Cloud Foundry application developer and platform engineer.

Cyrus Wadia for helping arrange the various permissions for us to write this book and to integrate portions of Pivotal content that help tell the Cloud Foundry story.

Pivotal Cloud Foundry Solutions and the **Application Transformation** practice at **Pivotal Labs** is the hidden voice behind this book. The numerous individuals, past and present, who make up the global PCFS + AppTx team, under the founding leadership of **Dino Cicciarelli, Joe Fitzgerald**, and **Matt Russell**, are the shoulders of giants that we stood upon to extend their work into this particular medium. They are the most coveted and elite Cloud Foundry solutions team in the world -- valued thought-leaders shaping the digital revolution and the transformation of so very many Fortune 1000 companies, government entities, and nonprofit organizations, who are in a position to bring about innovations that make a real impact and a better world for us all. We are grateful to each of you.

The entire **Packt** team for their guidance, insights, professionalism, and encouragement throughout the process of creating this book. They are the unsung team behind the book covers that influence and shape the global conversation on technologies such as Cloud Foundry that have the potential to change the world for the better. In particular, we would like to thank our editors **Devika Battike**, **Shrilekha Inani**, and **Prachi Sawant** for their extraordinary contributions to the book. Also, the efforts of **Judie Jose** and **Nipukumar Nath**, among so many others in the Packt team that helped along the way. Thank you all.

Pivotal, the **Cloud Foundry Foundation** and the **Cloud Foundry Community**. None of this would have existed without you. Your innovations, insights, and contributions are moving the needle toward a better, more innovative world, one Cloud Foundry foundation at a time. Thank you!

About the Reviewer

Sean Keery, Minister of Chaos at Pivotal, began hacking obscure video game systems at the age of 13. Sean then developed interpersonal skills while teaching snowboarding in Aspen. Nowadays we've got Cloud Foundry, choreography, containers and plenty of io. Cluster deployments and IaaS independence keep Sean occupied. His conference presentations can be found on YouTube. Follow Sean's tech ramblings on Twitter (@zgrinch). The daily commute is filled with podcasts and chipmunk bunny hops. Some family time, spicy food, a good book and wrecking the latest toys keep Sean busy at home.

www.PacktPub.com

For support files and downloads related to your book, please visit www.PacktPub.com.

Did you know that Packt offers eBook versions of every book published, with PDF and ePub files available? You can upgrade to the eBook version at www.PacktPub.com and as a print book customer, you are entitled to a discount on the eBook copy. Get in touch with us at service@packtpub.com for more details.

At www.PacktPub.com, you can also read a collection of free technical articles, sign up for a range of free newsletters and receive exclusive discounts and offers on Packt books and eBooks.

https://www.packtpub.com/mapt

Get the most in-demand software skills with Mapt. Mapt gives you full access to all Packt books and video courses, as well as industry-leading tools to help you plan your personal development and advance your career.

Why subscribe?

- Fully searchable across every book published by Packt
- Copy and paste, print, and bookmark content
- On demand and accessible via a web browser

Customer Feedback

I would like to dedicate this book to my mother, Margaret Farmer-Maguire—you are the inexhaustible well of eternal inspiration for your sons—a profile in persistence, always our happy and tireless warrior, inevitably creating outcomes that many would have thought impossible. Thank you for choosing me to be your son. An eternity of gratitude is not enough; thanks for all that you've done for our family.

– Rick Farmer

I would like to dedicate this book to my beloved late grandfather N. C. Mittal, parents, sisters, wife, and kids for their continuous encouragement and support. To my mom, Neena Jain, thank you for backing me and motivating me to try new things in life. To my wife and friend, Veenu, thank you for your love, patience, and enduring support. Without you all, I would not have been what I am now.

– Rahul Jain

I would like to dedicate this book to my wife, mother, beloved father and sister, and mentor Dr H. R. Wu and his wife. To my wife, Sharon, for being there for me and providing me with never-ending loving patience, support, guidance, ideas, and encouragement. To my parents and sister, thank you for your guidance and support. To my friend and mentor, Dr H. R. Wu and his wife, Mei, thank you both for your tireless support, guidance, and inspirational discussions. You all have made an important mark in the chapters of my life, to which these words can never truly express my heartfelt gratitude.

– David Wu

Table of Contents

Preface

Cloud Foundry is the open source platform to deploy, run, and scale applications. Cloud Foundry is growing rapidly and is one of the leading product that provides Platform as a Service (PaaS) capabilities to enterprise, government, and organizations around the globe. Giants such as Dell Technologies, GE, IBM, HP, and the US Government are using Cloud Foundry to innovate faster in a rapidly changing world.

Cloud Foundry is a developer's dream, enabling them to create modern applications that can leverage the latest thinking, techniques, and capabilities of the cloud, including these:

- DevOps
- Application Virtualization
- Infrastructure agnosticism
- Orchestrated containers
- Automation
- Zero downtime upgrades
- A/B deployment
- Quickly scaling applications out or in

This book will take readers on a journey where they will first learn Cloud Foundry basics, including how to deploy and scale a simple application in seconds. Readers will build their knowledge of how to create highly scalable and resilient cloud-native applications and microservices running on Cloud Foundry. Readers will learn how to integrate their application with services provided by Cloud Foundry and with those external to Cloud Foundry. Readers will learn how to structure their Cloud Foundry environment with orgs and spaces. After that, we'll discuss aspects of continuous integration/continuous delivery (CI/CD), monitoring, and logging. Readers will also learn how to enable health checks, and troubleshoot and debug applications.

By the end of this book, readers will have hands-on experience in performing various deployment and scaling tasks. Additionally, they will have an understanding of what it takes to migrate and develop applications for Cloud Foundry.

What is book covers

Chapter 1, *Cloud Foundry Introduction*, introduces users to Cloud Foundry by providing background on the product itself and some related concepts. The chapter focuses on Cloud Foundry architecture and containers.

Chapter 2, *Cloud Foundry CLI and Apps Manager*, walks through all the necessary steps to create an account on Pivotal Web Services (PWS) and use the Cloud Foundry CLI to push a simple application to PWS. The chapter also introduces the reader to the Apps Manager running on PWS.

Chapter 3, *Getting Started with PCF Dev*, presents the steps required to install and manage Pivotal PCF Dev on your local machine. It explains the differences between a fully provisioned Cloud Foundry deployment and PCF Dev.

Chapter 4, *Users, Orgs, Spaces, and Roles*, introduces the concepts around Org, Spaces, Roles, and Users to help the reader to structure and manage their Cloud Foundry deployment. It walks through the various Cloud Foundry CLI commands on how to create the Orgs, Spaces, Users, and Roles.

Chapter 5, *Architecting and Building Apps for the Cloud*, teaches the guiding principles used to develop cloud-native applications, as well as the techniques to migrate and modernize monolithic applications into cloud-native applications.

Chapter 6, *Deploying Apps to Cloud Foundry*, presents hands-on experience of creating and managing applications, routes, and services provided in the Cloud Foundry marketplace. It touches on buildpacks and how droplets are created when applications are pushed onto Cloud Foundry through the cf CLI.

Chapter 7, *Microservices and Worker Applications*, discusses microservice architecture design concepts in the context of Cloud Foundry and explains the worker application concept with a hands-on example. This chapter also explores the resiliency provided by the Cloud Foundry platform itself and provides guidelines on how to develop resiliency into the application using Spring Cloud Services, based on NetFlix OSS.

Chapter 8, *Services and Service Brokers*, takes a deep dive into the concepts of services, service brokers, and route services. It provides a working example, alongside a usable template for creating and managing custom service brokers. This will be leveraged in the chapter, with a demonstration of how easy it is to deploy the service broker, create a service instance, and bind it to a sample application.

Chapter 9, *Buildpacks*, introduces the various buildpacks provided by Cloud Foundry and walks through the process of consuming and managing the buildpacks. The chapter will dive into the inner working of buildpacks, followed by a walkthrough of creating a custom buildpack.

Chapter 10, *Troubleshooting Applications in Cloud Foundry*, provides insights into the different error codes and what they mean, including possible resolutions.

Chapter 11, *Continuous Integration and Continuous Deployment*, discusses continuous integration, continuous delivery, and continuous deployment strategies in the context of Cloud Foundry. This is followed by the concepts of zero downtime and A/B deployment strategies, which can be used to push new versions of an application into Cloud Foundry without disrupting the end user experience.

What you need for this book

This book assumes a medium level of understanding of the Mac OS X operating system. The book will go through a simple setup of Pivotal PCF Dev, which may require a basic understanding of networking and virtualization concepts.

Pivotal PCF Dev can be installed and run your local development machine. However, this book requires that you have enough resources on your local development machine to install PCF Dev. The minimum hardware requirements are as follows:

- CPU: 4 cores
- Memory: 8 GB RAM
- Disk space: 40 GB

In this book, you will need the following software list:

- Linux, Mac OSX or Windows Operating System
- VirtualBox
- Cloud Foundry CLI
- Git client
- Java 8
- Maven and Gradle build tools

Internet connectivity is required to install Pivotal PCF Dev and for DNS resolution. There are options to run PCF Dev in offline mode too.

Who this book is for

This book is intended for application developers, engineers, and architects who want to learn key aspects of running and developing applications on the Cloud Foundry platform. If you are seeking to migrate and modernize your applications to run on Cloud Foundry, this book is for you. This book is also ideal for anyone who is seeking to further their knowledge about Pivotal Cloud Foundry or as a reference guide during application development.

Conventions

In this book, you will find a number of text styles that distinguish between different kinds of information. Here are some examples of these styles and an explanation of their meaning. Code words in text, database table names, folder names, filenames, file extensions, pathnames, dummy URLs, user input, and Twitter handles are shown as follows: "To get a list of buildpacks currently installed on your target Cloud Foundry Foundation, type `cf buildpacks`".

A block of code is set as follows:

```
@SpringBootApplication
@EnableScheduling
@EnableDiscoveryClient
public class FortuneTellerApplication {
@Autowired
FortuneCookieGenerator fortuneCookieGenerator;
....
....
}
```

Any command-line input or output is written as follows:

```
$ cf apps
Getting apps in org pcfdev-org / space pcfdev-space as user...
OK

name requested state instances memory disk urls
spring-music started 1/1 1G 512M spring-music.local.pcfdev.io
```

New terms and important words are shown in bold. Words that you see on the screen, for example, in menus or dialog boxes, appear in the text like this: "click on the SCALE APP button."

Warnings or important notes appear like this.

Tips and tricks appear like this.

Reader feedback

Feedback from our readers is always welcome. Let us know what you think about this book-what you liked or disliked. Reader feedback is important for us as it helps us develop titles that you will really get the most out of. To send us general feedback, simply e-mail feedback@packtpub.com, and mention the book's title in the subject of your message. If there is a topic that you have expertise in and you are interested in either writing or contributing to a book, see our author guide at www.packtpub.com/authors.

Customer Support

Now that you are the proud owner of a Packt book, we have a number of things to help you to get the most from your purchase.

Downloading the example code

You can download the example code files for this book from your account at http://www.packtpub.com. If you purchased this book elsewhere, you can visit http://www.packtpub.com/support and register to have the files e-mailed directly to you. You can download the code files by following these steps:

1. Log in or register to our website using your e-mail address and password.
2. Hover the mouse pointer on the **SUPPORT** tab at the top.
3. Click on **Code Downloads & Errata**.
4. Enter the name of the book in the **Search** box.
5. Select the book for which you're looking to download the code files.
6. Choose from the drop-down menu where you purchased this book from.
7. Click on **Code Download**.

You can also download the code files by clicking on the **Code Files** button on the book's webpage at the Packt Publishing website. This page can be accessed by entering the book's name in the **Search** box. Please note that you need to be logged in to your Packt account. Once the file is downloaded, please make sure that you unzip or extract the folder using the latest version of:

- WinRAR / 7-Zip for Windows
- Zipeg / iZip / UnRarX for Mac
- 7-Zip / PeaZip for Linux

The code bundle for the book is also hosted on GitHub at `https://github.com/PacktPublishing/Cloud-Foundry-For-Developers`. We also have other code bundles from our rich catalog of books and videos available at `https://github.com/PacktPublishing/`. Check them out!

Downloading the color images for this book

We also provide you with a PDF file that has color images of the screenshots/diagrams used in this book. The color images will help you better understand the changes in the output. You can download this file from `https://www.packtpub.com/sites/default/files/downloads/CloudFoundryforDevelopers_ColorImages.pdf`.

Errata

Although we have taken every care to ensure the accuracy of our content, mistakes do happen. If you find a mistake in one of our books-maybe a mistake in the text or the code-we would be grateful if you could report this to us. By doing so, you can save other readers from frustration and help us improve subsequent versions of this book. If you find any errata, please report them by visiting `http://www.packtpub.com/submit-errata`, selecting your book, clicking on the **Errata Submission Form** link, and entering the details of your errata. Once your errata is verified, your submission will be accepted and the errata will be uploaded to our website or added to any list of existing errata under the Errata section of that title. To view the previously submitted errata, go to `https://www.packtpub.com/books/content/support` and enter the name of the book in the search field. The required information will appear under the **Errata** section.

Piracy

Piracy of copyrighted material on the Internet is an ongoing problem across all media. At Packt, we take the protection of our copyright and licenses very seriously. If you come across any illegal copies of our works in any form on the Internet, please provide us with the location address or website name immediately so that we can pursue a remedy. Please contact us at copyright@packtpub.com with a link to the suspected pirated material. We appreciate your help in protecting our authors and our ability to bring you valuable content.

Questions

If you have a problem with any aspect of this book, you can contact us at questions@packtpub.com, and we will do our best to address the problem.

1
Cloud Foundry Introduction

In this chapter, we introduce Cloud Foundry by providing background on the product itself and some related concepts that may be useful for those unfamiliar with it. We then dive deeper into the details of using Cloud Foundry from the application developers perspective in subsequent chapters.

In this chapter, we will cover the following topics:

- Why Cloud Foundry?
- What is PaaS?
- What is Cloud Foundry?
- What is Pivotal Cloud Foundry?

Why Cloud Foundry?

```
cf push
```

That's it. That is the essential answer to the question *Why Cloud Foundry?*, Anti-climatic, right? At least, until you understand the revolutionary leap that application development has taken as a result.

Without `cf push`, the typical application development cycle is convoluted and complex because often, much of the development activity is consumed by finding a place for your application to live and serve the world securely, reliably, and robustly. There are three problems that have impeded development:

- It is difficult to deliver applications that are valuable to you, your organization, and/or the world if you aren't able to focus on building the application itself. In some large organizations, developers have said that *80% of our efforts are getting infrastructure ready*. Imagine a day in which you only have to build your application, not assemble middleware; install application runtimes; or fiddle with an **operating system** (**OS**), **virtual machine** (**VM**), servers, storage, or networking.
- Application developers are not system administrators or system operators, nor should they be compelled to be. If you ask operators to develop code that one would expect from an application developer, most would likely decline. There are boundaries from their perspective. Both disciplines fall under IT, yes. Both are extremely technical roles, requiring deep expertise to be sure. Both do the heavy lifting required to ultimately make an application of some value available to an audience who needs it. However, the Dev versus Ops divide is wide and deep. There are fundamental specializations, concerns, and risks that drive behavior in both roles that creates an obvious and quite natural fracture line to follow when dividing the workload of getting applications up and running in production. Of course, both should work together, share, and learn techniques that are cross-functional and relevant to how to be more efficient and agile in their respective roles, such as **continuous integration and continuous deployment** (**CI/CD**). In the end, application developers thrive if they focus on developing applications and solving problems in that very difficult space, without the concerns of being a shadow platform engineer or operator.
- It is hard to build a consistent, reliable, secure, and highly available production environment. Much more so by stitching together compute, storage, and network capacity into a cohesive system that meets the demands of modern enterprises and the expectations of application consumers. All the while, providing the rigor and flexibility that enables developers to focus on developing applications with ease. VMware revolutionized the IT world with **server virtualization** in 1998. They abstracted away the boundaries of physical hardware into pools of virtual servers. This enabled us to make better use of the underlying hardware by distributing and fitting large, complex workloads over the physical boxes.

These are the problems that Cloud Foundry was made to address: ending the eternal battle of the developer's focus on apps versus operating and engineering the platform that those applications are run upon.

Cloud Foundry does this by bringing about enterprise-grade **application virtualization**. It does this by harnessing and orchestrating a symphony of containers into an elastically scalable distributed system comprising all of the components a given application needs to serve the world. This changes the game much the way VMware did with VMs and **server virtualization**. Cloud Foundry is a proven **application virtualization** platform that gives control back to the developer, allowing developers to focus on developing applications, instead of infrastructure operations.

 cf push was originally vmc push, which stood for VMware Cloud. Cloud Foundry was conceived at VMware in 2009 and born as an open source project in 2011. The original code for VMC can be found at https://github.com/cloudfoundry-attic/vmc.

What is PaaS?

Platform as a Service (Paas) is one of a number of terms in the taxonomy of cloud computing including **Infrastructure as a Service (Iaas)** and **Software as a Service (Saas)**.

While, generally, IaaS is server focused and SaaS is user focused, PaaS is developer focused. PaaS enhances developer productivity by enabling **application virtualization**, so there is a significant reduction in the need for developers to perform the undifferentiated heavy lifting associated with the *plumbing* that detracts from the actual work on application code and concerns. Often this is called **yak shaving**. For instance, it may include everything from installing application runtimes, dependencies, app packaging, staging, and deployment, to configuring deeper down the stack into infrastructure concerns such as configuring load balancers, networking, security, provisioning VMs—nearly anything that takes your focus off building a great application.

According to Jeremy H. Brown while at MIT around the year 2000, *yak shaving* is what you are doing when you're doing some stupid, fiddly little task that bears no obvious relationship to what you're supposed to be working on, but yet a chain of twelve causal relationships links what you're doing to the original meta-task. The term was coined by Carlin Vieri. The original email on the subject can be found at `http://projects.csail.mit.edu/gsb/old-archive/gsb-archive/gsb2000-02-11.html`.

The logo for the Twelve-Factor App at https://12factor.net © 2017 Salesforce.com. All Rights Reserved.

Heroku (`https://www.heroku.com`) is the name of one of the original trailblazers in PaaS. Available since 2007, Heroku is a cloud platform that enables developers to push applications into a hosted service on the internet. The idea was to focus developers on building applications, not infrastructure. Using insights gained by the Heroku team from operating a large platform with diverse applications running on it, Adam Wiggins and team formed the basis for what are now called **cloud-native** applications through their original Twelve-Factor App (`https://12factor.net`) patterns. They were motivated to raise awareness of some systemic problems seen in modern application development, to provide a shared vocabulary for discussing those problems, and to offer a set of broad conceptual solutions to those problems with accompanying terminology. We will discuss cloud-native apps, and further developments since the original Twelve-Factor App methodology was written, in future chapters. Additionally, Heroku's **buildpack** model is used for Cloud Foundry and will also be discussed a bit later in the book.

The Cloud Foundry definition of PaaS

In the cloud era, the application platform is delivered as a service, often described as PaaS. PaaS makes it much easier to deploy, run, and scale applications. Some PaaS offerings have limited language and framework support, do not deliver key application services, or restrict deployment to a single cloud. Cloud Foundry is the industry's open PaaS and provides a choice of clouds, frameworks, and application services.

Who are Pivotal and the Cloud Foundry Foundation?

In April 2013, Dell EMC and VMware formed a new company called **Pivotal**. Each parent company contributed people, software, products, and collateral that were not core to their own business to this new entity. This included 11 companies that had been acquired by the parent companies at one point or another. Soon after, with further investment from additional companies, such as General Electric, Ford, and Microsoft, Pivotal's mission focused sharply on transforming the way the world makes software.

Cloud Foundry, along with several other notable projects like the Spring Framework for Java (`https://spring.io`) and RabbitMQ (`http://www.rabbitmq.com`) for message brokering, were included in the Pivotal origin story.

The Pivotal logo. © 2017 Pivotal Software, Inc. All Rights Reserved.

Soon after its creation, Pivotal, together with other enterprise leaders, sought to create the Cloud Foundry Foundation to ensure the ongoing stewardship of the Cloud Foundry community and its open source software. The foundation was created as an independent non-profit under the Linux Foundation. Since its founding in January 2015, over 70 companies (`https://www.cloudfoundry.org/members/`) have joined the Cloud Foundry Foundation and continue the mission to *drive the global awareness and adoption of the Cloud Foundry open source project, to grow a vibrant community of contributors, and to create coherence in strategy and action across all member companies for the sake of the project.*

The Cloud Foundry Foundation exists to:

- Establish and sustain Cloud Foundry as the global industry standard PaaS open source technology with a thriving ecosystem
- Deliver continuous quality, value, and innovation to users, operators, and providers of Cloud Foundry technology
- Provide a vibrant, agile experience for the community's contributors that delivers the highest quality cloud-native applications and software, at high velocity with global scale

You can find more detail on the Cloud Foundry Foundation and its mission at https://www.cloudfoundry.org/foundation.

What is Cloud Foundry?

Cloud Foundry is a platform for developing and running cloud-native applications. It is a polyglot platform that allows you to deploy a myriad of applications written in many different computer languages — Java, Python, Node.js, Ruby, Go, .NET languages, and many more. Simply use the best language for the task at hand with the freedom of knowing that Cloud Foundry supports it.

The Cloud Foundry logo. © 2017 Cloud Foundry, Inc. All Rights Reserved.

Cloud Foundry is IaaS agnostic and open source. It abstracts away the underlying IaaS whether you run on VMware vSphere, Amazon Web Services (AWS), Google Cloud Platform (GCP), Microsoft Azure, OpenStack, or others. This means that true application portability is possible regardless of the infrastructure choices and it enables a consistent multi-cloud strategy — public, private, or hybrid.

Cloud Foundry application development requires software engineers to understand how to build and deploy cloud-ready applications. However, there is a little secret: your applications do not have to be fully cloud-native, Twelve-Factor applications to run on Cloud Foundry. Often existing applications will run just fine on Cloud Foundry with a few minor changes — if you know some simple recipes!

The easiest way to see if an application needs some changes to run on Cloud Foundry is simply to `cf push` the app. See what, if any, errors may arise. Then make corrections as needed, then `cf push` again. Iterate on that process until the app is running in Cloud Foundry. It is often surprising how little effort it takes to get an app to run on Cloud Foundry. And, in many cases, it is the middleware-specific customizations of the app code that are intended to integrate or launch the app on a given app server like WebLogic or WebSphere where some points of friction commonly are found in practice -- more so than the actual application functional code.

Cloud Foundry provides a highly available, scalable, and secure platform to deploy your application. And with autoscaling, your application can scale-out to accommodate surges in traffic and then scale-in once traffic subsides — automatically!

Here is a guide to Cloud Foundry at a glance:

- Initial release in 2011
- An open cloud-native platform (PaaS)
- Fast and easy to build, test, deploy, and scale apps
- Works with any language or framework
- Available as open source, commercial distributions, or hosted offerings
- Open source with an Apache license, hosted on GitHub
- Developers use the `cf` command-line utility to interact with a CF deployment
- The cf CLI (Command-Line Interpreter) is pre-built for Windows, Mac, and Linux
- The `cf` supports any language or framework through buildpacks

As a developer, Cloud Foundry does the following:

- Enables you to focus on building applications
- Moves you out of the VM provisioning game
- Allows you to recreate an application's runtime environment continuously
- Deploys and scales an application in seconds
- Externalizes and injects environment-specific dependencies
- Has an API that enhances release management productivity
- Uses containers to isolate apps and create *application virtualization*
- Manages your application's entire life cycle

The Cloud Foundry project code can be found at:

- `https://github.com/cloudfoundry/`
- `https://github.com/cloudfoundry-incubator/`

Cloud Foundry architecture

The Cloud Foundry architecture abstracts away many of the complexities of day-to-day application development to provide a rich and robust environment for deployment. Cloud Foundry handles many of the operational and infrastructural demands behind the scenes in a unified and consistent way so that Cloud Foundry operators and engineers can manage and maintain the platform without downtime in most cases, enabling rolling, zero-downtime upgrades, and patches to the platform without developers noticing anything going down. Scaling Cloud Foundry by adding more infrastructure is baked into the platform to enable growth over time as demand increases.

The Cloud Foundry platform is composed of a set of horizontally-scalable, distributed services. It includes tooling which automates and orchestrates the underlying infrastructure, providing an abstraction layer over IaaS platforms.

Cloud Foundry is very robust. It uses what can nominally be called Weak AI because of its narrow focus on maintaining a self-healing feedback loop under the hood via its release engineering and management tooling, called BOSH. For instance, when a virtual machine in Cloud Foundry is misbehaving, it is taken out of service and replaced quickly. This enables failure detection and recovery at any level: application, container, VM, or the entire Cloud Foundry Foundation when configured for **high availability (HA)**.

Perhaps the most unusual aspect of Cloud Foundry, from a platform engineer's perspective, is that it is infrastructure agnostic, meaning that an operator can run Cloud Foundry on a variety of IaaSes such as VMware vSphere, Amazon Web Services, Google Cloud Platform, Microsoft Azure, OpenStack, bare-metal servers, and others. This is as revolutionary as the concept of the write once, run anywhere dream of application portability that application developers sought with the slogan created by Sun Microsystems to illustrate the cross-platform benefits of the Java language. Cloud Foundry does this by using an abstraction, called a **Cloud Provider Interface (CPI)**, that translates a common set of infrastructure build commands into an IaaS-specific translation using an open source project called Fog (`http://fog.io`). Fog enables Cloud Foundry to avoid vendor lock-in, which constrains you to a single IaaS. Interestingly, many IaaS providers are adding support to Fog directly, such as the Google Compute Platform. As they do, Cloud Foundry enjoys this rich inheritance that will enable it to run on an ever-growing list of cloud providers as they become available and supported.

Weak AI versus **Strong AI**: Weak AI is non-sentient artificial intelligence that focuses on one narrow task, whereas Strong AI is a machine with the ability to apply intelligence to any problem, rather than just one specific problem. Most currently existing systems considered under the umbrella of artificial intelligence are weak AI at most.

The capabilities and the operational aspects of Cloud Foundry are truly remarkable, if not revolutionary, from a system operator's and platform engineering perspective.

BOSH is one of the most interesting components of the Cloud Foundry ecosystem. Although it sits firmly in the domain of the platform engineer, since it automates and directs the deployment of the Cloud Foundry components themselves, it is used to deploy and maintain a Cloud Foundry Foundation (installation). BOSH is an open source tool chain for release engineering, deployment, and life cycle management of large-scale distributed systems. If you are interested in looking at the operational side of Cloud Foundry, you can find out more about BOSH at `https://bosh.io` and find the open source code for it at `https://github.com/cloudfoundry/bosh`.

The Cloud Foundry platform provides key elements such as routing, container management, logging, and metrics, as well as application configuration, service catalog, and messaging built-in.

Cloud Foundry is a polyglot platform, in that you are free to use any programming language of your choosing to develop your application for deployment. It has built-in support for Java, .NET Core, Python, Ruby, Go, Node.js, and PHP and it can support more by adding a variety of buildpacks that contain everything needed for application runtimes in additional languages. Most buildpacks are open source and community-driven. They can be found at `https://github.com/cloudfoundry-community/cf-docs-contrib/wiki/Buildpacks#community-created`.

A simplified overview of the Cloud Foundry ecosystem:

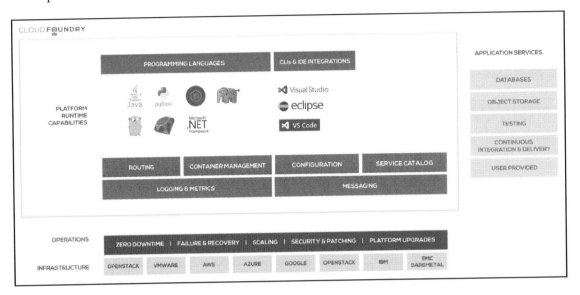

A high-level overview of the Cloud Foundry ecosystem. More detail can be found at https://cloudfoundry.org/ © 2017 Cloud Foundry, Inc. All Rights Reserved.

Additionally, there are **Command Line Interpreter (CLI)** and **Integrated Development Environment (IDE)** integrations for popular development tools such as Eclipse, Visual Studio, IntelliJ IDEA, and VS Code, among others.

What about connecting your application to services such as databases, message brokers, object stores, and so on? Most applications have dependencies on these types of externalities. Cloud Foundry addresses this necessity elegantly, providing several ways to address these capabilities, of course. We will discuss this in detail in future chapters.

A simplified overview of the Cloud Foundry platform architecture:

A conceptual overview of the Cloud Foundry platform architecture. More detail can be found at https://cloudfoundry.org/application-runtime/ © 2017 Cloud Foundry, Inc. All Rights Reserved.

The preceding figure shows the stack of infrastructure and BOSH that Cloud Foundry platform engineers use to install, manage, and maintain Cloud Foundry. There is the Cloud Foundry Application Runtime ™ (previously known as Elastic Runtime) inside the big box outline that is comprised of the various components. From the developer's perspective, this is Cloud Foundry. But from the holistic, systems view, it is but one part, albeit a very, very important part. The CF Application Runtime is exactly as the name implies:

The elastically scalable application runtime environment that stitches together the compendium of components needed to stretch across the underlying infrastructure resources to create and manage pools of compute, memory, datastore, blobstore, and networks to support the app-centric view of the world we call *application virtualization*. This includes all the orchestration, networking, containerization, management and control systems you might imagine are needed to pull together such a complex ballet of dynamic technology.

Primarily, these fall into the following categories:

- Routing
- Authentication
- Application life cycle management
- Application execution
- Platform services
- Messaging, metrics, and logging
- All of these are unified behind the Cloud Controller API, which enables RESTful integration with the CF Application Runtime through the Cloud Foundry CLI (a.k.a. the cf CLI) and other commercial **user interfaces** (**UI**) such as Pivotal Cloud Foundry's Application Manager web-based UI

We will unbox these in more detail in future chapters. Further information may be found at https://www.cloudfoundry.org/platform/.

Cloud Foundry security

Cloud Foundry enables a future-forward, cloud-based re-evaluation of long-held security fundamentals and assumptions because of the way its BOSH component works behind the scenes. This is an exciting time to rethink and reframe security in proactive ways that were not imaginable even a few years ago without the automation and feedback loops BOSH gives us. BOSH is constantly tearing down VMs that are no longer in good state or performing as expected, and recreating them on the fly. BOSH is always eliminating a plague that all infrastructure that is not fully automated will eventually encounter: *configuration drift*.

BOSH is always running on a feedback loop, validating the state of real-world infrastructure with the expected configuration. If there is drift, BOSH eliminates that bad apple and promptly replaces it with one that meets the exact specification of the configuration. This is a process called **repaving**. Repaving constantly ensures that we have smoothly paved underlying infrastructure that meets the needs of our Cloud Foundry Foundation and our applications. BOSH does this seamlessly behind the scenes with zero downtime to your application (provided you have at least two application instances running).

Configuration drift occurs naturally in data center environments when changes to software and hardware are made ad hoc and are not recorded or tracked in a comprehensive and systematic fashion. Often people, as varied as operators or developers, will log directly into a server or VM and make changes that will cause something to work with the tuned configuration of a server, but not work elsewhere if that change is not present. Often, that place is a production environment and the issue is not discovered until something has gone awry. Configuration drift is analogous to the insidiously phrased excuse of *It works on my machine*. This plagues developers who have fundamental, unaccounted for variations in their system configurations that enables a application to run **only** on their machine. We would probably hear that phrase less if we then immediately rack that particular machine into the data center and run it in production each time it is heard.

Because of this, a new way of thinking about security posture has become commonplace with the advent of the *three Rs of security*: repair, repave, and rotate.

These principles were first articulated by Justin Smith, a thought leader at Pivotal, in a presentation titled *Cloud Native Security: Repair, Repave, Rotate* in 2016, which can be found at `https://www.infoq.com/presentations/cloud-native-security`.

Justin defines cloud-native enterprise security as:

- **Repair**: Repair vulnerable software as soon as updates are available.
- **Repave**: Repave servers and applications from a known good state. Do this often.
- **Rotate**: Rotate user credentials frequently, so they are only useful for short periods of time. Minimizing the attack vector of time.

Cloud Foundry manages some of these for you already. And, it is improving rapidly as the three Rs have become a key element for the Cloud Foundry community to drive the cloud-based security posture story forward.

Cloud Foundry containers

Just as Cloud Foundry is changing the way of thinking about a proactive, modern, agile, and adaptable security posture that is constantly repairing, repaving, and rotating at the operational levels of the Cloud Foundry components, so too has the thinking about provisioning, scaling, and capacity management changed to reflect the dynamic and adaptable way in which Cloud Foundry enables containers to work.

In the past, at least in most enterprises, if you wanted infrastructure you would likely need to work your way through the circles of provisioning hell. Often the process looks something like this:

1. Request a server or VM to be provisioned or purchased.
2. Wait until that server or VM was provisioned.
3. In the meantime, you need to get to work building the app. So either,
    1. Find a box you can temporarily run under your desk as your app sandbox.
    2. Or, break out the credit card and provision some compute from a public cloud provider as a stopgap.
    3. Or, leverage some version of shadow IT that your organization turns a blind eye toward while the *normal* IT process runs the official gauntlet
4. Get the server racked in the data center or the VM spun up.
5. Get access and credentials to ssh and log in to the box.
6. Discover issues with the configuration.
7. Request remediation of the issues by the operations team.
8. Once everything is in order, install and configure your application runtime environment and middleware.
9. Finally, after week, months, or years, deploy your application to deliver the business or mission value it promised.
10. Find out that you are under-provisioned to handle demand -- then quickly start the process over again to get more capacity and compute to keep the app online and available as it grows.
11. Learn your lesson and *always* order way more capacity than you think you'll need, just in case, because it takes too long to bring more online once you're in production.

The last step is very common in large organizations with lots of processes and red tape. And, often as a result of protecting the scarce resources of servers racked in the data center and watts guzzled by those additional servers, organizations wind up vastly over-provisioned, meaning that they have more capacity taking up square footage in the data center than they need. In some organizations where this has been measured, the over-provisioning can be well over 40%. That is to say that over 40% of the racked servers can be un-racked and taken offline with no effect on the ability of the organization to provide a good home from which applications can serve their users.

This would be an entirely avoidable situation if it were not for the hard climb and time required by developers and operators to get through the process and red tape. The psychology that takes over is one of having long-lived pets. Because of the tremendous effort required to get these servers or VMs, developers in this situation *always* ask for more than they think will meet their immediate needs. They become attached and even if some of these servers have nothing on them yet, they defend them and protect them from reclamation, and rightfully so.

In large organizations, perhaps the hardest part of application development is getting into production. It is not unexpected in organizations of scale to wait a whole month, driving through road blocks step by step, until the production infrastructure is provisioned and has a dial tone to then finally deploy your application to the world. Cloud Foundry shortcuts that on the infrastructure side, but often there is still some much-needed improvement on the process red tape.

Part of the solution is to get rid of the servers as pets worldview that feeds this behavior. Containers are a good answer to this challenge. This is because they can be treated as disposable things that can be re-spun very quickly to enable our applications to scale-out automatically when demand is high and then scale-in once that demand dissipates, thus, always right-sizing our compute capacity and energy consumption to what we actually need at the time, and, eliminating the fear and headaches that one must always run through the thicket of ticket jungles to get more capacity when we need it.

What are containers?

Containers are ubiquitous in the cloud discussion. A good definition comes from **Amazon Web Services (AWS)**:

> *Containers are a method of operating system virtualization that allow you to run an application and its dependencies in resource-isolated processes. Containers allow you to easily package an application's code, configurations, and dependencies into easy to use building blocks that deliver environmental consistency, operational efficiency, developer productivity, and version control. Containers can help ensure that applications deploy quickly, reliably, and consistently regardless of deployment environment.*

> Source: AWS, What are containers? (`https://aws.amazon.com/containers/`)

Containers are great, but orchestrating and managing rolling security patches and upgrades without downtime is a very hard problem in most scenarios, leaving our applications open to vulnerabilities and exposing us to risks we may be unwilling to take.

Cloud Foundry makes containers work better by orchestrating them automatically. It does all of the difficult things that containers need to keep them updated, patched, happy, and healthy -- and, all with zero downtime. There are few other container-based PaaSes that can do this well in an enterprise or mission-critical setting at the current time.

Cloud Foundry containers are standards-based. The specification comes from the **Open Container Initiative (OCI)** (`https://www.opencontainers.org`). The OCI is a consortium of highly-visible organizations like Docker, Dell Technologies, Microsoft, IBM, Google, Red Hat, etc. that serve as the keeper of the flame for the `runC` library that Cloud Foundry uses as its primary container runtime library for Linux-based nodes. Commitment to this container interoperability standard by a wide variety of players enables Cloud Foundry to do interesting things to leverage the standard and expand the capability of the platform. For instance, Cloud Foundry can run Docker images from Docker repositories, such as Docker Hub. For more information, see `https://github.com/opencontainers/runc`.

This enables Cloud Foundry to run everything on Linux and Windows (any .NET core and most .NET classic) applications, to loading and running pre-baked Docker images with specific app runtimes and configurations.

What is Pivotal Cloud Foundry?

Pivotal Cloud Foundry™ or Pivotal CF™, commonly referred to as PCF, is currently the leading enterprise PaaS powered by Cloud Foundry. Many of the companies that comprise the Fortune 1000 use Pivotal Cloud Foundry internally as a part of their cloud portfolio offering. Using this particular Cloud Foundry distribution, they build their own cloud-native applications and migrate existing applications so that they can leverage many of the benefits of moving to a PaaS. It is because of this deep enterprise penetration and the higher likelihood of encountering Pivotal Cloud Foundry within the confines of business, government, and organizations that we will discuss some of the additional capabilities Pivotal Cloud Foundry provides above the open source Cloud Foundry release.

Pivotal Cloud Foundry delivers an always-available, turnkey experience for scaling and updating PaaS on multi-cloud public, private, or hybrid infrastructures such as VMware vSphere, Amazon Web Services, Google Cloud Platform, Microsoft Azure, and OpenStack.

As a commercial distribution of Cloud Foundry, it provides several significant additional features and a commitment to support the product that organizations are accustomed to from vendors. For instance, Pivotal Cloud Foundry provides extra tools to simplify installation and administration not included in the open source software product.

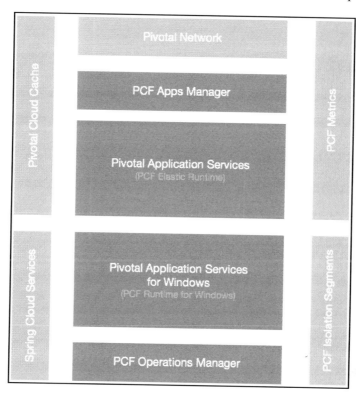

For instance, should you want to install a Cloud Foundry distribution on your own infrastructure, you would do the following at a high level:

1. Set up all external dependencies, such as an IaaS account, external load balancers, DNS records, and any additional components.
2. Create a manifest to deploy a BOSH Director.
3. Deploy the BOSH Director.
4. Create a manifest to deploy Cloud Foundry.
5. Deploy Cloud Foundry.

Source: Deploying Cloud Foundry at http://docs.cloudfoundry.org/deploying/index.html

This is initially a manual process that requires a good deal of BOSH and platform engineering expertise, although any platform engineer worth their salt would typically begin to automate a good deal of this process. However, it can be very difficult to get the distributed configuration of a large system composed of a variety of multiple VMs, network components, compute, IaaS access, storage, DNS, SSL certificates, and so much more described properly within the manifest file you must define, which BOSH then uses to build the Cloud Foundry foundation. Even getting to the starting line requires creating a manifest to deploy a BOSH Director which can be difficult if you are unfamiliar with the inner workings of BOSH; an interesting topic to be sure, but also deep and complex with a steep learning curve and commitment.

Building upon the foundation provided by the open source Cloud Foundry release (`https:/ /github.com/cloudfoundry/cf-release`), as one might expect, Pivotal Cloud Foundry adds many features atop of the open source version that have been driven and shaped by the needs of enterprise, government, and organizations to simplify the administration and day operations of Cloud Foundry.

Without belaboring the finer details of the differences between the open source and Pivotal distributions of Cloud Foundry, there are a few differences that are worth highlighting.

As mentioned previously, a good deal of expertise in BOSH is a prerequisite to installing the open source version of Cloud Foundry. Pivotal Cloud Foundry provides a simplified web-based UI for installing and managing the installation of Cloud Foundry and various components, such as the CF Application Runtime, and other services such as RabbitMQ, Redis, MySQL, and so forth as simplified service tiles. Ordinarily, each would require their own BOSH installation and manifest creation to deploy in a coherent way – a rather significant challenge if done manually. This UI is called Ops Manager and enables zero-downtime upgrades for the platform and services, along with simplified maintenance and changes to the deployment configurations underpinning the Pivotal Cloud Foundry Foundation.

A second significant difference between the open source and Pivotal versions of Cloud Foundry is developer-centric. Apps Manager is an administrative UI that enables developers to access many of the capabilities of the Cloud Foundry CLI in a more intuitive way. Apps Manager provides a visual way to configure and manage many of the critical features necessary to handle the daily ins and outs of managing your applications for scale, performance, settings, services, logging, and integrations such as autoscaling that are only available with the Pivotal Cloud Foundry distribution.

The Pivotal Cloud Foundry distribution provides additional support for cloud-native applications via much of the NetFlixOSS functionality under the guise of Spring Cloud and **Spring Cloud Services (SCS)**. This provides common pattern implementations that enhance resilience, ease of configuration, and high availability in the applications you design and deploy to Cloud Foundry, including service coordination and discovery, circuit-breaker patterns to prevent downtime, and other patterns that are particularly useful for microservices.

Another notable feature of the Pivotal distribution is the PCF Metrics dashboard, which presents easy access and visualizations of recent application events, metrics, and logging.

Pivotal Cloud Foundry components glossary

Pivotal Cloud Foundry components and what they do include:

- **Ops Manager**: A web interface for installing, configuring, upgrading, and scaling Pivotal CF and Pivotal Services
- **Apps Manager**: A web interface for working with Cloud Foundry and managing orgs, spaces, users, apps, services, routes, and so on
- **Pivotal Cloud Foundry Metrics**: A dashboard monitoring, event and logging component for applications running in PCF
- **Pivotal Services**: Managed services including autoscaling, MySQL, RabbitMQ, Redis, Spring Cloud Services, and so on

Other Cloud Foundry distributions and public providers

In addition to the commercial offering of Pivotal Cloud Foundry, the Cloud Foundry Foundation certifies additional platform providers to ensure consistency in the core Cloud Foundry components to ensure portability. The Cloud Foundry Certified PaaS certification requires certified offerings to actually use the software released by the Foundation's project teams. For more details on Cloud Foundry Certified Platform Providers, please see `https://www.cloudfoundry.org/provider-faq/`.

A partial list of provider offerings include:

- **AppFog from CenturyLink** (`https://www.ctl.io/appfog/`): CenturyLink's platform based on Cloud Foundry.
- **Atos Cloud Foundry** (`https://atos.net/en/solutions/application-cloudenablement-devops`): A commercially licensed and managed Pivotal Cloud Foundry.
- **GE Predix** (`https://www.predix.io/registration/`): An industrial internet offering of Cloud Foundry for IoT (Internet of Things devices) and analytics.
- **IBM Cloud** (`https://www.ibm.com/cloud/`): IBM's cloud platform based on Cloud Foundry, which provides access to IBM services, including Watson. Formerly called IBM Bluemix.
- **Pivotal Web Services** (`https://run.pivotal.io/`): Pivotal's public Pivotal Cloud Foundry. A fully managed version of Cloud Foundry that runs on a public cloud.
- **SAP HANA Cloud Platform** (`https://cloudplatform.sap.com/capabilities/runtimes-containers/cloud-foundry.html`): SAP's HANA cloud platform based on Cloud Foundry, which provides access to SAP services.
- **Swisscom Developer Portal** (`https://developer.swisscom.com/`): Swisscom's Application Cloud. A fully managed version of Cloud Foundry offered on a public cloud that stores all of your data in Switzerland.

A comprehensive list of Cloud Foundry Certified Platform Providers and their offerings can be found at `https://www.cloudfoundry.org/how-can-i-try-out-cloud-foundry-2016/`.

Summary

We explored how Cloud Foundry simplifies the development and deployment of scalable applications that are highly available. Focusing less on operational and administrative concerns of the platform enables application developers to instead transfer that effort into writing better code and improving the value of the features that make up the application.

We touched on a cloud-native application design which allows developers to take full advantage of a **Platform as a Service (PaaS)** like Cloud Foundry. And, found that leveraging Cloud Foundry opens up the possibility of quickly autoscaling applications to meet surges in demand while providing other benefits like zero-downtime deployments that would be difficult to accomplish in a traditional middleware-deployed environment.

Finally, we discussed some high-level differences between our open source Cloud Foundry distribution and a popular commercial distribution called Pivotal Cloud Foundry among other offerings that are available generally.

2
Cloud Foundry CLI and Apps Manager

In this chapter, we will explore the most common ways an application developer interacts with Cloud Foundry: the cf **Command Line Interface (CLI)** and the Apps Manager on **Pivotal Web Services (PWS)**. We will get acquainted with the basics of pushing applications to Cloud Foundry through both the cf CLI and the Apps Manager, and how they relate to each other.

Specifically, we'll cover the following:

- Creating a PWS account
- Installing the cf CLI
- Initial setup of the cf CLI
- The cf CLI help command
- Deploying an application to Cloud Foundry
- Accessing the Apps Manager on PWS

The cf CLI

Nearly every great leap in computing began at some point in a Terminal. Bathed in the glory of a text-based **User Interface (UI)**, the cf CLI issues commands made of user-typed text to an unseen program running behind the scenes performing an elaborate sequence of steps to execute the developer's will. The Command Line Interpreter, often mistaken as the Command Line Interface, is also abbreviated to the acronym CLI. Terminal-based CLI programs are a common daily tool in the system operator's world, but often less common in the world of application developers. The rise of **Integrated Development Environments (IDEs)** such as Eclipse, Visual Studio, and IntelliJ as places where all code is written and compiled, with productivity enhancers such as code suggestions and autocomplete, has reduced the need for developers to jump down to the level of the Terminal as often as their historic roots once required. The IDE is a great tool in the way that it abstracts away the Terminal commands by running them for the developer behind the scenes.

Depending on their background, a significant portion of application developers may shudder at the thought of using a CLI to deploy their application. Rest assured that there is indeed a nice UI for interacting with Cloud Foundry on Pivotal Web Services, called the Apps Manager. However, learning the cf CLI will serve you extraordinarily well once you begin automating away the time-consuming work of deploying applications with consistency and ease to various deployment environments (called **spaces** in Cloud Foundry parlance), from sandbox to User Acceptance Testing (UAT), to staging (pre-production), to production or whatever names you or your organization call them.

With the cf CLI, you get:

- Simplified CI/CD
- The ability to script automated tests, code, security, and compliance checks
- Zero Downtime Deployments (ZDD), known as blue-green deployments, which give you A/B testing as a side effect.
- Thorough troubleshooting when things go sideways with your application or deployment
- A comprehensive set of capabilities that a UI can only wrap a subset of without being too complex to work in a simplified way

When using the open source version of Cloud Foundry, the cf CLI is going to be the primary management tool for deploying and managing applications, managing service instances, organizations, spaces, domains, routes, users, and quotas. If you are using the Pivotal Cloud Foundry distribution, you will have the added use of the Apps Manager UI.

First, we will need a Cloud Foundry to work against and an easy way to get access to a Cloud Foundry deployment is by using Pivotal Web Services (PWS).

Second, we will install the cf CLI and explore some basic configurations and commands.

Third, we will push a simple test app to understand the basic flow of deploying apps to Cloud Foundry.

Fourth, we will explore the Apps Manager that PWS provides.

In the end, you'll have the following:

- Access to a Cloud Foundry foundation to push your code and attach services
- A Cloud Foundry CLI installed
- Access to the Apps Manager on PWS

What is Pivotal Web Services (PWS)?

Pivotal Web Services (PWS, pronounced **P-Dubs**), is one of the largest Pivotal Cloud Foundry foundations in operation. It is hosted on AWS and is an easy on-ramp to Cloud Foundry for developers to start with since it is publicly available over the internet. PWS is a fully managed version of Cloud Foundry that runs on a public cloud. You can get up and running immediately with a free trial subscription, without the need to use a credit card, which makes it a standout offering for those application developers wishing to learn and familiarize themselves with Cloud Foundry and the additional features provided by the Pivotal Cloud Foundry distribution.

Pivotal Web Services can be found on the internet at `https://run.pivotal.io`.

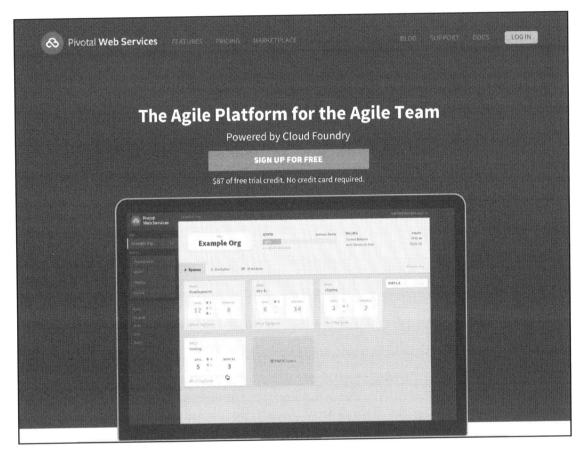

The Pivotal Web Services website. © 2017 Pivotal Software, Inc. All Rights Reserved.

At the time of writing, the Pivotal Web Services' free trial consists of:

- $87 USD credit for app usage for up to 1 year
- Up to 2 GB of memory to share across app instances
- Choice of free marketplace services to try
- Unlimited collaborators

Creating a PWS account

Creating a PWS account is a straightforward process. And, once you have access to PWS, you will be able to explore a large ecosystem of third-party services, such as databases, messaging, and metrics, which application developers can leverage when building their applications. With PWS, you can deploy, update, and scale your applications just as you would on any Cloud Foundry PaaS.

What you get when you register for PWS

When you register for a PWS account, a Cloud Foundry user account is created for you that gives you a Cloud Foundry *Org* and *Space*. All Cloud Foundry foundations will give you the same thing once your user account is created. We will go into detail about orgs and spaces in `Chapter 4`, *Users, Orgs, Spaces, and Roles*. For now, just think of orgs and spaces as simple organizing systems with the org at the top level, under which you will have several spaces, which are roughly equivalent to a deployment environment like a sandbox, development, QA, staging, prod, and so on, found in most enterprises to enable an application to progress up the chain of environments until they are finally promoted to production, where consumers will interact with the application.

Signing up

Start by opening `https://try.run.pivotal.io/gettingstarted` in your internet browser. This will take you directly to the PWS account creation screen to fill out the basic information needed to establish an account, as shown in the following screenshot:

A verification email will be sent to your email address that will provide you with a link to create your PWS account:

When you're ready to log in, open `https://login.run.pivotal.io/login` and it will open the sign in page, shown as follows:

Select **Pivotal Web Services** from the default set of apps that you get with your PWS account:

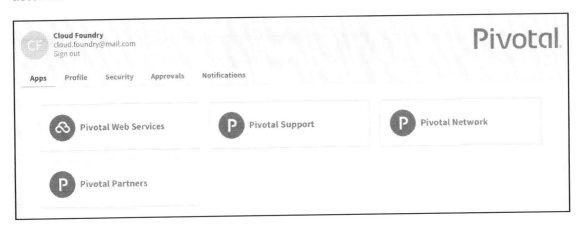

Give a name to your Org (in the following example, ours is called `cf-developers`) and then you'll see the Apps Manager UI with a default Space created, called **development**, to start deploying apps into:

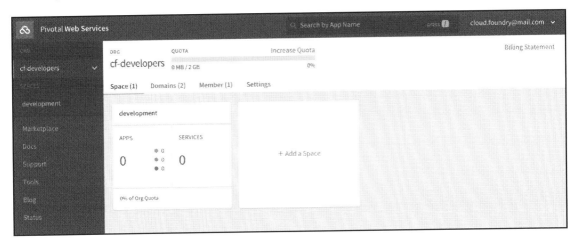

Installing the cf CLI

To install the cf CLI, go to `https://console.run.pivotal.io/tools`. Download and run the installer for your platform.

Verify the installation by opening a Terminal window and typing `cf --version`. With this, you now have a Cloud Foundry client that can communicate with any Cloud Foundry installation, including PWS.

 Make sure that you have the latest version of the cf CLI installed. There may be cases where a previously installed version of the cf CLI is already present. This will cause frustration if there have been significant changes in the tool since the previous version was installed.

If you are interested in alternative ways to install the cf CLI, there are a few additional possibilities, including:

- Downloading and installing it from GitHub
- Installing it using a package manager

 The cf CLI is written in the Go programming language so that it is a highly performant application. It is distributed as a self-contained binary with no external dependencies. If you are interested in the code for the cf CLI itself, you can find it at `https://github.com/cloudfoundry/cli`.

Downloading and installing from GitHub

Since Cloud Foundry is **open source software (OSS)**, you can download the latest release of components such as the cf CLI from GitHub and install them directly:

1. Go to `https://github.com/cloudfoundry/cli/releases`.
2. Download the installer for your platform, such as macOS X, Windows, Debian, or Red Hat.

Install the cf CLI by following the instructions for your operating system:

- **Install cf CLI on Windows**
    1. Unpack the `.zip` file.
    2. Double-click the `cf CLI` executable.
    3. When prompted, click on **Install**, and then **Close**.

- **Install cf CLI on macOS X and Linux**
    1. Open the `.pkg` | `.deb` | `.rpm` file.
    2. Follow the package installer wizard.
    3. When prompted, click on **Install**, then **Close**.

Install using a package manager

For Mac OS X users, you can use the `Homebrew` package manager. Homebrew bills itself as *the missing package manager for OS X*.

 You can find `Homebrew` at `https://brew.sh`—it is useful for much more than just installing the cf CLI. It also provides an easy way to simplify updating any tools you've installed using it through the command `brew update`.

```
$ brew tap cloudfoundry/tap
$ brew install cf-cli
```

For Debian - and Ubuntu-based Linux distributions:

```
# ...first add the Cloud Foundry Foundation public key and package
repository to your system
$ wget -q -O -
https://packages.cloudfoundry.org/debian/cli.cloudfoundry.org.key | sudo
apt-key add -
echo "deb http://packages.cloudfoundry.org/debian stable main" | sudo tee
/etc/apt/sources.list.d/cloudfoundry-cli.list
# ...then, update your local package index, then finally install the cf CLI
$ sudo apt-get update
$ sudo apt-get install cf-cli
```

Enterprise Linux and Fedora systems (RHEL6/CentOS6 and up):

```
# ...first configure the Cloud Foundry Foundation package repository
$ sudo wget -O /etc/yum.repos.d/cloudfoundry-cli.repo
https://packages.cloudfoundry.org/fedora/cloudfoundry-cli.repo
# ...then, install the cf CLI (which will also download and add the public
key to your system)
$ sudo yum install cf-cli
```

Initial setup of the cf CLI

After you've installed the cf CLI, verify that it works properly by typing the following command:

```
$ cf
```

If all goes well, you should see the cf CLI help text appear, looking something like this:

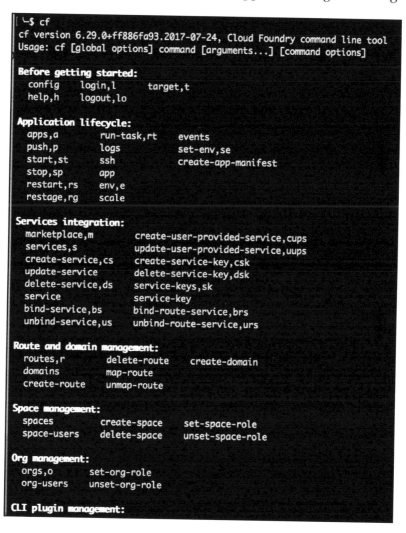

To see the version of the cf CLI that is installed, type the following command:

```
$ cf --version
```

The cf CLI help command

Perhaps the most useful command when starting out with the cf CLI is this:

```
$ cf help
```

This allows you to see the available CLI commands and understand their usage and syntax. The cf CLI enables you to control a wide range of commands that help you deploy and configure your applications on Cloud Foundry.

Finding cf CLI commands

Since there are many cf CLI commands available, it can be a bit overwhelming to find the command you are really interested in at a given point. If you have it available on your system, you can find commands containing cf CLI keywords using `grep`:

```
└$ cf help | grep "service"
  marketplace,m          create-user-provided-service,cups
  services,s             update-user-provided-service,uups
  create-service,cs      create-service-key,csk
  update-service         delete-service-key,dsk
  delete-service,ds      service-keys,sk
  service                service-key
  bind-service,bs        bind-route-service,brs
  unbind-service,us      unbind-route-service,urs
```

Command-specific help

With the cf CLI, commands can have specific subcommands that you can ask for help on to get more information.

To see the cf CLI syntax for specific commands, add `--help` or `-h` after the command, as shown here:

```
[ └$ cf api --help
NAME:
    api - Set or view target api url

USAGE:
    cf api [URL]

OPTIONS:
    --skip-ssl-validation      Skip verification of the API endpoint. Not recommended!
    --unset                    Remove all api endpoint targeting

SEE ALSO:
    auth, login, target
```

The official documentation for the cf CLI can be found at `http://docs.cloudfoundry.org/cf-cli`. It includes significant details on the various commands. Additionally, there is an official Cloud Foundry CLI reference guide that can be found at `http://cli.cloudfoundry.org/en-US/cf/`.

Deploying an application to Cloud Foundry

We now have our PWS account set up and working, and we also have our cf CLI installed and working. Now we just want to push a simple application to see it run on Cloud Foundry. To do that, we must do a few things:

1. Set the target Cloud Foundry instance so that our cf CLI knows where we are pushing our application bits.
2. Log in to the targeted Cloud Foundry instance using the cf CLI.
3. Push our simple app.

Targeting Pivotal cf API endpoint

What could make more sense than to target the Cloud Foundry instance you want to deploy your application into? To do that, you must set the Cloud Foundry API endpoint to which your cf CLI will issue commands. Behind the scenes, your cf CLI will have a back-and-forth conversation with the Cloud Foundry instance using RESTful calls. And, as with all RESTful calls, you must have an API endpoint to communicate with.

To set the API endpoint to PWS, type the following command in your Terminal:

```
$ cf api https://api.run.pivotal.io
```

You should see the API target set with feedback from the command line, like so:

```
 └$ cf api https://api.run.pivotal.io
Setting api endpoint to https://api.run.pivotal.io...
OK

api endpoint:   https://api.run.pivotal.io
api version:    2.89.0
```

If so, you have successfully targeted the PWS API endpoint and are ready to log in.

 If you are not using PWS or a Cloud Foundry instance that has all the necessary public SSL certificates in place, it is possible that you will see an SSL validation error when trying to target the API endpoint. This usually happens if your system uses self-signed certificates. If you see this, simply use the `--skip-ssl-validation` flag with the usual `cf api` command.

Logging into the Cloud Foundry API endpoint

We've told the cf CLI which Cloud Foundry endpoint to talk to using the `cf api` command; now we will use the `cf login` command to authenticate against that API endpoint. To do so, just type the following into your Terminal:

```
$ cf login
```

At this point, it will tell you which Cloud Foundry instance's API endpoint you are targeting and will prompt you for your username, which is often in the form of an email address, and the password you set up when you signed up for your PWS user account. Once you've entered that information, you'll see the targets set for the org and the space that you configured on your Cloud Foundry instance at PWS, like so:

```
┌ └$ cf login
API endpoint: https://api.run.pivotal.io

Email> cloud.foundry@mail.com

[Password>
Authenticating...
OK

Targeted org cf-developers

Targeted space development


API endpoint:    https://api.run.pivotal.io (API version: 2.89.0)
User:            cloud.foundry@mail.com
Org:             cf-developers
Space:           development
```

 We followed a two-step process to help familiarize you with what is
happening behind the scenes, by first targeting the Cloud Foundry
instance and then logging in to it. But there is a simple one-step process
you can use to do both at the same time in the future: use the `$ cf login
-a https://api.run.pivotal.io` command.

Pushing a simple application

Not only are we going to push a simple application to Cloud Foundry, we are going to push
the world's simplest Cloud Foundry application. You can't get any more basic than a
simple, static HTML page that displays the time-honored `Hello World!`.

Download the `app` with Git:

```
$ git clone
https://github.com/rickfarmer/worlds-simplest-cloud-foundry-app.git
```

If you don't have Git installed yet, you can download a ZIP file of the simple Cloud Foundry app at `https://github.com/rickfarmer/worlds-simplest-cloud-foundry-app/archive/master.zip`.

Navigate to the app directory:

```
$ cd worlds-simplest-cloud-foundry-app
```

Push the app to Cloud Foundry:

```
$ cf push
```

The app will be pushed to Cloud Foundry, and in the Terminal output you will see the URL to open in your browser in order to view the running application, like the following:

```
App helloworld-RANDOM-WORD was started using this command `$HOME/boot.sh`

Showing health and status for app helloworld-RANDOM-WORD in org cf-developers / space development as clou
d.foundry@mail.com...
OK

requested state: started
instances: 1/1
usage: 128M x 1 instances
urls: helloworld-random-word.cfapps.io
last uploaded: Mon Jul 31 05:11:17 UTC 2017
stack: cflinuxfs2
buildpack: staticfile_buildpack

     state    since                  cpu    memory      disk       details
#0   running  2017-07-30 11:11:36 PM 0.0%   0 of 128M   0 of 1G
```

In the preceding example output, the running app can be found at `http://helloworld-random-word.cfapps.io`.

Your deployment will be at a different random URL that is automatically generated for you to ensure it is unique among all the application URLs on PWS.

When you deploy this simple application, there will be some randomly generated words appended to the base name of the application to make a unique URL. In this case, this is done because every URL on a given Cloud Foundry instance must be unique for a deployed application. For example, with PWS it is likely that someone else reading this book will have used the application name as a URL already. To avoid this issue, a flag has been added to `manifest.yml` that does the random generation of the URL through `random-route: true`. More on the `manifest.yml` and the various configurations you can leverage with it will come later.

Opening the browser will reveal the world's simplest Cloud Foundry application in all its glorious simplicity:

Hello World!

Congratulations! You've just deployed an application to Cloud Foundry.

Accessing the Apps Manager on PWS

What is the Cloud Foundry Apps Manager?

- A web interface for managing organizations, spaces, apps, and other settings
- It offers a subset of the management features available through the cf CLI
- It provides you with a marketplace of services you can attach and leverage in your application development

Recall that, after signing up for the PWS account and logging in to it, we had a glimpse of the Apps Manager UI running at `https://console.run.pivotal.io`. Now with a simple app deployed, you can see the app named `hello world-RANDOM-WORD` running successfully in the Apps Manager.

The information includes the status, the number of instances running, when the app was last pushed, and the route, Cloud Foundry's term for the application URL:

The Apps Manager gives us a subset of the functionality of the cf CLI. Behind the scenes, it is talking to the same RESTful endpoint that the cf CLI talks to and is doing much of the same work for us. We won't spend a lot of time on the Apps Manager at this point since it only applies to Pivotal Cloud Foundry, but it is a standard interface for viewing some of the functionality available in the cf CLI, and for managing and deploying applications in a visual way for those who may be less comfortable with the command line.

The official documentation for Apps Manager can be found at `http://docs.run.pivotal.io/console`.

Summary

In this chapter, we touched on the Apps Manager which provides a user-friendly UI for common settings and commands related to the deployment and management of applications and services used in Cloud Foundry. We also took our first look at the cf CLI and found that it supports a wide range of commands for managing applications and related activities in Cloud Foundry.

Initial setup of the cf CLI is required prior to performing most development-related management tasks on Cloud Foundry. We found that the cf CLI is a tool that can be used with any of the various distributions of Cloud Foundry, including Cloud Foundry open source deployments, Pivotal Web Services, Pivotal Cloud Foundry, and PCF Dev (used for local development and deployment). And the cf CLI is used with other publicly available Cloud Foundry variants, such as IBM Cloud (formerly Bluemix), GE Predix, and more.

Getting Started with PCF Dev

3

TDD or test-driven development is essential to the 3 pillars of great software development:

- **Test-driven development (TDD)**
- **Continuous integration and continuous deployment (CI/CD)**
- **Pair programming**

However, to execute the TDD loop quickly and to make TDD worth doing from the moment their hands are placed on the keys, developers prefer to shorten the cycle of code deployments as much as possible. While balancing the necessity of running their code against a locally running environment that reliably mimics the production environment the code will eventually run in. And, with as few hops as possible over potentially latent or, in highly secured facilities, a nonexistent internet connection. And, just as importantly, to avoid much of the trouble and toil that arises from differences between these local environments where code is developed and the production environment from which the code will ultimately serve the world.

Enter PCF Dev.

PCF Dev enables you to push apps to PCF from day one of your project.

In this chapter, we will explore how to install Pivotal's PCF Dev to develop applications locally. We will cover the basics of PCF Dev and where it fits in your tool-belt as a Cloud Foundry application developer. Additionally, PCF Dev is another easy way to introduce yourself to Cloud Foundry application development or evaluate PCF without the overhead of installing a full Cloud Foundry foundation. Perhaps, most importantly, PCF Dev also allows you to iterate more quickly when developing CF apps. Enabling you to comfortably use TDD as part of your workflow. And, if you're already a CF developer, PCF Dev may be a simpler, faster alternative to BOSH-lite, which is another path to Cloud Foundry development that leans more toward Platform Engineers, Administrators, and Operators—particularly if you don't need to use BOSH to deploy additional products beyond Cloud Foundry. And, PCF Dev is an easy way to get started with Cloud Foundry with minimal fuss.

In this chapter, we will cover the following topics:

- A brief introduction to TDD
- Why PCF Dev?
- PCF technical requirements
- 20 minutes to cf push with PCF Dev
- Alternatives to PCF Dev

A brief introduction to TDD

Often, as developers, we prefer to run our applications locally as we develop them. This is a huge time saver in many cases as we rinse and repeat making updates or debugging while running our code through the well-worn TDD cycle of red, green, iterate. This means that, we start by creating a new test that proves some aspect of a feature that we want our code to have before the feature code is created—such that the test, when run, will fail (go red). We then create the actual feature code to satisfy the previously written test that enables the test to pass successfully (go green), followed by repeat iterations of debugging the feature code or creating more tests using the same workflow. The good side effect of TDD is that, not only do we end with code that works as intended—delivering on the promise of value the feature embodies; but, we also have clearly written tests that can serve as documentation for each feature.

With TDD, we get provable code that has many tests that can be run in an automated way each time we deploy and run our latest feature code. The most important outcome of creating provable code is that it enables us to make additions and changes to an existing codebase without ominous concerns that we will break the features that are already working well—causing failures that are hard to root out and correct. The TDD methodology creates a hedge against regression of the codebase into an unintentionally buggy state. In essence, when automating the test run, we have a living baseline of provable code that enables us to make changes with confidence—free from worry that we may have accidentally broken something else, somewhere else in the code and not have a clue as to what went wrong without digging deep into the recesses of a codebase that may have been written by someone else a long time ago.

Interestingly, there is this revolutionary, seismic rise of DevOps underway that is reshaping the way system operators, platform engineers, and administrators approach the building of infrastructures. With DevOps, they are now developing the infrastructure as code using the very same repeatable, idempotent, test-driven, and CI/CD automation-biased processes and techniques that application developers have been the practitioners of decades.

This is changing the IT world in fundamental ways, affecting processes and practices in place since the dawn of the Unix epoch on January 1st, 1970. Now, with the adoption of these development techniques, the traditional operational roles are transforming into those of Platform Reliability Engineers (PREs) that are hyperfocused and oriented toward increasing the reliability of these extremely complex platforms and infrastructures that are the axis around which the modern digital world rotates. They do this by creating the very same hedges against regression and reducing risk while delivering business value, the way any agile software development team does. By using the three pillars to drive operational excellence and resilience in the face of change.

This very approach is deeply encapsulated within the Cloud Foundry installation and day 1 processes. For instance, there are CI/CD pipelines that, not only install Cloud Foundry onto a given IaaS; but that generate the infrastructure itself into a standardized reference architecture, creating the networks, hardening the security, provisioning the capacity from memory to CPU to datastores, and so much more. And, there are pipelines that automate the ongoing Cloud Foundry day 2 management and maintenance processes as well—running continuously to perform automated upgrades and patches with zero downtime, backing up entire Cloud Foundry foundations, onboarding users, orgs and spaces into a given foundation, repaving the foundation, rotating credentials regularly, and many, many more. And, all of these pipelines are defined in yaml text files that are written like any other code, which is versioned and checked into a code repository—exactly as any application developer would do.

All the open source Pivotal Cloud Foundry pipelines can be found at: `https://github.com/pivotal-cf/pcf-pipelines` and `https://github.com/pivotalservices/concourse-pipeline-samples`.

Why PCF Dev?

A typical Cloud Foundry deployment, commonly referred to as a Cloud Foundry foundation, can be demanding on the infrastructure it needs to run on. Cloud Foundry requires a significant set of resources from the underlying Infrastructure as a Service (IaaS) it is deployed on, for example, vSphere, AWS, Azure, GCP, and so on. In addition, Cloud Foundry requires a good deal of specialized platform engineering expertise to deploy and properly configure it before the first `cf push` command can even be issued by an application development team.

The broad-stroke typical resources for common Cloud Foundry deployments can be heavy:

Pivotal Cloud Foundry minimally requires the following:

- More than 50 GB of memory
- More than 100 GB of disk space
- Minimally 2-6 physical CPU cores
- More than 1 hour to deploy (only once the infrastructure and other requirements are ready)

Open Source Cloud Foundry minimally requires the following:

- More than 48 GB of memory
- More than 50 GB of disk space
- Minimally 2-6 physical CPU cores
- More than 1 hour to deploy (only once the infrastructure and other requirements are ready)

And, these deployments are considered to be toy installations because they do not take into account strategies for **high availability** (**HA**) and **disaster recovery** (**DR**).

Note that Open Source Cloud Foundry deployments can be highly variable depending on the components one deploys and the capability desired. For instance, a given Cloud Foundry deployment may not include common services, such as Redis, MySQL, and RabbitMQ, that application developers find useful.

Clearly, a solution has to be available to enable developers to run Cloud Foundry on a single machine with much lower hardware specifications that also enables a tight TDD loop while reducing the barriers to entry into the Cloud Foundry game with reduced deployment complexity.

Even in the early days of Cloud Foundry development, there was a sincere recognition that it was difficult to run and administer a full-fledged foundation on a typical application developer's computer, and that a solution was needed to enable the fastest possible TDD loop for developers as they created code. And so it was that, initially, there was a neat little local version of Cloud Foundry called MicroCF or Micro Cloud Foundry.

Micro Cloud Foundry did a reasonable job as a stand-in for a full-blown Cloud Foundry foundation. There were some incompatibilities that would prevent an app developed using it from working seamlessly once it was deployed to the production foundation somewhere in the cloud. It was good enough when compared to running middleware locally, such as Web Logic Server (WLS) or WebSphere, where developers often assumed significant deltas would exist between local deployments and production deployments.

But, there were opportunities for the Cloud Foundry community to improve the tooling that application developers needed. In truth, MicroCF was relatively complex to deploy, requiring Ruby, and other dependencies to be installed and run. There were other limitations one would bump into that made it a bit frustrating to develop against MicroCF on certain occasions. Here, we find a pattern that we can learn from. There are great development practices that we can adopt for our applications from the developers and teams that actually create and write the code for Cloud Foundry and its tooling.

They are an interesting case study because they eat their own dog food. In essence, they always iterate and re-evaluate the current state of what they are creating in the context of the reality in which the product operates. This feedback loop informs improvements to be made in the next iteration of features. Much like the feedback loop of TDD—red, green, iterate. We will find that short, iterative feedback loops make all the difference in building software features and products in a low risk way that encourages the Spartan approach of only building what is minimally necessary to provide some defined business value. Also known as an MVP or Minimal Viable Product. This approach ensures that we follow the lean principles of software development.

It is not a coincidence that the team that builds the Cloud Foundry product at Pivotal follows the eat your own dog food philosophy of using their own tooling to reveal ways that they can improve it. That concept originated with the visionary executive Paul Maritz at Microsoft in the 1980s. Mr. Maritz would later become the CEO of Pivotal Software when the venture was originally spun-off and funded by EMC (now part of Dell Technologies), VMware, and **General Electric (GE)**.

Ultimately, MicroCF was deprecated as Cloud Foundry components began to be rewritten into the Go language from their original Ruby. The Cloud Foundry development team found that Ruby, which is not a compiled systems-level language, cracked at scale under the pressures of a complex system on the order of Cloud Foundry, which spins up many virtual machines bringing many systems-level complexities of the interwoven elements hidden beneath the covers. The Go language is a more recent systems-level, compiled language created by Google that has the potential to be used in place of other popular systems languages such as C and C++ while addressing some current weaknesses present in these languages.

The Cloud Foundry development team leveraged the advent of Go and the concept of continually re-evaluating the current state to build a feedback loop of continuous learning and experimentation opportunities. In practice, this becomes a microcosm of a virtuous cycle that happens iteratively all the time while pairing and writing tests as part of the 3 pillars of great software development.

To learn more about the Go language see: `https://golang.org`.

Once MicroCF was gone, the gap was filled more or less by a solution called BOSH-lite, which we will discuss briefly later in this chapter.

Did you know Cloud Foundry has an Attic? It is a place where all of the old code goes when it is retired from service. There are many historic milestones and interesting parts of the Cloud Foundry story that are put there in a kind of boneyard open to the public for perusal. The Cloud Foundry Attic can be found at: `https://github.com/cloudfoundry-attic/` and perhaps the most interesting code there is the VCAP project, which stood for VMware's Cloud Application Platform, which is the original version of Cloud Foundry dating back to around 2009. VCAP can be found at: `https://github.com/cloudfoundry-attic/vcap`.

The good news is that your timing for getting started with local Cloud Foundry development couldn't be better! There is now an excellent solution called PCF Dev created by Pivotal, which can be found at: `https://pivotal.io/pcf-dev`. You can develop locally against PCF Dev while providing a similar development experience as **Pivotal Web Services** (**PWS**) did that we used previously. And, it only requires 3 GB to 6 GB of memory to be free. Contrast this with the previously mentioned minimum requirements of Pivotal Cloud Foundry and Open Source Cloud Foundry deployments:

Pivotal Cloud Foundry minimally requires the following:

- 3 GB of memory is listed as a requirement; but, in practice, you'll want at least 8 GB (16 GB recommended) on your machine
- 20 GB of disk space
- 1 physical CPU core
- About 10-20 minutes to deploy (once you have the pre-requisites in place)

About 10-20 minutes to deploy PCF Dev is impressive considering the complexity of Cloud Foundry. We'll put this to the test shortly.

And, as for production environment parity, Pivotal makes a clear statement: If an application runs on PCF Dev, it runs on PCF with no modifications in almost all cases—this is another huge upside to PCF Dev as an application developers' dream solution to local development. This is because it uses the same components under the hood as a full Cloud Foundry foundation.

Comparing PCF Dev to Pivotal Cloud Foundry

To see the depth of PCF Dev when compared to PCF and CF, Pivotal maintains a comparison list. You can find the latest compatibility statement for PCF Dev by Pivotal, along with a comprehensive feature comparison at: `https://docs.pivotal.io/pcf-dev/index.html#comparison-to-pcf`.

	PCF Dev	PCF	CF
Space required	20 GB	100 GB+	50 GB+
Memory required	3 GB	50 GB+	variable
Deployment	cf dev start	Ops Manager	bosh create-env
Estimated time-to-deploy	10 Minutes	Hour+	Hour+

Out-of-the-Box Services	Redis MySQL RabbitMQ	Redis MySQL RabbitMQ GemFire	N/A
PAS	✓	✓	✓
Logging/Metrics	✓	✓	✓
Routing	✓	✓	✓
Compatible with CF CLI	✓	✓	✓
Deploy apps with any supported buildpack	✓	✓	✓
Supports Multitenancy	✓	✓	✓
Diego Support	✓	✓	✓
Docker Support	✓	✓	✓
User-Provided Services	✓	✓	✓
High Availability		✓	✓
Integration with 3rd party Authorization		✓	✓
BOSH Director (That is, can perform additional BOSH deployments)		✓	✓
Day Two Lifecycle Operations (For example, rolling upgrades, security patches)		✓	✓
Ops Manager		✓	
Apps Manager	✓	✓	
Tile Support		✓	
Developers have root-level access across cluster	✓		
Pre-provisioned	✓		
Does not depend on BOSH	✓		

For Cloud Foundry application developers, a few additional things stand out on this list about PCF Dev:

- Apps Manager is included, which gives you a nice web-based user interface to interact with Pivotal Cloud Foundry for deploying and managing your applications.
- Redis, MySQL, and RabbitMQ are included as default services that you can write applications against.
- Docker support is included.
- BOSH is not included, which means that you do not have all of the platform operations capabilities that make Cloud Foundry the highly manageable and highly available production environment that doesn't fall over easily. So, be especially cautious, PCF Dev is truly only for development. Don't depend on it for important workloads, such as production applications. With PCF Dev, the guardrails and safety bumpers are taken off in order to slim down the deployment to run on a single virtual machine.

PCF Dev technical requirements

In order to install and run PCF Dev, there are few pre-requisites:

- The cf CLI needs to be installed; see `Chapter 2`, *Cloud Foundry CLI and Apps Manager*.
- A current version of VirtualBox needs to be installed. The latest installation distribution and instructions for your operating system can be found at: `https://www.virtualbox.org/wiki/Downloads`.
- An internet connection to automatically resolve wildcard URLs into PCF Dev.

The ability to resolve wildcard DNS is a fundamental necessity for the Cloud Foundry magic to work. If you expect to be in a location where internet access is not available, you can configure a local DNS server on your PCF Dev local machine to handle wildcard DNS resolution. As such, the offline option requires some additional configuration. The details of an offline DNS resolution configuration using DNSmasq (`http://www.thekelleys.org.uk/dnsmasq/doc.html`) for OS X and Ubuntu or `Acrylic` for Windows can be found at: `https://docs.pivotal.io/pcf-dev/work-offline.html`. For Ubuntu, further detail on DNSmasq configuration can be found on the LeaseWeb Labs blog at: `https://www.leaseweb.com/labs/2013/08/wildcard-dns-ubuntu-hosts-file-using-dnsmasq/`.

20 minutes to cf push with PCF Dev

A premium has been placed on reducing the complexities of a Cloud Foundry installation when it comes to PCF Dev. PCF Dev starts as a cf CLI plug-in that is downloaded from PivNet that extends the capability of the cf CLI that was previously installed on your system. The 10-20 minutes separating you from your first local cf push is highly dependent on the speed of your internet connection, because the first time PCF Dev is started, it will download a 4 GB virtual appliance that installs as a 20 GB virtual image into the VirtualBox application running on the local machine.

Installing PCF Dev

Use the following steps to install PCF Dev on your local machine:

1. Open the URL for PCF Dev on PivNet using: `https://network.pivotal.io/products/pcfdev`.

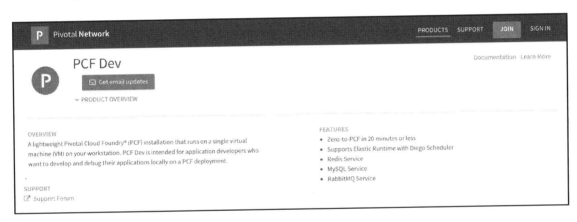

2. Download the latest version of the PCF Dev CLI plug-in for your operating system, which will be in the following format:

    `pcfdev-VERSION-PLATFORM.zip`

3. Unzip the ZIP file:

```
$ unzip pcfdev-VERSION-osx.zip
```

4. Navigate to the folder it unzipped into using PowerShell (Windows) or a Unix Terminal (OS X or Linux).

5. Run the PCF Dev binary. This will install the PCF Dev plug-in for the cf CLI. Upon successful installation, you'll see a message like this:

```
Plugin successfully installed. Current version: X.XX.X. For more
info run: cf dev help
```

6. Validate that the PCF Dev plug-in is working properly by running the cf dev help command:

```
$ cf dev help
NAME:
    dev - Control PCF Dev VMs running on your workstation

ALIAS:
    pcfdev

USAGE:
    cf dev SUBCOMMAND

SUBCOMMANDS:
    start Start the PCF Dev VM. When creating a VM, http proxy env
vars are respected.
    ...
```

7. Start PCF Dev by running the cf dev start command:

```
$ cf dev start
```

Note: If you have issues running the cf dev start command. It may be an internet proxy issue that is preventing you from downloading the PCF Dev OVA file remotely from PivNet, or that your PCF dev plugin version does not match the latest one available. The OVA file is the virtual appliance that will run on our local machine in VirtualBox, so we will need it to proceed with PCF Dev.

The PCF Dev CLI plug-in must be able to connect to PivNet at: https:// network.pivotal.io to download the OVA file. You can test if your machine can download the file using a curl command to get a response back from PivNet it using:

```
$ curl https://network.pivotal.iodf
```

- If you do not get back a successful response, it is likely that your local environment variable, `https_proxy`, is not set to use a proxy server that will let you access `https://network.pivotal.io` from your local machine. For comparison, try successfully getting the universal internet example page using `curl https://example.com` to see if some sites are blocked while others aren't. If the internet proxy is the issue, you'll want to get a proxy setting that allows traffic to PivNet or connect to a network without a proxy.

- If there is not an issue with the internet proxy blocking traffic to PivNet, then make sure that you are using the latest versions of both the cf CLI and the cf CLI PCF Dev plug-in from PivNet. Differences in the installed cf and plug-in versions may cause some incompatibility issues on occasion.

- If these are at the latest versions for both, and, you have ruled out that it is not an internet proxy issue — you can manually download the PCF Dev OVA file from `https://network.pivotal.io/products/pcfdev#/releases/1622` that matches your PCF dev plug-in version and then run it manually. To do this, the steps are:

  1. Find the corresponding OVA version for your plug-in by running the `cf dev version` command. This will give you information similar to PCF Dev version 0.28.0 (CLI: 5cda315, OVA: 0.547.0).

  2. Download the listed OVA file version manually from PivNet at: `https://network.pivotal.io/products/pcfdev#/releases/1622`.

  3. Finally, run the command `cf dev import /path/to/ova` to install your PCF Dev environment. If all goes well, you are now able to proceed using `cf dev start`.

8. The first time you start PCF Dev, it may prompt you to log in to your PivNet account:

```
Please sign in with your Pivotal Network account.
Need an account? Join Pivotal Network: https://network.pivotal.io

Email>

Password>
```

9. Once logged in, the first time you'll be prompted to accept the **End User License Agreement (EULA)**; if you agree to the terms, you can hit the *Y* key to continue:

```
PRE-RELEASE END USER LICENSE AGREEMENT
This Pre-Release End User License Agreement ("Pre-Release EULA") is
an agreement to license Pre-Release Software between Licensee and
Pivotal Software, Inc. ("Pivotal"). Unless otherwise set forth in a
signed agreement between Pivotal and Licensee, by downloading,
installing or using Pre-Release
Software, Licensee is agreeing to these terms.
...
[<up>, <previous>] Scroll up
[<down>, <next>] Scroll down
[y] Accept
[n] Do Not Accept
```

10. At this point, the first time you run the `cf dev start` command, the virtual appliance is downloaded, installed, and run using the VirtualBox application. You'll see activity similar to the following as it performs the steps needed to get PCF Dev started and ready to go for deploying your applications:

```
Downloading VM...
Progress: |=====================>| 100%
VM downloaded.
Allocating 4096 MB out of 16384 MB total system memory (5565 MB
free).
Importing VM...
Starting VM...
Provisioning VM...
Waiting for services to start...
7 out of 58 running
7 out of 58 running
7 out of 58 running
7 out of 58 running
40 out of 58 running
```

```
56 out of 58 running
58 out of 58 running
```

```
is now running.
To begin using PCF Dev, please run:
    cf login -a https://api.local.pcfdev.io --skip-ssl-validation
Apps Manager URL: https://apps.local.pcfdev.io
Admin user => Email: admin / Password: admin
Regular user => Email: user / Password: pass
cf dev start 69.83s user 180.36s system 5% cpu 0:10:35.59 total
```

Once installed and running, PCF Dev will show the login and other relevant information such as URLs to use. Be sure to take note of the information. You'll need it later to continue working with PCF Dev.

Exploring PCF Dev

With a proper PCF Dev installation complete, we can now log into it and treat it like any other Cloud Foundry foundation we would deploy an application on.

Since PCF Dev is only accessible on the local machine; it comes with a preconfigured set of user credentials, URLs, endpoints, Orgs, and Spaces that you can use for your development.

These credentials are displayed upon the successful start of PCF Dev using the `cf dev start` command.

For instance, consider the following list that defaults to the values given:

- API endpoint: `https://api.local.pcfdev.io`
- Apps Manager URL: `https://apps.local.pcfdev.io`
- An Admin user with the Email: `admin` and Password: `admin`
- A Regular user with the Email: `user` and Password: `pass`
- An Org for apps to be named: `pcfdev-org`
- With a Space for deploying the apps to be named `pcfdev-space`

With this information in hand, the first thing we will want to do is log into our PCF Dev foundation using the following command:

```
$ cf login -a https://api.local.pcfdev.io --skip-ssl-validation
```

This will prompt us to enter our login information. To begin with, we will use our regular user, with the email> user, who does not have administrative privileges to the foundation to keep things simple.

 You'll see a prompt to enter an email>. This can be confusing since it can be any unique identifier for what is more accurately described as a username that you will use to log in to Cloud Foundry. Email is a certainly a common choice; but, not the only form of username accepted, as you can see.

The Terminal will look something like the following once we are logged in properly:

```
API endpoint: https://api.local.pcfdev.io

Email> user

Password> pass
Authenticating...
OK

Targeted org pcfdev-org

Targeted space pcfdev-space
API endpoint: https://api.local.pcfdev.io (API version: 2.82.0)
User: user
Org: pcfdev-org
Space: pcfdev-space
```

By default, the regular user is assigned to the Org called pcfdev-org and Space pcfdev-space.

To keep it simple, we can deploy our sample app here. In the later chapters, we'll discuss orgs and spaces in more detail, along with how to create new orgs and spaces to help layout your development and deployment targets and workflows.

Deploying a test application to PCF Dev

Scott Frederick, the renowned Spring Java and Cloud Foundry Guru—who is well-known for his far-reaching contributions to both the Cloud Foundry and Spring Java communities early in the Cloud Foundry era—developed what is perhaps the best known and most common Java application used to test a Cloud Foundry foundation. We will leverage the Spring Music test application to validate that our PCF Dev foundation works. One reason for Spring Music's popularity is that the app has the interesting property of allowing developers to change the backing datastore dynamically from the default in-memory database included in the Spring Music app itself to any of a number of potential backing datastores that Cloud Foundry leverages as services, an important Cloud Foundry concept that we will explore in greater detail in the upcoming chapters.

Being a Java application, you'll want to ensure that you have the appropriate version of the Java JDK installed on your system to run Spring Music. You can install Java JDK from `http://www.oracle.com/technetwork/java/javase/downloads/jdk8-downloads-2133151.html`.

If you are unfamiliar with Java development, be sure that your **Java Standard Edition (Java SE)** installation is the **Java Development Kit (JDK)** version that a Java developer would use to develop code. Not the **Java Runtime Environment (JRE)** that does not include the term JDK. The JDK version includes both the JRE that Java programs run on, as well as, the Java Developer Kit tooling that is used to make Java programs. That's not confusing at all, right?

Detailed information covering the Spring Music application can be found at: `https://github.com/cloudfoundry-samples/spring-music`.

Clone and build the Spring Music App

In order to get a deployable version of the Spring Music application, we will need to download it from a code repository online and build it. We do this, as follows:

1. Clone the Git repository that contains the Spring Music application using the following command:

   ```
   $ git clone https://github.com/cloudfoundry-samples/spring-music
   ```

2. Navigate to the spring-music directory:

   ```
   $ cd ./spring-music
   ```

3. Assemble the Spring Music app using a Windows PowerShell or a Unix Terminal using the following,

   On Unix-like platforms such as Linux and macOS X that do not yet have Gradle installed, use:

   ```
   $ ./gradlew clean assemble
   ```

   Unix-like platforms such as Linux and macOS X that do have Gradle installed, use:

   ```
   $ gradle clean assemble
   ```

   On Windows use the gradlew.bat batch file, using:

   ```
   $ gradlew clean assemble
   ```

4. Deploy the spring-music application to PCF Dev using the following code:

   ```
   cf push --hostname spring-music
   ```

5. You'll see the `cf push` command doing quite a bit of work, until it finally concludes with some output, like the following:

```
...
requested state: started
instances: 1/1
usage: 1G x 1 instances
urls: spring-music.local.pcfdev.io
last uploaded: Sun Nov 12 08:53:46 UTC 2017
stack: cflinuxfs2
buildpack: container-certificate-trust-store=2.0.0_RELEASE java-
buildpack=v3.13-offline-
https://github.com/cloudfoundry/java-buildpack.git#03b493f java-
main open-jdk-like-jre=1.8.0_121 open-jdk-like-memory-
calculator=2.0.2_RELEASE spring-auto-reconfiguration=1.10...

     state since cpu memory disk details
#0 running 2017-11-12 02:57:23 AM 0.0% 328.9M of 1G 170M of 512M
```

6. Now that we have the app deployed, we can view it using the cf CLI, just as we did with PWS in the previous chapter using the `cf apps` command:

```
$ cf apps
Getting apps in org pcfdev-org / space pcfdev-space as user...
OK

name requested state instances memory disk urls
spring-music started 1/1 1G 512M spring-music.local.pcfdev.io
```

And, also as we did previously with PWS, we can open the Apps Manager web UI to view the applications deployed into our PCF Dev foundation by opening its URL. In the case of PCF Dev that is `https://apps.local.pcfdev.io/`.

If you haven't yet trusted the dynamically created, self-signed certificates that the PCF Dev start process generated, you'll see various SSL certificate issues that warn you about the validity of your PCF Dev from both the Apps Manager in the browser, as well as, at the cf CLI when you log in to the PCF Dev API endpoint. You may have noticed that, initially, we logged into PCF Dev using the cf login command with the `--skip-ssl-validation` flag to bypass the SSL warning at the command line, as follows:

```
$ cf login -a https://api.local.pcfdev.io --skip-ssl-validation
```

Logging into the Apps Manager at the URL `https://apps.local.pcfdev.io/` without trusting the PCF Dev installation will yield a warning like this:

You can choose to bypass the warning in the browser. For example, in Google Chrome, you can click on **Advanced** and **Proceed to apps.local.pcfdev.io (unsafe)**. If you prefer not to deal with bypassing the SSL warnings in the cf CLI and the web browser every time you use them, you can trust the PCF Dev installation using the `cf dev trust` command. This will add the PCF Dev self-signed certificate into your OS certificate store. It will likely require you to authorize adding it to the certificate store using your user or an admin account on your computer.

To trust PCF Dev, run the following command:

```
$ cf dev trust
***Warning: a self-signed certificate for *.local.pcfdev.io has been
inserted into your OS certificate store. To remove this certificate, run:
cf dev untrust***
```

As noted in the warning message, you can later run the `cf dev untrust` command to remove the certificate from your OS certificate store.

You can then log out of the PCF Dev endpoint using the following command:

```
$ cf logout
Logging out...
OK
```

And then log in again without the `--skip-ssl-validation` flag, instead of using only the following command:

```
$ cf login -a https://api.local.pcfdev.io
```

Similarly, you can log in to the Apps Manager UI using the regular user credentials to see the app deployed there:

Once logged into Apps Manager, you can see that one app has been pushed:

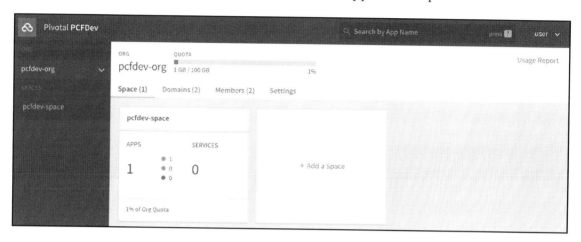

Behind the scenes, the Apps Manager is running as any other application would in Cloud Foundry. If you're interested in seeing it run, just switch over from the `pcfdev-org` into the system org. The system org is where you can get a peek at some of the applications that make up Cloud Foundry itself, recursively running on Cloud Foundry to manage Cloud Foundry functionality. Inception, anyone?

Clicking on the box labeled APPS drills down to display the currently deployed applications. Here we can see that Spring-Music was deployed with the hostname `spring-music`, which places it at the URL `http://spring-music.local.pcfdev.io`:

Clicking on the Spring Music URL will open the Spring Music App in your web browser. And, then clicking on the information icon in the upper-right corner enables us to see which datastore Spring Music is using as a data source at the moment. Since we do not yet have our services configured, Spring Music has defaulted to the profile for the Cloud using an in-memory database. As we'll find when we get to services, we can easily attach applications to a variety of services that are available in the Cloud Foundry Service Marketplace.

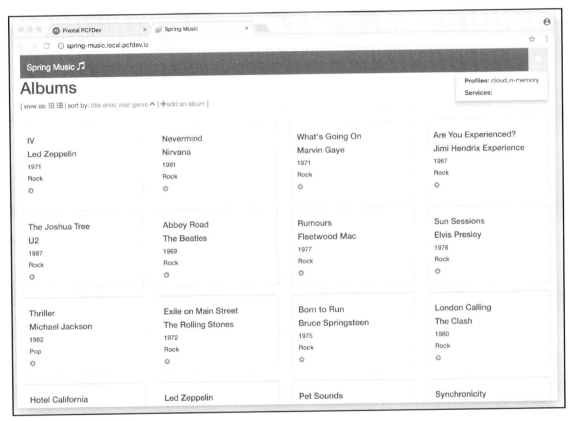

Congratulations! You have now proven that your local Cloud Foundry foundation of PCF Dev is able to run a test application—the same way you were able to push and run a test application in PWS on the public internet.

PCF Dev housekeeping

Behind the scenes PCF Dev is running many containers in a single virtual machine that is hosted on the VirtualBox application you installed on your computer to begin with. If you'd like a peek behind the curtain, you can open the VirtualBox app and see that you really are running a Cloud Foundry foundation on a single virtual machine. From the VirtualBox UI, it looks something like this:

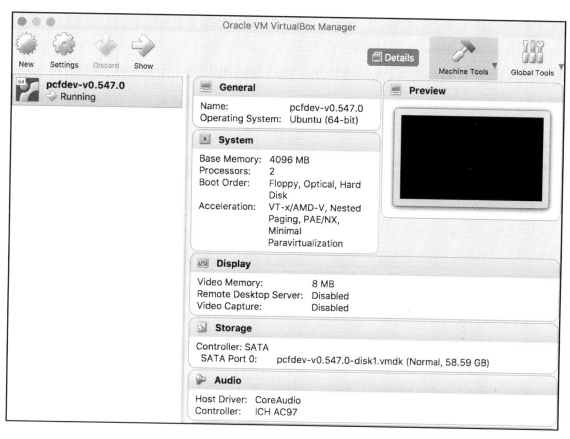

Since VirtualBox is running behind the scenes, it may be easy to forget that the PCF Dev VM is cranking away in the background consuming some of the memory that would otherwise be available to your machine for other things.

As such, we will now see some handy housekeeping commands that will help you manage your PCF Dev installation.

Stop

```
$ cf dev stop
```

This will shut down the PCF Dev VM while preserving all of the data you've added to it.
The following is the typical output from this command:

```
$ cf dev stop
Stopping VM...
PCF Dev is now stopped.
```

The result in VirtualBox is as follows:

Use `cf dev start` to restart a stopped PCF Dev VM.

Suspend

```
$ cf dev suspend
```

This saves the current state of the PCF Dev VM to disk and then stops the VM. The following is the typical output from this command:

```
$ cf dev suspend
Suspending VM...
PCF Dev is now suspended.
```

Resume

```
$ cf dev resume
```

This resumes the PCF Dev VM from a suspended state. The following is the typical output from this command:

```
$ cf dev resume
Resuming VM...
PCF Dev is now running.
```

Destroy

```
$ cf dev destroy
```

This deletes the PCF Dev VM and destroys all of the data it has with it. The following is the typical output from this command:

```
$ cf dev destroy
PCF Dev VM has been destroyed.
```

Status

```
$ cf dev status
```

Sometimes, you may lose track of whether the PCF Dev VM is still running or not. This will tell you the status of the PCF Dev VM. The following is the typical output from this command:

```
$ cf dev status
Running
CLI Login: cf login -a https://api.local.pcfdev.io --skip-ssl-validation
```

```
Apps Manager URL: https://apps.local.pcfdev.io
Admin user => Email: admin / Password: admin
Regular user => Email: user / Password: pass
```

Alternatives to PCF Dev

Until PCF Dev became available, the open source product BOSH-lite was a good solution to get started with Cloud Foundry. However, BOSH-lite is more BOSH-centric and, as such, requires a bit of BOSH expertise to deploy Cloud Foundry. BOSH is billed as an open source tool for release engineering, deployment, lifecycle management, and monitoring of distributed systems. Cloud Foundry doesn't actually require that BOSH be used to deploy it. And, conversely, BOSH is not strictly for deploying Cloud Foundry. It is a generalized tool that can be used for deploying and keeping any distributed system running and healthy. However, the two tools are like peanut butter and chocolate—really good together.

BOSH is a major tool in the Platform Engineers toolbox. Less often now, are BOSH and BOSH-lite tools that a Cloud Foundry application developer would use at the beginning of their Cloud Foundry learning process given the advent of PCF Dev. PCF Dev is a more suitable starting point because it focuses heavily on the sweet spot of developer concerns such as app deployment, services, logging, metrics, and local development. PCF Dev handles much of the heavy lifting needed when getting started with Cloud Foundry development, enabling you to get to the application development work more quickly while largely eliminating the operational work required to stand up your local deployment environment using a tool such as BOSH-lite. All of this is an accelerator for a developer, and it helps shorten the time to deploy the app code, instead of necessitating tinkering under the hood of the platform the app will run on.

All of this is not to say that BOSH and BOSH-lite are not interesting. Quite the opposite. They are extremely interesting technologies and a topic that goes very, very deep if one feels compelled to peel back the cover and examine the cogs and wheels that make the intricacies of highly available and robust distributed systems, such as Cloud Foundry, tick like a well made Swiss timepiece. But, this is a topic deserving its own separate treatment.

Beyond BOSH-lite, there is little else at the current time that gives a developer a quick and easy path to having a local Cloud Foundry available to work against when developing cloud-native code.

Further reading

More information on PCF Dev can be found at the product site: `https://pivotal.io/pcf-dev`.

Pivotal has a PCF Dev walkthrough available online at: `https://pivotal.io/platform/pcf-tutorials/getting-started-with-pivotal-cloud-foundry-dev/introduction`.

PCF Dev can be downloaded from PivNet at: `https://network.pivotal.io/products/pcfdev`.

If you would like to examine the code that makes up PCF Dev, the open source repository can be found on GitHub at: `https://github.com/pivotal-cf/pcfdev`.

Summary

In this chapter, we installed a local machine version of Cloud Foundry called PCF Dev. Then, we logged into it and pushed an app to verify that it worked. We did this to shorten our development and debugging cycle, which generally consists of the time-tested practice of TDD for writing great code that is resistant to regression failures. Using TDD, we follow the workflow of red, green, iterate until our code is feature complete.

We examined the key differences between PCF Dev and other distributions of Cloud Foundry. PCF Dev is a convenient addition to your Cloud Foundry development toolkit. This ensures that you are creating applications that are highly likely to run with little to no modification of your production foundation of Cloud Foundry.

4
Users, Orgs, Spaces, and Roles

Cloud Foundry enables platform operators to organize the Cloud Foundry deployment as per their organizational structure and add users with various capabilities through roles. A Cloud Foundry deployment can be structured around **Organizations (Orgs)** and **Spaces**. It is very important to understand the concepts of organizations and spaces, so you can design your Cloud Foundry deployment as per your company's requirements.

In this chapter, we will explore the most common ways to design an Org and a Space, understand **roles**, and grant access to users to an Org or a Space on **Pivotal PCF Dev**. We will be using the cf CLI and the Apps Manager to create an org, a space, a user, and assign role(s) to them.

Specifically, we'll cover the following:

- Creating an Org
- Creating a Space
- Adding users
- Assigning roles to users

Organizations (Orgs)

An Org can be considered to be the name of an **Application Group**, **Product Group**, or **Business Unit**. An Org consists of computing resources and spaces. Each Org has a default resource quota that is shared by multiple spaces. Orgs can be maintained by a single or multiple users, who then can manage the Org and can create resource quotas for each space.

Create an Org using Apps Manager

To create an Org using the Apps Manager running on PCF Dev, log in to the Apps Manager by accessing `https://apps.local.pcfdev.io` with the admin user account. Use the PCF Dev login information to connect to the Apps Manager:

```
~ >>> cf dev status
Running
CLI Login: cf login -a https://api.local.pcfdev.io --skip-ssl-validation
Apps Manager URL: https://apps.local.pcfdev.io
Admin user => Email: admin / Password: admin
Regular user => Email: user / Password: pass
```

Figure 1: PCF Dev login information

The default details to connect to the Pivotal PCF Dev are:

To begin using PCF Dev, please run:

```
cf login -a https://api.local.pcfdev.io --skip-ssl-
validation
```

Apps Manager URL: `https://apps.local.pcfdev.io`

Admin user => Email: `admin` / Password: `admin`

Regular user => Email: `user` / Password: `pass`

Upon signing in, click on the drop-down menu under the Org on the left pane, and select **+Create a New Org**:

Figure 2: Select the option to Create a New Org

Now, provide an Org name, which can be the name of the Application Group, the Business Unit, or the Product Group, whatever the case may be. Once you define the name, select the **CREATE ORG** button. For illustration purposes, we will create an Org with the name `cf-my-first-org`:

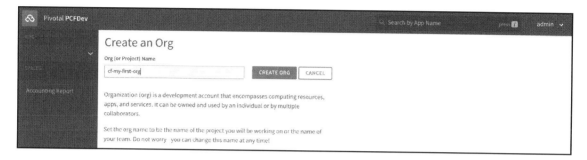

Figure 3: Create an Org

Once the Org has been created, you will see the success message, and the Org will be initialized with the default quota of 100 GB RAM on the Pivotal PCF Dev:

Figure 4: Create Org successful

The default domains will be listed under the **Domains** tab:

Figure 5: List the default domains under an Org

Congratulations! You have successfully created your very Org `cf-my-first-org` using the Apps Manager on PCF Dev.

Create an Organization (Org) using the cf CLI

The Orgs can also be created using the cf CLI. To do this, we will login to the PCF Dev environment by executing the `cf login -a https://api.local.pcfdev.io --skip-ssl-validation` command.

Before we move further, let's take a look at the help text on how to create an Org. We will execute the `cf create-org --help` command:

```
[~ >>> cf create-org --help
NAME:
    create-org - Create an org

USAGE:
    cf create-org ORG

ALIAS:
    co

OPTIONS:
    -q      Quota to assign to the newly created org (excluding this option resul
ts in assignment of default quota)

SEE ALSO:
    create-space, orgs, quotas, set-org-role
```

Figure 6: Help command on how to create an Org using cf CLI

Now, in order to create the Org, we need to execute the `cf create-org ORG-NAME` command, where the `ORG-NAME` would be the name of the Application Group, the Business Unit, or the Product Group.

For illustration purposes, we will create an Org with the name `cf-my-first-org`:

```
~ >>> cf create-org cf-my-first-org
Creating org cf-my-first-org as admin...
OK

Assigning role OrgManager to user admin in org cf-my-first-org ...
OK

TIP: Use 'cf target -o "cf-my-first-org"' to target new org
```

Figure 7: Create an Org using the cf CLI

If the Org already exists, then the cf CLI will not **re-create** the Org and will respond with a friendly message that the `Org cf-my-first-org already exists`:

```
~ >>> cf create-org cf-my-first-org
Creating org cf-my-first-org as admin...
OK
Org cf-my-first-org already exists
```

Figure 8: Output when an Org already exists using the cf CLI

Congratulations! You have successfully created your very Org `cf-my-first-org` using the cf CLI on PCF Dev.

List Orgs using the cf CLI

Once you have successfully created your Org, you can now list all of the Orgs to verify all of the Orgs you have access to. This is done by executing the `cf orgs` command:

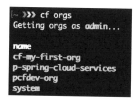

```
~ >>> cf orgs
Getting orgs as admin...

name
cf-my-first-org
p-spring-cloud-services
pcfdev-org
system
```

Figure 9: Listing all the Orgs using the cf CLI

Based on the Business Unit or the Application Group, the Cloud Foundry administrator or the user with the Org Manager role can add new `wildcard` domains by clicking on the **ADD DOMAIN** button and following the instructions. Once the Cloud Foundry administrator creates an Org, it's in an active state. The Cloud Foundry administrator can de-activate the Org if the Application, Product Group, or Business Unit has misused it, haven't paid for their usage, or no longer need the Org.

Spaces

A Space is where the applications are pushed to. All service bindings are created and managed within a space. Spaces can be mapped to a specific environment, such as development, testing, integration, or production. Spaces can also be mapped to a sub-team under the Business Unit, Application, or Product Group. Services used by applications are scoped by Spaces. Developers push their applications into Space and then continue to develop and maintain their applications in the same space.

If a given Space requires a different resource quota than the one defined at the Org, then the Cloud Foundry administrator or the Org Manager of that Org can create a custom resource quota and assign it to Space.

Creating a Space using the Apps Manager

Now, let us look at how to create a Space using the Apps Manager on Pivotal PCF Dev. We begin by logging in to `https://apps.local.pcfdev.io/` with the PCF Dev user account admin.

Select the `cf-my-first-org` from the ORG dropdown from the top left menu:

Figure 10: Targeting a Space in the cf-my-first-org Org using the Apps Manager

Now click on the **Add a Space** button, specify the **Spaces** name as `development`, and hit the **SAVE** button:

Figure 11: Creating a development Space in the cf-my-first-org Org using the Apps Manager

If the Space creation is successful, then you should see the Space listed under the `cf-my-first-org` org:

Figure 12: Creation of development space using the Apps Manager is a success

Congratulations! You have successfully created your very first Space under the `cf-my-first-org` using the Apps Manager on PCF Dev.

Creating a Space using cf CLI

To create a Space using the cf CLI on Pivotal PCF Dev, we need to login first. To do this, we need to specify the Cloud Foundry API endpoint of PCF Dev, which is `https://api.local.pcfdev.io` and also skip the SSL validation:

```
[~ >>> cf login -a https://api.local.pcfdev.io --skip-ssl-validation
API endpoint: https://api.local.pcfdev.io

Email> admin

Password>
Authenticating...
OK
```

Figure 13: Login to PCF Dev using cf CLI

Next, select the `cf-my-first-org` from the Org list presented to you on the command line, and hit *Enter*:

```
Select an org (or press enter to skip):
1. cf-my-first-org
2. p-spring-cloud-services
3. pcfdev-org
4. system

Org> 1
Targeted org cf-my-first-org



API endpoint:   https://api.local.pcfdev.io (API version: 2.82.0)
User:           admin
Org:            cf-my-first-org
Space:          No space targeted, use 'cf target -s SPACE'
```

Figure 14: Select the cf-my-first-org from the options presented upon successful login

Note in the preceding output that the Org does not have space. In order to create a Space with the name `development`, we execute the command `cf create-space development`:

```
[~ >>> cf create-space development
Creating space development in org cf-my-first-org as admin...
OK
Assigning role RoleSpaceManager to user admin in org cf-my-first-org / space dev
elopment as admin...
OK
Assigning role RoleSpaceDeveloper to user admin in org cf-my-first-org / space d
evelopment as admin...
OK

TIP: Use 'cf target -o "cf-my-first-org" -s "development"' to target new space
```

Figure 15: Create development space under cf-my-first-org Org using cf CLI

If the Space with the name development already exists, you will get a message, `space development already exists`:

```
[~ >>> cf create-space development
Creating space development in org cf-my-first-org as admin...
OK
Space development already exists
```

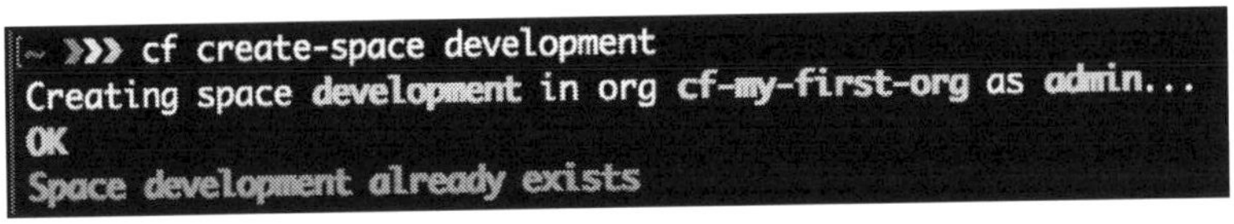

Figure 16: Output from the cf CLI when the development space already exists

Lastly, we target the Space by executing `cf target -o ORG -s SPACE`. In this case, `cf target -o cf-my-first-org -s development`:

```
[~ >>> cf target -o cf-my-first-org -s development
api endpoint:   https://api.local.pcfdev.io
api version:    2.82.0
user:           admin
org:        .   cf-my-first-org
space:          development
```

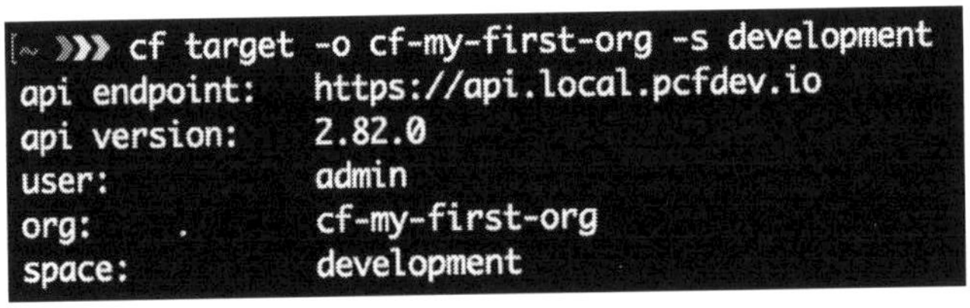

Figure 17: Using cf CLI to target to the org cf-my-first-org and the space development

Congratulations! You have successfully created your very first Space under the `cf-my-first-org` using the cf CLI on PCF Dev.

List spaces using the cf CLI

Once you have successfully created your Space under the Org, you can now list all of the spaces that belong to the Org.

This is done by executing the command `cf spaces`:

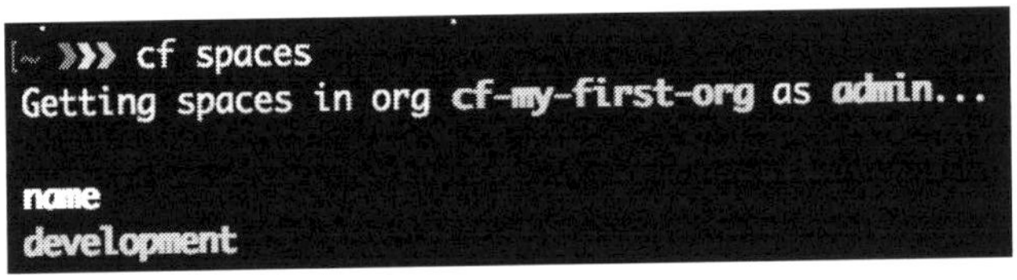

```
[~ >>> cf spaces
Getting spaces in org cf-my-first-org as admin...

name
development
```

Figure 18: List all the spaces under the cf-my-first-org using the cf CLI

You need to ensure you have set the `cf target -o ORG` before you run the command listed previously.

User accounts

A **user account** allows a user to log in to Cloud Foundry and perform certain operations that are limited by the roles assigned to them by the **Cloud Foundry Administrator**.

The user accounts can be created at an Org or Space level, based on the role they play in the organization. The same user can administer the Org and Space, or can be restricted to pushing applications to a given Space or Spaces.

Additionally, a user can span across multiple spaces in an Org, and under each Space, they can be controlled by the Space role.

Create a user using the cf CLI

Let us take a look at how to add a user to our `cf-my-first-org` Org in Pivotal PCF Dev. To do this, we need to specify the Cloud Foundry API endpoint of PCF Dev, which is `https://api.local.pcfdev.io`, and also skip the SSL validation:

```
[~ >>> cf login -a https://api.local.pcfdev.io --skip-ssl-validation
API endpoint: https://api.local.pcfdev.io

Email> admin

[Password>
Authenticating...
OK
```

Figure 19: Login to the PCF Dev using cf CLI

Next, select the `cf-my-first-org` from the Org list presented to you on the command line:

```
Select an org (or press enter to skip):
1. cf-my-first-org
2. p-spring-cloud-services
3. pcfdev-org
4. system

Org> 1
Targeted org cf-my-first-org

Targeted space development


API endpoint:   https://api.local.pcfdev.io (API version: 2.82.0)
User:           admin
Org:            cf-my-first-org
Space:          development
```

Figure 20: Select the Org and Space upon successful login using cf CLI

Since there is just one space, the cf CLI will target the space development. If we had more than one space, then the cf CLI would prompt you to choose the Space you would like to target to.

We will now create our first user by executing the command `cf create-user USERNAME PASSWORD`. For example, let us create a user, `John`, with the password `welcome`, by executing `cf create-user John welcome`:

```
[~ >>> cf create-user John welcome
Creating user John...
user John already exists
OK

TIP: Assign roles with 'cf set-org-role' and 'cf set-space-role'.
```

Figure 21: Create user John with a default password using the cf CLI

By executing this command, we have registered a user in Cloud Foundry, but when the user **John** logs in to the **Apps Manager**, he will not have access to any Org or Space:

Figure 22: user John has no access to any orgs or spaces

Congratulations! You have created your first user using the cf CLI. In the next section, we will discuss the various roles that exist in Cloud Foundry, and then assign one of them to the user John.

Roles

The **roles** restrict what a user can do within a Cloud Foundry Org or Space. The roles are predefined and managed within CloudFoundry.

Users are assigned the roles by the Cloud Foundry Administrator, Org Manager, or Space Manager. Only users with administrator privileges can create new user accounts.

Roles that can be assigned to users at the **Org level** are:

- OrgManager
- BillingManager
- OrgAuditor

Roles that can be assigned to users at these **Space level** are:

- SpaceManager
- SpaceDeveloper
- SpaceAuditor

Let's look at what each of the roles can perform.

OrgManager role

A user with the **OrgManager** role can perform the following functions:

- Invite and manage the user permissions at the Org and the Space level
- Create and manage the quotas at the Org and the Space level
- Add private domains
- Create and manage spaces. He can also delete the Spaces.

BillingManager role

A user with the **BillingManager** role can perform all read-only operations for billing purposes, like:

- Viewing users and their roles assigned to an Org
- View Org quotas
- View the application instances, application status, service instances, and the bindings between the application and the services

OrgAuditor role

A user with the **OrgAuditor** role can perform the following functions:

- View all of the users and roles assigned to the Org and Space
- View all the Org quotas

SpaceManager role

With the **SpaceManager role**, a user can perform the following functions:

- Invite and manage the user permissions at the Space level
- View Org quota plans
- View and edit space
- View the application instances, application status, application resources, service instances, and the bindings between the application and the services

SpaceDeveloper role

A user with the **SpaceDeveloper** role can perform the following functions:

- View all the Space users and their roles
- View Org quota plans
- View all of the spaces under the Org
- View the application status, number of instances, service bindings, and resources allocated to each application
- Deploy, run, and manage applications
- Create and bind services to applications
- Assign routes, scale application instances, memory allocation, and disk limits of applications
- Rename applications

SpaceAuditor role

With the **SpaceAuditor** role, a user can perform the following functions:

- View users and roles
- View Org quota plans
- View all of the spaces under the Org
- View the status, number of instances, service bindings, and resource use of applications

Assigning roles to a user using cf CLI

Let us now assign the OrgManager role to the user, John, that we created in the previous section, for the Org `cf-my-first-org` and also assign the SpaceDeveloper role for the development space under the Org, using the cf CLI on Pivotal PCF Dev.

To do this, we need to specify the Cloud Foundry API endpoint of PCF Dev, which is `https://api.local.pcfdev.io`, and also skip the SSL validation:

```
[~ >>> cf login -a https://api.local.pcfdev.io --skip-ssl-validation
API endpoint: https://api.local.pcfdev.io

Email> admin

Password>
Authenticating...
OK
```

Figure 23: Login to PCF Dev using cf CLI

Next, select the `cf-my-first-org` from the `ORG` list presented to you on the command line, followed by the development space:

```
Select an org (or press enter to skip):
1. cf-my-first-org
2. p-spring-cloud-services
3. pcfdev-org
4. system

Org> 1
Targeted org cf-my-first-org

Targeted space development


API endpoint:   https://api.local.pcfdev.io (API version: 2.82.0)
User:           admin
Org:            cf-my-first-org
Space:          development
```

Figure 24: Select the Org and Space upon successful login using the cf CLI

Since there is just one space, the cf CLI will target the space development. If we had more than one space, then the cf CLI would prompt you to choose the Space you would like to target to.

Now, we will assign the OrgManager role to the user John by executing `cf set-org-role USERNAME ORG ROLE`, for example, `cf set-org-role John cf-my-first-org OrgManager`:

```
[~ >>> cf set-org-role John cf-my-first-org OrgManager
Assigning role OrgManager to user John in org cf-my-first-org as admin...
OK
```

Figure 25: Assign user John the OrgManager role using cf CLI

We will now log in to the Apps Manager on PCF Dev as the user John, and verify John is able to view the Org `cf-my-first-org`. So connect to `https://apps.local.pcfdev.io` and log in with the username `John` and password `welcome`:

Figure 26: Login to the Apps Manager with John's credentials

Navigate to the **Members** section to verify the role assigned to the user John. We should see the role is OrgManager:

Figure 27: Viewing all the members and their permissions under the cf-my-first-org Org

Since we have not assigned John any roles in the development space, he should have no roles selected for him. We can verify this by navigating to the development space and selecting **Members**:

Figure 28: Viewing all the members and their permissions under the development Space

Let's get back to the cf CLI and assign the SpaceDeveloper role to John. This is done by executing `cf set-space-role USERNAME ORG SPACE ROLE`, for instance, `cf set-space-role John cf-my-first-org development SpaceDeveloper`:

```
[~ >>> cf set-space-role John cf-my-first-org development SpaceDeveloper
Assigning role RoleSpaceDeveloper to user John in org cf-my-first-org / space de
velopment as admin...
OK
```

Figure 29: Assign SpaceDeveloper role to user John using cf CLI

Refresh the Apps Manager and verify John's role in Apps Manager. At this time John should have the SpaceDeveloper role assigned:

Figure 30: Viewing members and their permissions under the development space using Apps Manager

At this point, `John` can perform the operations of an OrgManager for the `cf-my-first-org` Org. He can also perform the activities of a **SpaceDeveloper** in the development space.

You can see how simple it is to onboard new users to use Cloud Foundry. If your Cloud Foundry installation is configured with an external user store, like Active Directory or SAML, then the users will need to login first and then contact the Cloud Foundry platform operator to assign to an appropriate role to the user. All roles are managed within Cloud Foundry.

Summary

In this section, we discussed creating Org, Spaces, and user accounts using the cf CLI and the Apps Manager. We looked into the different types of roles supported within Cloud Foundry and learned how to do role assignment to users using the cf CLI.

5
Architecting and Building Apps for the Cloud

Chapter 1 of this book introduced the Pivotal Cloud Foundry architecture. This followed on with the basics of the Cloud Foundry command line interface and then the concepts of Orgs, Users, Spaces, and Roles. In the proceeding chapters, we'll look at deploying applications and various advanced topics for Cloud application development. However, before we proceed, we need to know how an application should be developed for the Cloud. Questions arise as to what does the ideal application on the Cloud foundry should look like? How does one even build applications for the Cloud? What are the application design considerations and best practices? How and what does it take to move an existing application to Cloud Foundry? By the end of this chapter, you will be able to answer these questions.

This is a very important chapter that will define how one can develop their application that will take advantage of Cloud Foundry. We will cover the topics:

- What is a cloud-native application?
- Principals of cloud-native design
- Application migration and the journey to achieving cloud-native design
- Application modernization techniques
- Application modernization and your organization

This is indeed a chapter with a lot of content but, once mastered, it will be both liberating and rewarding as you move towards developing your Cloud application.

What is a cloud-native application?

A cloud-native application is one that wholly embraces the traits and behavior of a Cloud platform, independently of its underlying infrastructure. Such applications are effectively highly scalable and operate in a resilient and consistent manner throughout its lifecycle.

Let us take a dive into this definition. A Cloud platform is one that operates over or is built into a Cloud infrastructure. Cloud Foundry, as described in Chapter 1, is such a platform that offers the benefits of the orchestration of containers over a number of cells (Virtual Machines), which offers the capability for application scaling, resiliency, and consistency. Application/horizontal scaling enables efficient leveraging of resources on an infrastructure, in a way that application instances could be scaled up or down to cater for varying levels of incoming traffic loads. This would maximize the utilization of the infrastructure. Contrary to this is the concept of vertical scaling, where scaling here means to increase/decrease physically available resources to an application. Traditionally, this entails increasing the physical server hardware such as RAM to provide more memory for an application. We'll see later that Cloud Foundry enables vertical scaling by tuning applications to a fixed numerically allocated resource, such as memory. This would still be bounded by the physical amount of resources available on the infrastructure.

Resiliency provides a means to recover from application crashes or unpredictable infrastructure issues. This is achieved by the shutting down and starting up of cells and containers. Finally, consistency provides a means for applications to operate with a known fixed environment that is always consistent across all cells and containers. This all leads to predictable behavior of applications in execution over its lifetime, during and after development. As such, it is important to note that a cloud-native application can either be green-field or brown-field. It's a matter of whether or not an application falls into the abovementioned definition.

Aside from inheriting the benefits of consistency provided by a platform, having an application deployed on a Cloud platform does not automatically deem it to be cloud-native. Applications must be architected and implemented to leverage the scaling and resilient benefits. Scaling should be performed so that it results in an efficient use of infrastructure resources. To have, say, a monolithic application running on Cloud Foundry with horizontal scaling may not be an efficient means of leveraging the infrastructure's resources.

Ideally, the monolithic application should be decomposed or architected into sufficiently optimally sized units such that this would enable fine-grained scaling of an application, for example, if a particular application's single function, such as 'search', experiences a high load, only that function should be scaled up. This is on the contrary to having an entire monolithic application scaled up, which leads to inefficient use of infrastructure resources. The additional issue of not having optimally decomposed units is that a monolithic application may not be scalable at all and would fail to operate once scaled.

Resiliency, on the other hand, ensures that an application, in its entirety, does not stop functioning or cause data integrity issues, while offering a potentially improved user experience. A simplistic example, in this case, would be updating a monolithic application. Updating the application directly would result in downtime. An alternative would be to utilize a green-blue deployment strategy and scale up the number of instances. For a monolithic application, this would potentially result in a very high resource usage dictated by the number of application instances, or cause the application to crash because it wasn't architected to be scalable. The ideal and efficient scenario would be, again, to follow a decomposition strategy mentioned for scaling, using an architectural pattern known as Microservices. We shall discuss this in further detail in `Chapter 7`, *Microservices and Worker Applications*. Nonetheless, with Microservices, it would be possible to efficiently update a small portion of the application without bringing it down entirely, albeit with limited functionality, when implemented with a circuit breaker pattern. We could take a step further and marry this approach with a green-blue deployment strategy, which would lead to infrastructure resource efficiency and the zero-downtime update of applications.

The principles of cloud-native design

There are 12 guiding principles for Cloud application design known as the 12-factor app. These 12 principles were originally formulated by Heroku, which offered guidance to develop cloud-native applications. More recently, three additional principles were proposed by Hoffman, which led to cloud-native application design for secure and actively profiled API centric Microservices. Some parts of the original 12 principles have also been expanded upon to clarify and address recent successful architectural approaches. We also introduce one additional principle in this book. We describe the 16 principals in the proceeding sections.

One codebase, one application

The original principle was *Codebase*, which described, in the broader scope, a process of having a single codebase deployable for different environments, such as QA and production. This was expanded upon to encompass the need for a single loosely coupled, highly cohesive codebase. For a developer, this makes it easier to create CI/CD pipelines. In addition, the single code base makes it easy to onboard new developers and ensure code that is much easier to maintain.

API First

This was not part of the original 12-factor principles. The concept introduces the concept of the **Application Programming Interface (API)** First approach to an application design. Design of the application begins at the seams that define a contract on what and how other applications would interact with your application. This defines the purpose, resulting in an application that is independent, unique and easily understood in its ecosystem. It is only then that the application is implemented to this contract. For the developer, this means that they already know what their service responsibilities are and they can easily understand what functionality other services have which are exposed to them. This makes application development much easier once responsibilities are understood, leading to code that is much easier to maintain.

Dependency management

As part of the original 12-factor principle, it mandates that an application's dependencies should be clearly defined and not rely on a system-wide packaging/location. For example, don't rely on some location on disk, like `/usr/local/lib`, or the **Global Assembly Cache (GAC)** for **.NET** Applications, where dependency location is known and expected to always exist. This is because these locations are unlikely to be set up or exist when migrating to a Cloud platform. In modern dependency management, we have *Maven/Gradle/NuGet* for Java and .NET applications, respectively, where dependencies are defined and are pulled in during a build. Later in `Chapter 9`, *Buildpacks*, we will explore the concept of buildpacks, which set up dependency frameworks and runtime support, needed to build and/or run an application, on a Cloud platform such as *Cloud Foundry*. With this principle, dependencies and the versions are known upfront to all developers working on the codebase. This also makes it easier for onboarding new developers. There is no mistake between different dependency versions for each developer and the environments that they are run on.

Design, build, release, and run

This principle describes the concept that each phase should be executed as isolated independent steps. In the 15 principles, this was broadened to include an initial design phase. This clarified the need for defining the dependencies needed for the application. In essence, the design phase declares the dependencies. The build phase pulls together the dependencies to produce a build artifact with a build number. The release phase combines the build artifact with application or environment specific configurations, and tags the output with some versioning for tracking/audit purposes and finally, the run phase defines the process of launching and running the application. The run phase is usually the responsibility of a Cloud platform, but consideration is needed for situations where applications may need to be run locally on a development machine. A popular approach to versioning has been the semantic versioning approach, which follows the major.minor.patch release number. More details can be found at the semantic versioning specification at: `http://semver.org/`.

The end goal of this principle is the high level of confidence of reproducing a build output. There should not be the issue of the *build worked on my machine*, it should not require additional interventions or have different resultant builds. In general, this principle should be automated with the use of CI/CD pipelines. For the developer, this leads to released executables that are traceable back to the build source, leading to easier auditing and debugging purposes.

 In exceptional cases, it may not always be possible to have identical builds from the same source code, for example, Field-Programmable Gate Array (FPGA) firmware are not guaranteed to be identical after each build. In these instances, an additional associated build number would be highly advantageous for comparative benchmarks and audits.

Configuration, credentials, and code

In the original 12 principles, this was entitled *Configuration*. The principle requires that an application's configuration is externalized to environment variables. This enables an application to be configurable without the need to modify a release. This is especially useful in automating the build-release process. Credential and code were included in the 15 principles to provide a clear demarcation of credentials and configuration from code. There should be no hard-coded credentials and no configuration in the code. These should be externalized for the purposes of configurability and to ensure sensitive information is not revealed should the source code be made public deliberately or accidentally.

While we have discussed the externalizing configuration to environment variables, there still remains the issue of version controlling the configuration change or cleanly adjusting sets of configuration to a specific purpose, for example for QA, development, or production. One such solution is to utilize configuration servers. *Spring Cloud Configuration Server* is one such instance, which allows sourcing of configuration to environment variables from a server that points to a git repository holding the configuration for the given run environment. A git repository of the configuration means that changes of configuration can be tracked and safely adjusted. For the developer, this enables them to focus solely on code development and that they can be assured that the configuration and credentials are decoupled and will be consistent across all environments and other developers.

Logs

As part of the original 12 principles, Logs dictate that logging output should be treated as event streams and should be simply emitted out via standard out and standard error. The benefits of this principle are three-fold. The first is that applications are simplified and no longer need to implement the intricacies of storing logs. Instead, all management and processing of logs are handled externally by the Cloud platform and external tools. This simplifies the application's code and potentially reduces the risk of bugs, and simply enables the developer to focus on the application to deliver the intended business value. The second is the support for horizontal scaling. Should an application be scaled horizontally and that the logging was managed by the application, developers would need to introduce logic to handle the identification of which application instance a log comes from. Thirdly, an application running on the Cloud cannot make assumptions about how much space is available in a container and how long stored content will last on the disk of the container. The container is ephemeral and hence, any stored content will disappear. By deferring the logging stream externally to the cloud platform, storage, processing, and viewing of logs can be done independently from the application itself. For the developer, this ultimately liberates them from additional work to ensure that the logs are retained. The only responsibility, that they have, is to ensure that error conditions and any other loggable aspect of their application are emitted. This also has the side benefit of having code that is less complex.

Disposability

As is in the original 12 principles, disposability refers to an application's ability to be started up and shut down gracefully, within both scenarios in a rapid manner. Disposability is a requirement due to the ephemeral nature of Cloud applications. Simply put, an application should be shut down and started up quickly so that it can be ready to handle incoming traffic. At the same time, applications should be shut down gracefully, so that any critical information in an application is not lost or corrupted. For the developer, this places a good constraint on them to ensure that code is efficient for startup and shutdown. In addition, any code that they write should ensure that quick and graceful shutdowns can be achieved.

Backing services

Backing services is part of the original 12 principles. All backing services should be treated as bound/attached resources. A backing service is simply any service that is consumed by an application. A bound/attached resource is simply the connection between an application and a backing service. Some example backing services include data stores (*MySQL*, S3), caching (*Redis*), and messaging (*RabbitMQ*). In essence, an application bound to some backing service should not have code that is specific to that type of backing service. The generic nature of the implementation will enable backing services to attached/detached at will. Such scenarios enable administrators to quickly and reliably replace failing backing services without needing to code updates or the redeployment of applications. For the developer, this requires them to write code that is decoupled from service resources. This leads to code that is much easier to test.

Environment parity

Originally called the dev/prod parity in the 12 principles, the goal was to ensure that gaps between development and production were small or non-existent. This has been expanded to be *Environment parity* to achieve the goal that the application when built and released as per guidelines, should '*work anywhere*' in any related environment. There are three factors known to affect parity, and they are *time, people*, and *resources*. The **time** relates to the situation where an application takes days, weeks, or even months to go into production. By then, multiple changes or factors (business, bug fixes, external, and so forth) may have affected the outcome of the application to go into production. By reducing the time, it is possible quickly identify issues, deliver the intended business value, and iterate. The second factor, **people**, describes the discrepancy between the developer and the DevOps team that deploy the application, in a large enterprise. Reducing the gap between these people would give better environment parity.

Ideally, the developer should be the same person that deploys the application. However, this is not always practically possible, especially in some private Cloud situations. The alternative would be to have the developer be closely involved in the deployment of the application in production. Or, better yet, utilize CI/CD pipelines and automate the whole process. The less human intervention, the better the consistency and predictability of the deployment. The third and final factor, **resources**, relates to the differences in resources used for development versus that used in production. For example, a developer may use a memory database for development, while in production, a real database such as SQL Server is used in the place. This may bring about some differences in performance and application behavior. For environment parity, the resources between these stages should be identical. By following the *8th principle: Backing Services* with the *5th principle: configuration, credentials, and code*, it is possible to model your application to be bound with any resources at will and have the same type of database (for example, an SQL Server), but different instances where needed to be configured for either development or for production. Later in this book, we shall discuss services, which will allow you to quickly spin up databases, or other types of resources that are available for use in your application. The key takeaway from this principle is that anything you do differently between environments will only increase the gap of difference. The goal is to avoid introducing these differences as much as possible, where practicable. This principle affects development teams, platform teams, and the organization as a whole. Platform teams must ensure resources and environments, such as QA, development, and production are identical throughout the organization. For development teams, it enables a cadence of rapid releases that enable them to iterate on their code much faster without concern of environment differences. Consistency gives confidence to all teams and enables faster determination of issues. For the organization, this leads to breaking down of silos between teams, leading to faster, innovative development.

Administrative processes

This principle describes the requirement for running administrative and maintenance tasks, such as database migrations as a separate process within the same production environment as the application. The code for the administrative task should be shipped with and be run against the release for the same given codebase and configuration. This makes sense because the administrative tool should do what the application does/works with for the given release. However, depending on the Cloud platform, one should evaluate and consider the best course for performing the administrative tasks. For example, on Cloud Foundry, it would not be practicable to run the administrative task as a separate spawned process with an instance of an application in the same container. The application itself may be scaled up to multiple instances, or there is no guarantee how an application would behave/live for the duration of the administrative process. The former scenario may introduce complexities to the handling of the administrative task relative to each instance.

The latter, on the other hand, should an application instance fail, may forcibly cause the entire container to be shut down. A possible solution, in this case, would be to introduce some administrative application with a restful API, that is deployed within the same environment and run when required. For the developer, this removes the need for administrative code within the application itself and thus, the codebase is simpler and easier to maintain.

Port binding

The original 12-factor principle states that services should be exported via port binding. Basically, the container itself should not require the injection of a web server so that the application can be web facing. The application itself should hold the web service and bind to a given available port from the container. From a developer's perspective, it means being able to receive a port number, instantiate a web server from some web server library, and bind them together. However, given the nature of existing enterprise applications, this may not always be practicable and may still require some form of lightweight web server. Therefore, the constraints by this principle would, in some cases, need to be relaxed. For developers, this relaxed constraint liberates them from the need to have web service code in the codebase. On Cloud Foundry, an example would be running the classic .NET framework using the **hosted webcore (HWC)** buildpack. As you will learn later, buildpacks provide the necessary support runtime needed to build and run an application. In this instance, HWC is essentially the core of *IIS* under the hood, which receives an assigned port number from the container and hosts the .NET framework application.

Stateless processes

This was called *Processes* in the original 12-factor principle and stated that an application's processes should be stateless and share nothing. **Stateless processes** here means that a single process should not expect to retain any state information, whether it is on a container's disk or its memory, since there is no guarantee that information will be retained. Should state need to be retained, it should be done so externally to the application through backing services, such as *Redis*. **Share nothing** processes relate to when more than one process runs concurrently in the container. A good practice would be to avoid sharing and storing state between these processes; this makes the application less complex and easier to maintain. Again, utilize an external backing service to store state information, should this be required.

Finally, in Hoffman's 15 principles, it was contended that, while the original 12 principles were more relaxed with having multiple processes within a container, it is better to have only a single process per container. For the developer, this will lead to a simpler application that is easier to maintain and will better position their application for scaling and is durable in handling data integrity in the presence of ephemeral containers.

Concurrency

This principle, as per the original 12, describes the requirement for an application be scaled horizontally, using principles 12 and 7. In doing so, this will result in processes that share nothing, stateless and disposable, which make them prime candidates for efficient horizontal scaling. The alternative to horizontal scaling is vertical scaling, whereby an application's underlying server/system is scaled by increasing its CPU or RAM. In general, the **stateless processes** follow a *Unix process model* that enable developers to architect their application in such a way that enables them to divide the workloads as separate independent programs and scale them accordingly (`https://en.wikibooks.org/wiki/A_Quick_Introduction_to_Unix/Files_and_Processes`). In more current architectural models, Microservices have a division work that is well defined and each Microservice in itself is a single application that can be individually and horizontally scaled. For the developer following this principle, it will lead to having code that is less complex and easier to maintain without the need to have cached information between itself and its dependent or calling services.

Telemetry

This principle is an addition to the 12 principles and describes the need for metrics and monitoring of applications. The deployment of applications on the Cloud generally means a reduced accessibility to a running instance to perform some form of debugging or diagnostic. One should consider what information they will need to capture in order to monitor and diagnose issues and performance of an application. For the developer and platform teams, this provides them with immediate insights into their applications requirements, future capacity plans, and potential application issues. In general, the types of information can be categorized into three types:

- **Application Performance Monitoring (APM)**: This consists of a stream of events output by your application and captured by external tools to give information on how well your application is performing. The indicators/markers in the event stream, in order to provide the performance information, is set by you.

- **Domain-specific telemetry**: This is a stream of events output by your application and used by analytic tools to provide specific information to your business.
- **Health and system logs**: This is a stream of event data from your Cloud platform that provides indicators such as application startup, shutdown, scaling, and any periodic health checks.

Authentication and authorization

While not part of the original 12 principles, authentication and authorization describes the requirement for applications to be secure in order to be cloud-native. Before we delve further, let us define authentication and authorization. Authentication is the act of knowing *who you are*, that is, your login credentials. Authorization is the process of rules that determine what *you are allowed or not allowed* to act on for a target resource, that is, the permissions. In knowing this, every API endpoints should be secured with **role-based access control (RBAC)**. Every incoming request should be authenticated and, have associated, authorization that determines whether or not the incoming request has permission to access the endpoint. Modern application development technologies are available to assist the developer with this. The **Single Sign-On (SSO)** (`https://www.techopedia.com/definition/4106/single-sign-on-sso`) concept along with *OAuth2* (`https://en.wikipedia.org/wiki/OAuth`) authorization standard, are such ideas that can be put together to achieve this goal. For all teams, this principle gives confidence that applications and resources are secure.

Graceful fault tolerance

While not part of the original 12 or Hoffman's 15 principles, this book introduces a new principle that dictates that a cloud-native application should be both graceful and fault tolerant. While testing should always be in place to pick up on issues before release, it is still possible that test coverages are not 100% and corner cases are missed. Any failing components of an application should not bring down the entire application or cause data integrity issues. In addition, such failure should be graceful. A graceful failure should not crash a user's system/browser and should instead provide friendly information of the failure. Concurrently, this failure should be logged and alert the development teams involved. The circuit breaker is one such design pattern that could be implemented to achieve this. For the developer, this enables their application to handles failures so that they do not propagate and cause data integrity issues, while at the same time, have rapid feedback on such failures.

Application migration and the journey to cloud-native design on Cloud Foundry

As briefly mentioned previously, a cloud-native application needs not be a new application from scratch, that is a green-field application; we can achieve a cloud-native from existing monolithic applications. In the context of business: what's important for application migration is to deliver business value and receive a return on investment from that, rapidly, with critical application feedback, which mitigates a number of project risks. We can apply this concept using the *cloud-native maturity model*. This model serves as a good indicator to benchmark an application's evolution to the epiphany of cloud-native design.

 Your application doesn't have to be cloud-native in order to be deployed and running on Cloud Foundry.

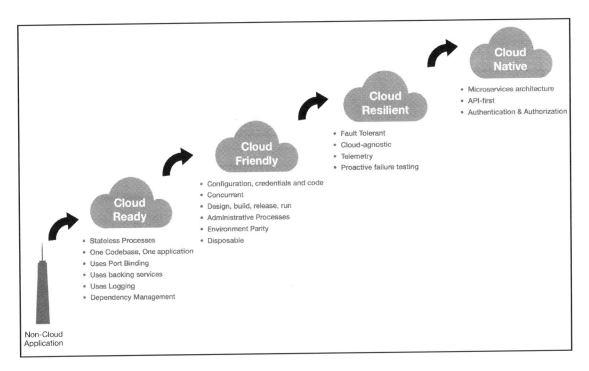

Figure 1: The cloud-native maturity model

As can be seen in the preceding figure, the cloud-native maturity model follows the 16 guiding principles of cloud-native design. To achieve the first phase, one would look at how they can move an existing monolithic application to the Cloud with minimal changes up to and including those mentioned above. To achieve the subsequent phases, a number of refactoring steps would need to be performed. We call this the application modernization steps. Modernization is the process of applying the 16 principles to a monolithic application and decomposing it into microservices. Techniques for resilient cloud-native applications are discussed in Chapter 7, *Microservices and Worker Applications*.

Becoming Cloud Ready

Great! We now know what the 16-principles are and the cloud-native maturity model. But, how does one start this monumental task? As mentioned earlier, it is not always necessary to follow any of the principals to have an application running on a Cloud Platform. The simplest path is to follow a test-driven-development approach and push your application, see what happens, fix, and iterate. However, in a structured investigative approach, one way is to initially do nothing to the application and first map out the structure of your application, for example:

- What are the software dependencies?
- What is/are the language frameworks?
- What are the system requirements?
- What are the data stores and resource services that your application consumes?
- How does one start the application?

Broadly speaking, the goal is to **lift-and-shift** the entire application over to a new platform, for example, Cloud Foundry. Here, we are assuming that the operating system and development language are identical on the new platform. Think of your monolithic application as a building. It has a base foundation to support it, it has an entrance door to let you enter and potentially, there are other exits, some giant satellite dish for TV, phone lines and windows to so for visibility. Understand your application's base foundation. Thereafter, understand its inputs and outputs. Once these are listed out, what are the compatible features between the existing application foundation to the new platform's foundation? What incompatible features can be replaced? Do the same for the inputs and the outputs. If needed, write small chunks of test programs for each feature and run it on the new platform to determine its compatibility.

Once the mapping is complete, we can start moving the monolithic application to the platform. By this stage, you will need to choose the right buildpack for your application. Take small steps first and those that have a minimal impact on the code and minimal side-effects. For a Cloud Ready result, we could use the following staged approach:

1. **Dependency management**: Switch your application to a dependency management tool, if not done so already. Your application should still run on your existing server/platform. If there are dependencies that are not available as a tool, try to package this dependency with your application, if practiceable and legal to do so.

2. **One codebase, one application**: Ensure that there is only a single application. Separate these out into a different repository if feasible. Additional setup scripts should not be run initially on the Cloud platform. Setup scripts here refer to standing up of application hosting servers and disk resources, and so on. These should be internalized into the application code or deprecated and allow the Cloud Platform buildpacks to handle this for you.

3. **Port binding**: Ensure your application can receive a port number from the new platform and bind to it. This will enable your application to receive and output information.

4. **Logging**: Switch all debugging outputs to `stdout` or `stderr`. Depending on the complexity of your application, you may wish to separate this step into two parts. Some applications may output debug logs and auditing logs to a database or file. The first is to switch the output of general debugging information to `stderr`. If feasible, the second is to handle the audit logs. We really would like to separate audit logs for now because they could convolute the debugging output to assist your migration process. There are a few ways at this stage to handle this. Either:

    1. Tag auditing logs with some tag, such as Audit and then output to `stdout`. Thereafter, when you view the logs you could filter out the Audit tagged logs.

    2. Leave auditing logs alone and let it continue to write to the disk/database.

    3. Or, switch off logging of auditing logs. Both options **2** and **3** defers the logging refactor until we commence the Backing Services and Stateless processes refactoring. Be aware of option **2**, that the ephemeral disk of a container has limited disk space and may cause exceptions relating to out of disk space.

5. **Backing services**: Treat all output and input resource services as a dependent service to your application. Your application should be able to know the dependent services upfront and set up the necessary software dependencies/drivers to operate within your application. We'll learn more about services in the later chapters.

6. **Stateless processes**: With backing services ready, your application can easily connect to dependent services to ensure a stateless process. As mentioned, a stateless process should not retain state in the running application instance process. There should be no files written to or read from the local disk. Auditing logs should be stored in some database. Other stateful information, such as session cookies should be cached on some caching backing service such as Pivotal Cloud Cache, Redis, Couchbase, and so on.

7. **Configuration, credentials, and code**: This falls into the next phase, being Cloud Friendly, however, it is recommended that at least the credentials are not in the code and are not checked into a source code repository! You could either standup some secrets management tool as a backing service and read in the credentials, for example, using HashiCorp's Vault, or store encrypted credentials and utilize some external decryption service within your organization to get the credentials.

By this stage, your application should be able to operate at a minimum on the new Cloud Platform. You may wish to iterate through the steps above again to see if there are any additional refactors, to make your application *Cloud Ready* tight. The next stage is looking at more specific application modernization steps.

Modernizing the monolith

The approach of modernizing an application towards cloud-native maturity leads to an application that is highly scalable and resilient. We discussed how a cloud-native application could scale a component of an application rather than scaling the entire application. Consider the scenario where a search component, that represents 50 Megabytes of memory used, of a monolithic application that requires 1 Gigabyte of memory. The monolithic application then experiences double the load on the search component. Naturally, we would scale the instance by two, which would result in 2 Gigabytes of memory used in total. If we were to extract out the search component as a Microservice, we would be able to able to scale only the search component.

In an ideal world, ignoring potential memory setup overheads of a separate microservice application, it would mean that we would have had only increased the total application memory usage to 1.1 Gigabytes. That's a significant 45% saving of memory usage. There are, of course, costs associated with refactoring code, such as introducing new bugs. However, these can be mitigated with automated CI/CD pipelines and test-driven-development.

To modernize an existing monolithic application to be cloud-native, several techniques are available at hand. An in-depth discussion of these techniques deserves an entire book on its own, however, we shall discuss a common approach here.

The common approach to modernizing the monolith is as follows:

1. Stop adding any new features to the existing monolithic application.
2. Create all new features as microservices.
3. Add Anti-corruption layers between the monolithic application and new microservices.
4. Perform monolith strangling.

In general, the first and foremost step of application modernization is to stop adding new features into the monolithic application itself. New features should instead be developed as Microservices that will communicate with the monolith. The question arises, however, is how to enable the communication between a microservice to a monolithic application? The **anti-corruption layer** (ACL) pattern is an answer to this. The basic premise is that a monolith should look like an existing microservice to the new microservice. Next, when there are no new features to add, monolith strangling is employed to identify and extract existing code that can be refactored out of the monolith as a microservice. Naturally, we would then need to re-visit the ACL pattern to provide the communication between the monolith and the new microservice, and also remove any existing ACL's that are no longer required, that is, we extract a new microservice from the monolith that once had an ACL and is no longer needed now. This process continues until the monolith is fully decomposed or if there is of no further value to continue decomposition. *Figure 2*, presents a possible flow path for approaching application modernization:

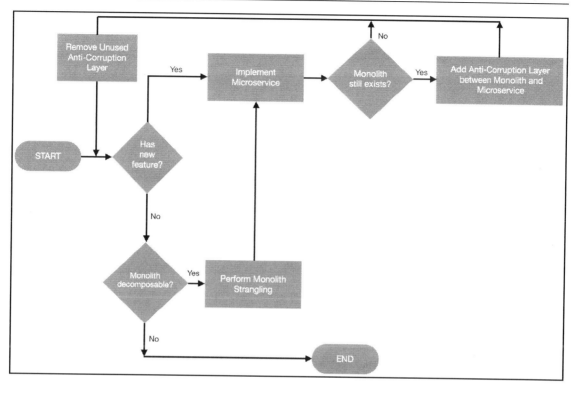

Figure 2: A flow path for application modernization

Anti-corruption layer

The **anti-corruption layer** (**ACL**) is a pattern from the book *Domain-Driven Design* by Eric Evans. The concept describes the situation when one has two systems that need to communicate with each other and that if they're incompatible, there needs to be a delegated layer of communication to ensure requests and responses are understood by both systems. The ACL consists of 3 components: a facade, an adapter, and a translator. The facade, as its name suggests, is a component facing or built into the monolith. The monolith uses this as a means of publishing its functionality. The adaptor component publishes service endpoints to the monolith to be available to external microservices.

The translator is a component that would act as a translation layer to convert request and response models between the monolith and the new Microservice. *Figure 3* describes this visually:

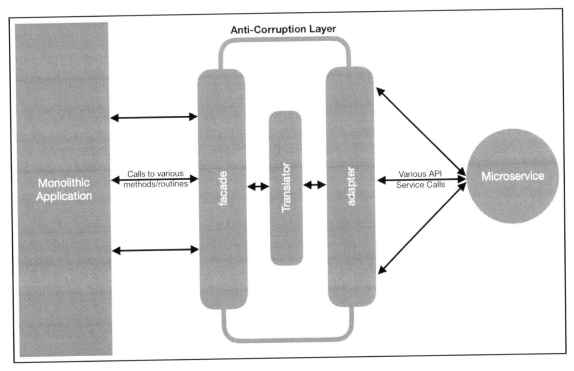

Figure 3: The anti-corruption layer pattern between a monolith and a microservice

Strangling the monolith

The process of strangling the monolith is to identify parts of the monolith that can be extracted as a microservice. Chapter 7, *Microservices and Worker Applications*, shall describe this in further detail in terms of defining a microservice. Once a candidate Microservice is identified, it is extracted as a new microservice and a new anti-corruption layer is introduced to provide communication with the monolith. *Figure 4* shows this in action:

In some literature, the monolith application is sometimes referred to as the *big ball of mud*.

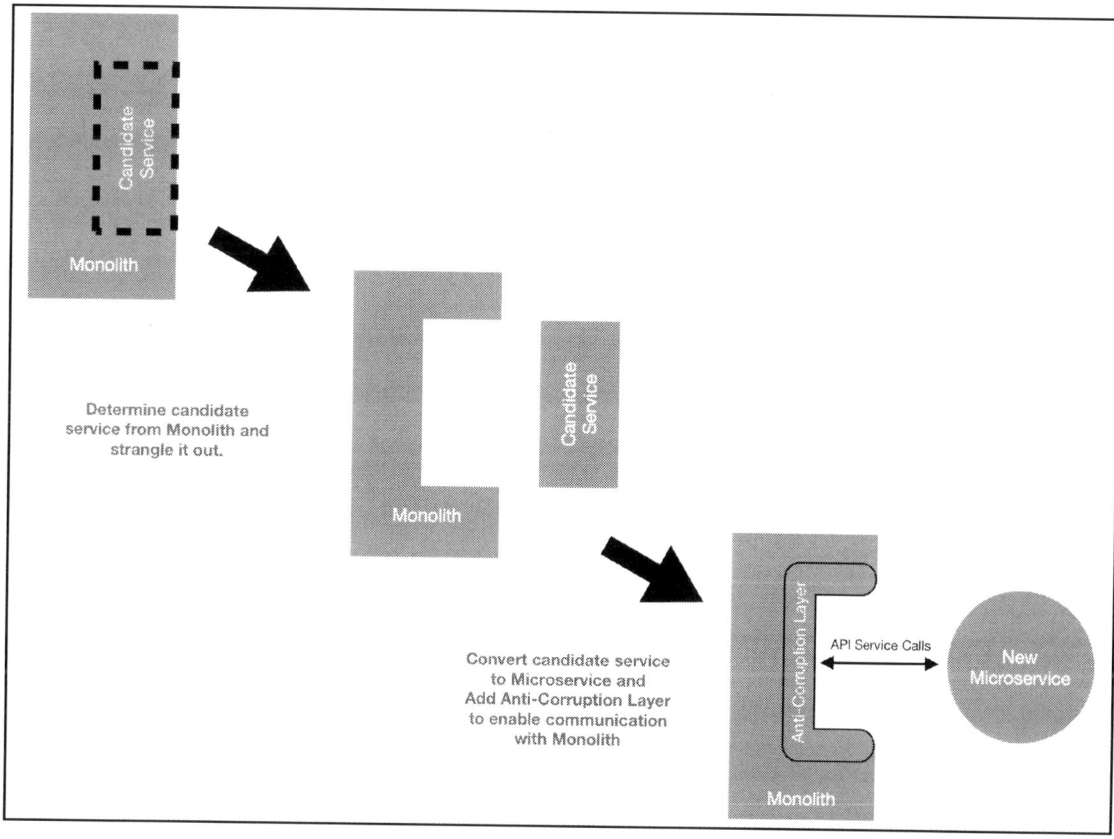

Figure 4: Strangling the monolith

How does one define what a candidate service is? A common approach is through understanding the business capabilities within an application to form bounded contexts, from which microservices are defined with a hard, contractual boundary to which it intercommunicates with the monolith and potentially other microservices. This candidate service should be isolated and not be sharing resource services, such as databases, between other microservices and the monolith. This is commonly known as domain-driven design and is well presented in the book, *Domain-Driven Design*, by Eric Evans, that assists in the determination of business capabilities in an application to be defined as services.

Application modernization and your organization

In order for a true realization of adopting cloud-native design and applying modernization to an application, a number of changes are required in an organization. The first, obvious one is through adopting CI/CD pipelines while the subsequent changes involve changing the organization itself.

In Dr. M. E. Conway's paper, entitled *How Do Committees Invent?*, published in 1967, an observation, informally described by Dr. Conway, the relation between organization's structure and the design of systems in that organization is discussed:

Any organization that designs a system (defined more broadly here than just information systems) will inevitably produce a design whose structure is a copy of the organization's communication structure.

Essentially, in the context of software development, the structure of an application usually follows an organization's structure. For example, enterprise IT has traditionally been organized into siloed structures such as software development, release management, IT operations, and systems administration. The outcome is such that personnel in each department are experts in their domain and have their own set of tools, vocabularies, communication styles and target performances, that is, they are siloed. Collaboration between these departments is usually sub-optimal due to their differences. In the context of an application, we see this reflected as database tier, MVC tier, service-engine tier, and so on. This inevitably leads to an application design whereby it is difficult to deploy some innovative change in one tier without affecting the others.

In a generic sense, the breaking down of silos, or desilofication, is an important, contributing step towards change in an organization. It is a process of breaking down barriers and encouraging communication between teams in an organization to share a wealth of culminated knowledge and skills, leading to an acceleration of innovation. One example of this is using shared knowledge and skills to solve problems. Consider a rather simplistic hypothetical scenario where a developer is building a critical software module to lock a door on a product. How does one determine that the software module reliably locks a chamber door to enable safe operation of a product? For software, this would work, but measuring and proving reliability over a longer term may be difficult, that is, it takes one bug to take out the entire reliability of the module.

Even worse, the failed software module reports that the door is locked, when it is still opened and the product continues to operate. This would present a hazardous situation for a user. One solution is to engage alongside a mechanical and electrical engineer to build a physical locking mechanism that could physically disconnect power when the door is open, of which the developer would work closely with to integrate software detection of the lock, for reporting purposes. The developer's work is simplified and they can now focus on other aspects of the software. Even if the software detection fails, the door is still physically locked and the product either operates or not. Of course, this may bring in new factors to consider, but the whole idea is that there is no silo between teams and a problem is quickly solved through collaboration, leading to a faster potential for delivery of the product to the market.

This is the idea leading to DevOps, to bring together a state of commonality of ideas, tools, vocabularies, communication styles and so on, which enable the common goal of delivering an outcome rapidly and safely.

This change is not simple alone and coming up with an organization structure up-front that works is usually difficult and can be costly. The solutions employed by organizations wishing to take on cloud-native architectures is to use the *Inverse Conway Maneuver* proposed by *Leroy* and *Simon* in 2010, in their article entitled *Dealing with creaky legacy platforms*, whereby rather than coming up with an organizations change upfront, determine an application architecture that works and change the organization around that. However, these changes may in fact even fall naturally into place for organizations adopting cloud-native design, so their culture is open to change and adopts a fail-fast approach to innovation. Essentially, an organization undergoing technology-driven change is driving their customer's preferences and behaviors. Ultimately, this will drive change to the organization itself or it will face the consequence that competing organizations will innovate faster and take the lead, as is well put in the *GE annual report* in 2000:

...when the rate of change inside an institution becomes slower than the rate of change outside, the end is in sight. The only question is when.

References

- Kevin Hoffman, *Beyond the Twelve-Factor App*, O'Reilly, 1st Ed., ISBN: 978-1-491-94401-1, Apr. 2016
- Matt Stine, *Migrating to Cloud-Native Application Architectures*, O'Reilly, 1st Ed., ISBN: 978-1-491-92679-6, Feb. 2015
- Duncan C. E. Winn, *Cloud Foundry*, O'Reilly, 1st Ed., ISBN: 978-1-491-94059-4, Jan. 2016
- Melvin E. Conway, *How Do Committees Invent?*, F.D. Thompson Publications, Datamation Magazine, 1968
- Jonny Leroy & Matt Simons, *Dealing with creaky legacy platforms*, Cutter IT Journal, Dec. 2010
- Jason Bloomberg, *DevOps Insight into Conway's Law*, Cortex Newsletter, 22 June 2015, Retrieved from `https://intellyx.com/2015/06/22/devops-insights-into-conways-law` on October 2017
- General Electric, GE Annual Report 2000, Relishing Change, Page 4, Retrieved from `https://www.ge.com/annual00/download/images/GEannual00.pdf` on October 2017
- Eric Evans, *Domain-Driven Design: Tackling complexity in the heart of software*, 17th print, ISBN:978-0-321-12521-7, June 2011

Summary

In this chapter, we discussed architecting and building apps for the cloud. In particular, we have learned about what is cloud-native application is and what the 16 guiding principles are that will lead us to a cloud-native application. More importantly, we looked at how we can migrate existing applications to the cloud, the cloud-native maturity model and the concept of application modernization, its techniques and how it affects your organization. In the next chapter, we'll look into how to deploy applications onto Cloud Foundry!

6
Deploying Apps to Cloud Foundry

In the last chapter, we had visited the concepts of architecting and building apps for Cloud. This chapter explores the deployment of apps onto Cloud Foundry. It will enable you to understand how to deploy applications and have them running on Cloud Foundry.

By the end of this chapter, you will know the following:

- What you will need before you push an application to Cloud Foundry
- What are buildpacks and how they are used during deployment
- What are services and how to create them
- How to deploy apps onto Cloud Foundry
- How to update a deployed application
- What happens when an app is deployed on Cloud Foundry
- How to scale applications
- How to access application logs
- Using Apps Manager

Pushing your first application to Cloud Foundry

In order to have applications running on Cloud Foundry, we must first be able to deploy them on Cloud Foundry. Colloquially, *push it to the cloud* is what you will hear and read to denote deploying the application to the cloud. The magic command to do this is:

```
cf push
```

That's it! There are of course a number of parameters that you will need, such as specifying the application name and perhaps other settings that may be needed for the application to run. However, before proceeding to push an application to Cloud Foundry, there are a number of prerequisites that must be fulfilled beforehand.

What you need before you push

The important minimum prerequisites before you push an application to Cloud Foundry are:

1. Ensure your application is supported by Cloud Foundry and/or has the necessary buildpack.
2. Ensure your application is *Cloud Ready*. While this is not strictly necessary, it will make starting development on the cloud easier by preventing occurrences of issues that would otherwise impede you.
3. If you do have any backing services that will be consumed by your application, ensure they are instantiated. You will learn more about this later in this chapter.
4. Enable debug output of your application, if you are still developing your application.
5. Exclude any extraneous files from the push that are not needed to run the application. Optionally, you should consider separating static assets as a separate app or retrievable as resource assets, if practical to do so.
6. You have the cf CLI installed and have initialized it to point to a target Cloud Foundry Controller, through `cf login` in the `pcfdev-org` using the *development* space.

We described the concept and suggested steps to achieve *Cloud Ready* in `Chapter 5`, *Architecting and Building Applications for the Cloud*. For completeness, we will summarize the minimum *Cloud Ready* steps here:

- **Stateless process**: No permanent disk access.
- **One codebase, one application**: There is only a single application that is being pushed. There should be no additional executable servers that run beforehand or startup scripts.
- **Port binding**: The application is port agnostic and receives it from Cloud Foundry.
- **Backing services**: The app treats and consumes all resources as a backing service.
- **Logging**: At the minimum, all error and event messages are output to `stdout` or `stderr`.
- **Dependency management**: All dependencies are included or listed for retrieval through Maven/Gradle/Nuget (as is supported by a buildpack).

Services

In `Chapter 5`, *Architecting and Building Applications for the Cloud*, one of the necessary requirements for achieving *Cloud Ready* applications were backing services. A backing service, or service for short, is quite simply any networked service that an application will consume. For example, *MySQL, SQL Server*, and *S3 Blob* stores for *DataStores, RabbitMQ* for messaging and emailing services. Note that when we say service, it corresponds to a *blueprint* of that service. In order for applications to use the service, we must create an instance of the service, or what we call a service instance. Once these service instances are created, an application instance can use these once they are bounded.

That is, these services are actually accessed by application code through some URL or some other form of a locator that potentially require credentials, that is, this could be some form of connection string. When this happens, we say that *an application is now bounded to a service instance*. For the following examples, it is assumed that you are using PCF Dev and it is using the admin user. In a real-world scenario, not all users, and some Orgs themselves, have permissions to create and bind services.

Ideally, your application should be able to connect to one of these types of services and just use it as is. A key concept for service abstraction for your application is for it to know the service as *what it actually does* rather than know *what it is*. For example, your application requires a database to write to. It would be great if it knew it only had to deal with writing and reading data from a database, rather than the implementation intricacies of dealing with a MySQL or an SQL Server. That way, you could just swap between the two if you really needed to (just keep in mind about *Principle 9*: *Environment Parity*, don't do this between development and production environment). A tool for this is an **Object-Relational Mapping (ORM)** Framework, such as *Hibernate* and *EntityFramework*, which could read the database connection information from a bound database backing service and consume the database if it is supported.

In this section, we'll cover questions such as *How do I know what backing services are available for me to use*? *How do I create one of these services and bind it to my application*?

Listing the available services to create

There are two ways we can source a service. One is from what we call the *marketplace* and another is through a *user-provided service*. The marketplace is simply a listing of available services on your foundation and to your Org, and may hold services with plans that are free of charge on your platform or it can hold services published by some service provider, which may have an associated subscription cost for each given plan. The services listed in the marketplace are implemented through the Service Broker API, so you can also create your own custom services if need be. The user-provided service is simply a user service that provides the binding connection configuration to your service that is external to Cloud Foundry. You'll learn more about services, user-provided services and the service brokers in Chapter 8, *Services and Service Brokers*.

The command `cf marketplace` will list out the available services on your foundation.

The cf CLI has some shorthand commands. The marketplace is one such command with a shorthand. Try typing and executing `cf m`.

```
[~ >>> cf marketplace
Getting services from marketplace in org pcfdev-org / space development as user...
OK

service      plans             description
local-volume free-local-disk   Local service docs: https://github.com/cloudfoundry-incubator/local-volume-release/
p-mysql      512mb, 1gb        MySQL databases on demand
p-rabbitmq   standard          RabbitMQ is a robust and scalable high-performance multi-protocol messaging broker.
p-redis      shared-vm         Redis service to provide a key-value store

TIP:  Use 'cf marketplace -s SERVICE' to view descriptions of individual plans of a given service.
~ >>>
```

Figure 5: A list of available services on our foundation when running the command cf marketplace

Figure 5 shows the output of the available services after we run the marketplace command. Column-wise, from left to right, we see the service name, the service plans, and the description of the service. In this case, on our PCF Dev environment, we see the local volume for local disk access (PCF Dev only!), `p-mysql` for MySQL database, `p-rabbitmq` for RabbitMQ messaging service, and `p-redis` for key-value caching. The associated plans show the available capacity or service level agreements that a service can provide. Depending on the service provider, some of these plans may incur a cost.

Creating a service

Before proceeding with the foll, ensure that you have the permissions to create and bind services. For the following examples, also check that you are logged in as an *admin* user on PCF Dev. Otherwise, you will receive a `You are not authorized to perform the requested action` error message.

To create a service, run the `cf create-service <SERVICE_NAME> <PLAN> <INSTANCE_NAME>` command. Here, SERVICE_NAME and PLAN refer to the service name and plan names found in the list from the marketplace, respectively. The INSTANCE_NAME is the name of the instantiated service. You will need this instance name later in order to bind this service to an application. Note that you can also use the shorthand, `cf cs`.

So, let's instantiate a MySQL database with on a 1 GB capacity plan and call this `my-database-service`. The command to do this would be:

```
cf create-service p-mysql 1gb my-database-service
```

```
[~ >>> cf create-service p-mysql 1gb my-database-service
Creating service instance my-database-service in org pcfdev-org / space development as admin...
OK
~ >>>
```

Figure 2: The result of executing the cf create-service command to instantiate a MySQL 1 GB database plan called my-database-service

To see the status of the service and to see a list of instantiated services, we can perform the following command:

```
cf services
```

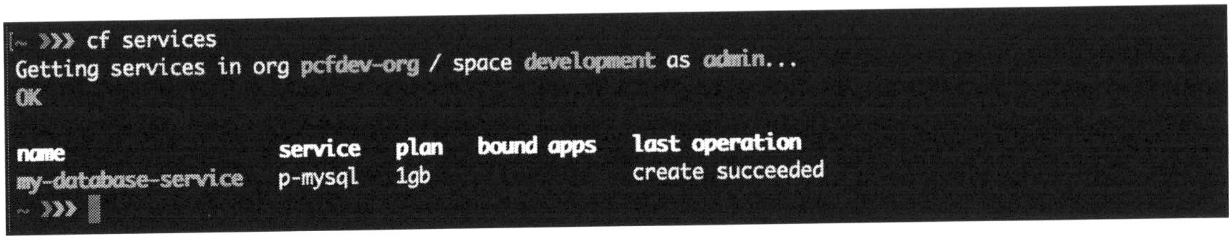

Figure 3: The result of executing the cf services command to list the instantiated services

Figure 3 shows the output of the command. We can see that our service, `my-database-service`, has been instantiated with the status `create succeeded`. It is possible for other services to take longer to instantiate. This would show the last operation to be in a pending state. At the moment, there is nothing listed under `bound apps` because we have not performed binding of the database service to our application.

To see more details about our instantiated service, we can run the following command:

```
cf service my-database-service
```

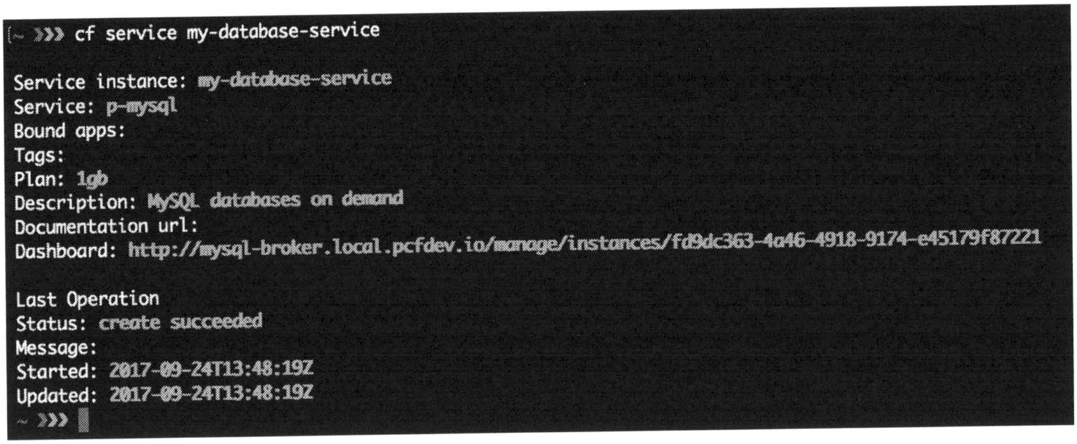

Figure 4: Retrieving more information about the instantiated my-database-service

To bind `my-database-service` to an application, we need only to run:
`cf bind-service <APP_NAME> <SERVICE_INSTANCE_NAME>`.

This will bind an application named `APP_NAME` to a service named `SERVICE_INSTANCE_NAME`. Alternatively, this can be specified in a CF Push manifest file, which we will cover later in this chapter.

 Although our command example shows how to bind to a single application, it is possible to bind to many applications within the same Org or same Space. You will learn later in this book that a service instance scope is within an Org or in some instances, depending on the service broker registration, restricted to space. Again, we'll discuss more on service brokers later in this book.

Of course, at the moment, we don't have an application deployed on Cloud Foundry yet. So, let's jump on to the next section to start pushing an application to Cloud Foundry.

 You will learn later, that, after the process of binding a service to an application, a **JSON** environment variable will be updated with an entry called `VCAP_SERVICES`, containing the service configuration and potentially random credentials. These credentials and configuration do change and are not guaranteed to be always the same for each bind. This JSON environment variable is specific to each application and also contains another section called `VCAP_APPLICATION`, which contains application information. It is from this environment variable data structure that the application reads in its' configuration. You can see this environment variable with the command `cf env <APP_NAME>`.

Buildpacks

In order to deploy and successfully run an application on Cloud Foundry, a buildpack is required to ensure that the necessary runtime support for your application is set up, along with your application during the push. Essentially, a buildpack consists of a set of tools, potential runtime components, and scripts that are programmed to retrieve dependencies required by the application for a given language; move the compiled output to some run location, compile the code, and/or configure the application for running in the container.

From a developer's perspective, a buildpack brings out the polyglot benefits of Cloud Foundry. It enables the development of applications using different supporting types of languages with consistent versioned dependencies. From a platform team's perspective, all dependencies are consistent throughout all environments, such as development and production. There is no need to snowflake dependency and framework setup for different development teams.

To get a list of buildpacks currently installed on your target Cloud Foundry Foundation, type `cf buildpacks`:

```
~ >>> cf buildpacks
Getting buildpacks...

buildpack             position   enabled   locked   filename
java_buildpack        1          true      false    java-buildpack-offline-v3.13.zip
ruby_buildpack        2          true      false    ruby_buildpack-cached-v1.6.37.zip
nodejs_buildpack      3          true      false    nodejs_buildpack-cached-v1.5.32.zip
go_buildpack          4          true      false    go_buildpack-cached-v1.8.1.zip
python_buildpack      5          true      false    python_buildpack-cached-v1.5.18.zip
php_buildpack         6          true      false    php_buildpack-cached-v4.3.31.zip
staticfile_buildpack  7          true      false    staticfile_buildpack-cached-v1.4.5.zip
binary_buildpack      8          true      false    binary_buildpack-cached-v1.0.11.zip
dotnet-core_buildpack 9          true      false    dotnet-core_buildpack-cached-v1.0.15.zip
~ >>>
```

Figure 5: Typing cf buildpacks will retrieve a list of buildpacks currently installed on your Cloud Foundry Foundation

An installed Cloud Foundry platform is commonly referred to as a *foundation*. Usage: **Q:** *How many foundations do you have?* **R:** I have 500 foundations. [Naturally, the asker will respond in shock or skepticism].

You will learn more about installing additional buildpacks, creating buildpacks, and other various advanced topics dealing with buildpacks later in this book. For now, the most important part of this chapter is how to do we use the buildpack with our push command. Well, generally we don't, because it should just work! The `cf push` command will automatically detect the application type and associate the correct buildpack with it. Each buildpack has a detection script that will determine the whether the buildpack is compatible to use with the application through the presence of some application files. For example, the HWC .NET framework buildpack will be used when there is a presence of a `Web.config` file.

While `cf push` does the buildpack detection automatically, we can speed up the push process by specifying the buildpack we want to use with the `cf push` command through the −b parameter. This will force skip the detection process. To use the −b parameter, type the following command: `cf push myapp −b binary_buildpack`. The buildpack name used with the −b command is the same name as those listed using the `cf buildpacks` command. Alternatively, instead of specifying the buildpack name, a URI (Uniform Resource Identifier) can be used instead. For example, `cf push myapp −b https://github.com/cloudfoundry/binary-buildpack` specifies that `myapp` will use the binary buildpack downloaded from the specified Github URL.

Deploying your first app onto cf using the cf CLI

We discussed buildpacks and services. We instantiated a service to use, but we need to bind it to an application that is deployed on Cloud Foundry first in order to use it. This section will now show you how to deploy the application. For demonstration purposes, this section will use the Hello Spring Cloud sample application. The *Hello Spring Cloud* is a simple *Java* web API application that uses the *Spring Cloud Connectors* library in order to inspect the bounded services and display their connection status.

To deploy our first sample application, do the following steps:

1. This project requires *Maven*, a tool for building and managing *Java* projects. If not done so already, download *Maven* from: `https://maven.apache.org` and follow the installation instructions on the site.

2. Download or git clone the Hello Spring Cloud repository at `https://github.com/Cloud-Foundry-For-Developers/hello-spring-cloud.git`.

3. If the sample application was downloaded, extract the contents of the ZIP file to a directory.

4. Change into the `Hello Spring Cloud` directory and run `mvn clean package` to build the application.

5. Type and execute `cf push`.

```
~/hello-spring-cloud >>> cf push
Using manifest file /Users/damu/hello-spring-cloud/manifest.yml

Creating app hello-spring-cloud in org pcfdev-org / space development as admin...
OK

Creating route hello-spring-cloud-calisthenical-padeye.local.pcfdev.io...
OK

Binding hello-spring-cloud-calisthenical-padeye.local.pcfdev.io to hello-spring-cloud...
OK

Uploading hello-spring-cloud...
Uploading app files from: /var/folders/45/n3wsmxkj61n4vssl53q3lr7h0000gn/T/unzipped-app185161434
Uploading 24M, 137 files
Done uploading
OK

Starting app hello-spring-cloud in org pcfdev-org / space development as admin...
Downloading ruby_buildpack...
Downloading dotnet-core_buildpack...
Downloading java_buildpack...
Downloading go_buildpack...
Downloading python_buildpack...
Downloaded python_buildpack
Downloading php_buildpack...
Downloaded java_buildpack
Downloaded ruby_buildpack
Downloading staticfile_buildpack...
Downloading binary_buildpack...
Downloaded dotnet-core_buildpack
Downloaded go_buildpack
Downloading nodejs_buildpack...
Downloaded php_buildpack
Downloaded binary_buildpack
Downloaded nodejs_buildpack
Downloaded staticfile_buildpack
Creating container
Successfully created container
Downloading app package...
Downloaded app package (30.7M)
Staging...
-----> Java Buildpack Version: v3.13 (offline) | https://github.com/cloudfoundry/java-buildpack.git#03b493f
-----> Downloading Open Jdk JRE 1.8.0_121 from https://java-buildpack.cloudfoundry.org/openjdk/trusty/x86_64/openjdk-1.8.0_121.tar.gz
       (found in cache)
       Expanding Open Jdk JRE to .java-buildpack/open_jdk_jre (1.3s)
-----> Downloading Open JDK Like Memory Calculator 2.0.2_RELEASE from https://java-buildpack.cloudfoundry.org/memory-calculator/trusty
       /x86_64/memory-calculator-2.0.2_RELEASE.tar.gz (found in cache)
       Memory Settings: -Xss349K -XX:MetaspaceSize=104857K -Xms681574K -Xmx681574K -XX:MaxMetaspaceSize=104857K
-----> Downloading Container Certificate Trust Store 2.0.0_RELEASE from https://java-buildpack.cloudfoundry.org/container-certificate-
       trust-store/container-certificate-trust-store-2.0.0_RELEASE.jar (found in cache)
       Adding certificates to .java-buildpack/container_certificate_trust_store/truststore.jks (0.3s)
-----> Downloading Spring Auto Reconfiguration 1.10.0_RELEASE from https://java-buildpack.cloudfoundry.org/auto-reconfiguration/auto-r
       econfiguration-1.10.0_RELEASE.jar (found in cache)
Exit status 0
Staging complete
Uploading droplet, build artifacts cache...
Uploading droplet...
Uploading build artifacts cache...
Uploaded build artifacts cache (108B)
Uploaded droplet (76.1M)
Uploading complete
Destroying container
Successfully destroyed container

0 of 1 instances running, 1 starting
1 of 1 instances running

App started


OK

App hello-spring-cloud was started using this command `CALCULATED_MEMORY=$($PWD/.java-buildpack/open_jdk_jre/bin/java-buildpack-memory
-calculator-2.0.2_RELEASE -memorySizes=metaspace:64m..,stack:228k.. -memoryWeights=heap:65,metaspace:10,native:15,stack:10 -memoryInit
ials=heap:100%,metaspace:100% -stackThreads=300 -totMemory=$MEMORY_LIMIT) && JAVA_OPTS="-Djava.io.tmpdir=$TMPDIR -XX:OnOutOfMemoryErro
r=$PWD/.java-buildpack/open_jdk_jre/bin/killjava.sh $CALCULATED_MEMORY -Djavax.net.ssl.trustStore=$PWD/.java-buildpack/container_certi
ficate_trust_store/truststore.jks -Djavax.net.ssl.trustStorePassword=java-buildpack-trust-store-password" && SERVER_PORT=$PORT eval ex
ec $PWD/.java-buildpack/open_jdk_jre/bin/java $JAVA_OPTS -cp $PWD/. org.springframework.boot.loader.JarLauncher`

Showing health and status for app hello-spring-cloud in org pcfdev-org / space development as admin...
OK

requested state: started
instances: 1/1
usage: 256M x 1 instances
urls: hello-spring-cloud-calisthenical-padeye.local.pcfdev.io
last uploaded: Sun Sep 24 16:41:29 UTC 2017
stack: cflinuxfs2
buildpack: container-certificate-trust-store-2.0.0_RELEASE java-buildpack=v3.13-offline-https://github.com/cloudfoundry/java-buildpack
.git#03b493f java-main open-jdk-like-jre=1.8.0_121 open-jdk-like-memory-calculator=2.0.2_RELEASE spring-auto-reconfiguration=1.10...

     state     since                cpu    memory          disk           details
#0   running   2017-09-24 11:42:04 AM  0.0%  229.3M of 256M  157M of 512M
~/hello-spring-cloud >>>
```

Figure 6: Performing cf push on the Hello Spring Cloud application

Congratulations! You have just pushed your first application to Cloud Foundry! *Figure 6* shows the output of executing `cf push` on the *Hello Spring Cloud* project. We'll go through this in further detail later in this chapter. But for now, let's run the application and see it in action. Simply copy the URL and paste it into a browser address bar. The URL in *Figure 6* is `hello-spring-cloud-calisthenical-padeye.local.pcfdev.io`, but you may have a different URL:

Figure 7: Output of the Hello Spring Cloud application without any bound services

Figure 7 shows the output of the Hello Spring Cloud application. What's with all the bad URL and invalid address messages, you might be asking? This error is due to the fact that we haven't bound any services to our application. We'll get this fixed soon. First, let's discuss whats happening during an application deployment.

Applications versus application instances

Be careful how these are used. Right now, we've talked about deploying an application. An application in Cloud Foundry here describes the actual application that was deployed on Cloud Foundry. An application instance is an instantiation of the application. It means an application can have multiple application instances running. This is similar to the previous discussion on services and service instances. This is an important differentiator once we start looking into scaling applications.

The phases of application deployment

From *figure 6*, we can see a number of things are happening during an application deployment. We can separate this into several phases:

1. **Manifest read**: This phase reads in a YAML configuration file that contains the cf push parameters. By default, the file is called `manifest.yml` and is included in the same location as your application source. Using a manifest file is optional. Without it, you will need to perform cf push with the application name and any other parameters on the CLI. If the YAML file does not exist, this step is skipped during the deployment process.

2. **Application entry creation**: This phase creates an application record for the given Org and Space for the given current user. At this stage, metadata is also stored. The metadata here contains parameters relating to the memory and disk size, application instance count and a specific buildpack, if it was input.

3. **Route creation**: This phase creates a URL route to your application. The route is optional and can be skipped if your application does not require a route.

4. **Route mapping**: After creating a route, it is mapped to your application.

5. **Application file upload**: The application files are now uploaded. For new deployments, all files specified for deployment are uploaded. Subsequent deployments, for example, you modify the application and rebuild and re-push will perform a hashing process that enables the deployment process to perform a differencing comparison. Only files that differ will be uploaded.

6. **Buildpack detection**: After the application files are uploaded, the buildpack detection process is performed. This means that all buildpacks available on your platform are downloaded and compared against the application files to determine the best fit buildpack to use. This can be skipped by implicitly declaring the buildpack you wish to use before performing a push.

7. **Staging**: Using the input buildpack, all dependencies are pulled/pooled and applications maybe built with a given stack to produce a droplet.

8. **Droplet upload**: The droplet is now stored into an internal blobstore.
9. **Application launch**: The application is launched by submitting it to an internal bulletin board system that starts a bidding process in Diego that queries and receives a response for the next candidate Diego cell that is ready to run the application.

 Diego is the heart of Cloud Foundry that performs the orchestration of containers. A Diego cell is a type of virtual machine having an operating system, such as Linux.

The Droplet

Later in this book, you will learn in-depth about buildpacks, but for now, we'll brieflydiscuss the process. Once an appropriate buildpack is associated with the application, it proceeds to package the buildpack, with the application source or binary on a target stack. A stack is a prebuilt root filesystem for a targeted supported OS. In this book, the stack is `cflinuxfs2`. For Windows, this will be `Windows2012R2` or the upcoming `Windows2016`. This package is stored as an intermediate tarball droplet and a request to a Diego cell is made to start a container to begin a staging process. The staging process takes in the intermediate droplet and runs a number of buildpack scripts that would pull in the dependencies, the runtime framework, and may compile the application to produce an executable. The stack remains, alongside with the application executable dependencies frameworks and is re-packaged into a final droplet. This droplet is stored/cached internally on Cloud Foundry and is copied out to be used by Diego Cells for each launch of an instance of an application.

Re-deploying the application

To re-deploy an application, after some modifications, simply execute `cf push` and that's it! You will notice that the push process may be slightly faster as most of the application has already been created and won't need to be re-created.

 You will learn that there are some things that are retained when you re-deploy an application. In particular, if a specified start command is used with cf push, for example, `cf push -c ".\application"`, this won't change after successive calls to cf push! You will need to call `cf push -c "null"` to clear this start command or delete the application and re-deploy.

To make things interesting, it is also possible to re-deploy an application onto Cloud Foundry with a different name. Simply call `cf push <NEW_APP_NAME>`. This is very useful in instances where you may wish to test some modification of code and compare that with a previous version. This also gives rise to the possibility of performing green-blue deployments in an automated deployment pipeline. We'll learn more about green-blue deployments later in this book in `Chapter 11`, *Continuous Integration and Continuous Deployment*.

Binding a service to the application

So, let's now bind our service, `my-database-service`, from the previous section and see what happens. Run the command, as follows:

```
cf bind-service hello-spring-cloud my-database-service
```

```
~ >>> cf bind-service hello-spring-cloud my-database-service
Binding service my-database-service to app hello-spring-cloud in org pcfdev-org / space development as admin...
OK
TIP: Use 'cf restage hello-spring-cloud' to ensure your env variable changes take effect
~ >>>
```

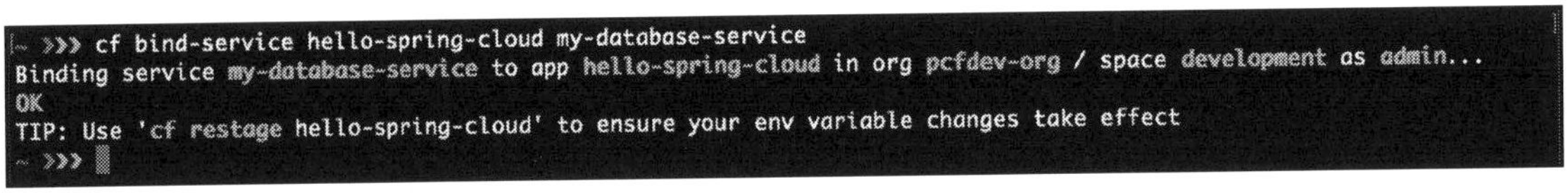

Figure 8: The result of performing servicing binding between the Hello Spring Cloud application and the my-database-service

This command will bind the service, named `my-database-service`, that we created earlier to our application named `hello-spring-cloud`. If we refreshed our browser for the same application page, you might be surprised to find that it would show up to be the same *Figure 7*. This is because we performed the connection; however, the application itself has not read in the new bounded service information and instantiated the necessary objects to perform the read. To resolve this, we need only to call `cf restart hello-spring-cloud` to relaunch the application on Cloud Foundry.

```
[~ >>> cf restart hello-spring-cloud
Stopping app hello-spring-cloud in org pcfdev-org / space development as admin...
OK

Starting app hello-spring-cloud in org pcfdev-org / space development as admin...

0 of 1 instances running, 1 starting
0 of 1 instances running, 1 starting
0 of 1 instances running, 1 starting
1 of 1 instances running

App started


OK

App hello-spring-cloud was started using this command `CALCULATED_MEMORY=$($PWD/.java-buildpack/open_jd
k_jre/bin/java-buildpack-memory-calculator-2.0.2_RELEASE -memorySizes=metaspace:64m..,stack:228k.. -mem
oryWeights=heap:65,metaspace:10,native:15,stack:10 -memoryInitials=heap:100%,metaspace:100% -stackThrea
ds=300 -totMemory=$MEMORY_LIMIT) && JAVA_OPTS="-Djava.io.tmpdir=$TMPDIR -XX:OnOutOfMemoryError=$PWD/.ja
va-buildpack/open_jdk_jre/bin/killjava.sh $CALCULATED_MEMORY -Djavax.net.ssl.trustStore=$PWD/.java-buil
dpack/container_certificate_trust_store/truststore.jks -Djavax.net.ssl.trustStorePassword=java-buildpac
k-trust-store-password" && SERVER_PORT=$PORT eval exec $PWD/.java-buildpack/open_jdk_jre/bin/java $JAVA
_OPTS -cp $PWD/. org.springframework.boot.loader.JarLauncher`

Showing health and status for app hello-spring-cloud in org pcfdev-org / space development as admin...
OK

requested state: started
instances: 1/1
usage: 256M x 1 instances
urls: hello-spring-cloud-calisthenical-padeye.local.pcfdev.io
last uploaded: Sun Sep 24 16:41:29 UTC 2017
stack: cflinuxfs2
buildpack: container-certificate-trust-store=2.0.0_RELEASE java-buildpack=v3.13-offline-https://github.
com/cloudfoundry/java-buildpack.git#03b493f java-main open-jdk-like-jre=1.8.0_121 open-jdk-like-memory-
calculator=2.0.2_RELEASE spring-auto-reconfiguration=1.10...

     state     since                     cpu     memory            disk             details
#0   running   2017-09-24 05:10:46 PM    0.0%    225.4M of 256M    157M of 512M
~ >>>
```

Figure 9: The result of executing cf restart on Hello Spring Cloud App after binding a service

The *Figure 9* shows that the application was successfully restarted after binding `my-database-service`. Go back to the browser and reload the application page:

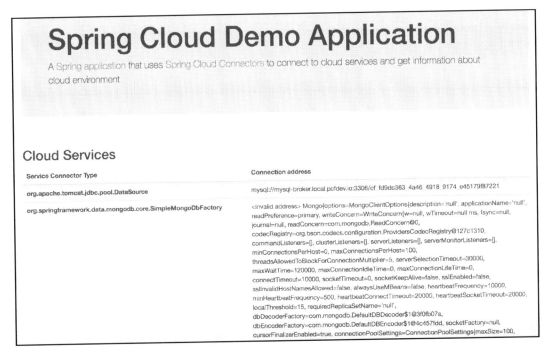

Figure 10: The output of the Hello Spring Cloud application after binding it with the my-database-service

Notice in *Figure 10* that the connector type `org.apache.tomcat.jdbc.pool.DataSource` is now populated with the resultant entry `mysql://mysql-broker.local.pcfdev.io:3306/cf_fd9dc363_4a46_4918_9174_e45179f87221`, instead of `<bad url>` as seen in *Figure 7*. This visually shows that our service was successfully bounded and detected by the application, thanks to the *Spring Cloud Connector*.

Restaging applications versus restarting applications

By now, you will have wondered why we used `cf restart` instead of `cf restage` as advised in *Figure 8*.

`cf restart` will request a **Diego cell** to take a compiled droplet, unpack it, and run it in a container. A restart is only necessary when an application needs to re-run to take in the new configuration and it should be used in situations where a service is bounded to an application for the first time, or if there is an update to the `cf env` environment variable.

Running `cf restage` will request a Diego cell to recompile the droplet as discussed previously, unpack it and run it in a container. A restage is used when there are environment variable changes in the staging of the application on Cloud Foundry. For example, changing environment variables that affects a Buildpack. The Java buildpack has an environment variable, `JBP_CONFIG_OPEN_JDK_JRE`, that can be used to change the jvm memory. Changing the memory setting and performing a `cf restart` will not take in the change, because it uses a droplet that already has the previous environment variable settings for `JBP_CONFIG_OPEN_JDK_JRE`. A restage is in order to re-compile the droplet with a buildpack that takes in the new changes.

Manifest files

Manifest files are optional push configuration files. It simplifies the process of pushing an application to Cloud Foundry by placing all of the push settings in a file, which would otherwise require a user to input through command line arguments. By default, `cf push` will automatically look for a file called `manifest.yml` located in the same directory as the application files. If you have a different YAML file, this can be overridden using `cf push -f <path-to-manifest-file>`. Alternatively, the manifest file can be ignored by running `cf push <APP_NAME> [<PARAM1>...<PARAMn>] --no-manifest`. By ignoring the manifest file, it would mean that all push parameters must be specified! An important concept to note is that **the command line arguments always take precedence over the manifest file**. For example, calling `cf push -i 2`, will force the push process to ignore the number of instances specified in the manifest and instead create two instances.

Let's look inside the `hello-spring-cloud` application manifest:

```
~/hello-spring-cloud >>> cat manifest.yml
---
applications:
- name: hello-spring-cloud
  instances: 1
  host: hello-spring-cloud-${random-word}
  path: target/hello-spring-cloud-0.0.1.BUILD-SNAPSHOT.jar
~/hello-spring-cloud >>> █
```

Figure 11: The content of the manifest.yml for the Hello-Spring-Cloud application

The first line `---` signifies the beginning of a YAML file. The keyword `applications` is an attribute to represent the set of applications to be pushed. It is, therefore, possible to have multiple applications specified in one manifest file to be pushed. The next keyword, `- name`, is the name of the application on Cloud Foundry. The keyword, `instances`, signify the number of instances to be vertically scaled to on this application. The `host: hello-spring-cloud-${random-word}`, represents the route hostname to be used. Note that there is a `${random-word}`, which basically will append some random words to the route URL. Finally, a `path` is the attribute to tell `cf push` where on the local disk, the files are to be deployed on Cloud Foundry. A number of other attributes can be found at: `https://docs.cloudfoundry.org/devguide/deploy-apps/manifest.html`. One particular attribute of interest not in *Figure 11* is the services attribute. This attribute enables the association of applications to one or many existing service instances as required. The only requirement is that the services are instantiated first.

From an organization's perspective, the push process can be standardized by manifest files, which would fit nicely into automated CI/CD pipelines. For development purposes, these manifests can be overridden through the command line.

Monitoring and managing the applications

So far, we deployed our application onto Cloud Foundry. However, the next steps will involve steps on how we can manage and monitor our applications. This can be done in two ways, either through Apps Manager or through the cf CLI. You've already learned how to log on to Apps Manager to create Orgs, Spaces, and add users. With Apps Manager, you are also able to monitor and manage applications as well. We'll explore how to do that in this section. For possible scripting purposes, you may also take the cf CLI route to create, manage, and monitor your application.

Monitoring and managing the application using cf CLI

Using the cf CLI is just as easy as using Apps Manager. This section will show you how key cf CLI commands are used to manage and monitor your application on Cloud Foundry. We'll split this section into two parts. The first is the monitoring of applications and the second is the management of applications.

Monitoring your application

In monitoring our applications, we like to see a snapshot health and status of our applications and also potentially dive deeper to see and debug our application output. There are two parts to monitoring your application. The first is seeing the application status and the second is using logs. With these tools, it is possible for a developer to easily determine applications that are failing or have the potential to fail. In addition, the log feature assists developers to evaluate and debug applications. This is valuable to an organization because developers no longer need to request to access logs and monitoring information. The whole platform, once configured, can be securely self-serviced, which enables rapid development of applications.

Listing all of the applications in a space

First, let's find our application. Run the command `cf apps`:

```
~/hello-spring-cloud >>> cf apps
Getting apps in org pcfdev-org / space development as admin...
OK

name               requested state   instances   memory   disk   urls
hello-spring-cloud started           2/2         512M     512M   hello-spring-cloud-calisthenical-padeye.local.pcfdev.io
~/hello-spring-cloud >>>
```

Figure 12: cf apps will assist in listing all applications that are deployed on your foundation

As in *Figure 12*, we see the `hello-spring-cloud` application has two instances and 512 Megabytes of memory, as we had scaled this in the last section.

Getting the health and status of your application

To see the health and status of our application, run the command `cf app hello-spring-cloud`:

```
~/hello-spring-cloud >>> cf app hello-spring-cloud
Showing health and status for app hello-spring-cloud in org pcfdev-org / space development as admin...
OK

requested state: started
instances: 2/2
usage: 512M x 2 instances
urls: hello-spring-cloud-calisthenical-padeye.local.pcfdev.io
last uploaded: Mon Sep 25 16:12:39 UTC 2017
stack: cflinuxfs2
buildpack: container-certificate-trust-store=2.0.0_RELEASE java-buildpack=v3.13-offline-https://github.com/cloudfoundry/java-buildpack.git#
03b493f java-main open-jdk-like-jre=1.8.0_121 open-jdk-like-memory-calculator=2.0.2_RELEASE spring-auto-reconfiguration=1.10...

     state     since                   cpu    memory          disk          details
#0   running   2017-09-25 11:13:21 AM  0.3%   303.6M of 512M  157M of 512M
#1   running   2017-09-25 11:13:24 AM  0.3%   304.9M of 512M  157M of 512M
~/hello-spring-cloud >>>
```

Figure 13: cf app hello-spring-cloud shows the current health and status of our application

The health and status output give more details about our application. In particular, the buildpack information, the status and resource usage of each application instance.

Viewing application logs

The next part of monitoring our application is viewing the logs of our application. Run `cf logs hello-spring-cloud --recent`:

```
~/hello-spring-cloud >>> cf logs hello-spring-cloud --recent
Connected, dumping recent logs for app hello-spring-cloud in org pcfdev-org / space development as admin...

2017-09-25T11:13:23.04-0500 [APP/PROC/WEB/1]OUT       - @ConditionalOnMissingBean (types: org.springframework.boot.web.client.RestTemplateB
uilder; SearchStrategy: all) did not find any beans (OnBeanCondition)
2017-09-25T11:13:23.04-0500 [APP/PROC/WEB/1]OUT    WebMvcAutoConfiguration matched:
2017-09-25T11:13:23.04-0500 [APP/PROC/WEB/1]OUT    WebMvcAutoConfiguration#hiddenHttpMethodFilter matched:
2017-09-25T11:13:23.04-0500 [APP/PROC/WEB/1]OUT       - @ConditionalOnMissingBean (types: org.springframework.web.filter.HiddenHttpMethodFi
lter; SearchStrategy: all) did not find any beans (OnBeanCondition)
2017-09-25T11:13:23.04-0500 [APP/PROC/WEB/1]OUT       - @ConditionalOnProperty (spring.mvc.formcontent.putfilter.enabled) matched (OnProper
tyCondition)
2017-09-25T11:13:23.04-0500 [APP/PROC/WEB/1]OUT       - @ConditionalOnMissingBean (types: org.springframework.web.filter.HttpPutFormContent
Filter; SearchStrategy: all) did not find any beans (OnBeanCondition)
2017-09-25T11:13:23.04-0500 [APP/PROC/WEB/1]OUT    WebMvcAutoConfiguration.WebMvcAutoConfigurationAdapter#defaultViewResolver matched:
2017-09-25T11:13:23.04-0500 [APP/PROC/WEB/1]OUT       - @ConditionalOnMissingBean (types: org.springframework.web.servlet.view.InternalReso
urceViewResolver; SearchStrategy: all) did not find any beans (OnBeanCondition)
2017-09-25T11:13:23.04-0500 [APP/PROC/WEB/1]OUT    WebMvcAutoConfiguration.WebMvcAutoConfigurationAdapter#requestContextFilter matched:
2017-09-25T11:13:23.04-0500 [APP/PROC/WEB/1]OUT    WebMvcAutoConfiguration.WebMvcAutoConfigurationAdapter#viewResolver matched:
2017-09-25T11:13:23.04-0500 [APP/PROC/WEB/1]OUT    WebMvcAutoConfiguration.WebMvcAutoConfigurationAdapter.FaviconConfiguration matched:
2017-09-25T11:13:23.05-0500 [APP/PROC/WEB/1]OUT    SecurityFilterAutoConfiguration:
2017-09-25T11:13:23.05-0500 [APP/PROC/WEB/1]OUT       Did not match:
2017-09-25T11:13:23.05-0500 [APP/PROC/WEB/1]OUT          - @ConditionalOnClass did not find required classes 'org.springframework.security.
web.context.AbstractSecurityWebApplicationInitializer', 'org.springframework.security.config.http.SessionCreationPolicy' (OnClassCondition)
2017-09-25T11:13:23.05-0500 [APP/PROC/WEB/1]OUT    SendGridAutoConfiguration:
2017-09-25T11:13:23.05-0500 [APP/PROC/WEB/1]OUT       Did not match:
2017-09-25T11:13:23.05-0500 [APP/PROC/WEB/1]OUT          - @ConditionalOnClass did not find required class 'com.sendgrid.SendGrid' (OnClass
Condition)
2017-09-25T11:13:23.05-0500 [APP/PROC/WEB/1]OUT    SessionAutoConfiguration:
2017-09-25T11:13:23.05-0500 [APP/PROC/WEB/1]OUT       Did not match:
2017-09-25T11:13:23.05-0500 [APP/PROC/WEB/1]OUT          - @ConditionalOnClass did not find required class 'org.springframework.session.Ses
sion' (OnClassCondition)
2017-09-25T11:13:23.05-0500 [APP/PROC/WEB/1]OUT    SitePreferenceAutoConfiguration:
2017-09-25T11:13:23.05-0500 [APP/PROC/WEB/1]OUT       Did not match:
2017-09-25T11:13:23.05-0500 [APP/PROC/WEB/1]OUT          - @ConditionalOnClass did not find required classes 'org.springframework.mobile.de
vice.site.SitePreferenceHandlerInterceptor', 'org.springframework.mobile.device.site.SitePreferenceHandlerMethodArgumentResolver' (OnClassC
ondition)
```

Figure 14: cf logs hello-spring-cloud --recent shows the most recent log output from the hello-spring-cloud application

Alternatively, it is possible to follow the output of the logs. Run `cf logs hello-spring-cloud`:

```
~/hello-spring-cloud >>> cf logs hello-spring-cloud
Connected, tailing logs for app hello-spring-cloud in org pcfdev-org / space development as admin...
```

Figure 15: cf logs hello-spring-cloud waits and provides an immediate output of the logs

In *Figure 15*, the `cf logs` command was run without the `--recent` option. This means that the logs are now being tailed and will output once there is some activity occurring with the application. This approach is very useful for debugging applications. To get some output, let's enter our application from the browser and see what happens:

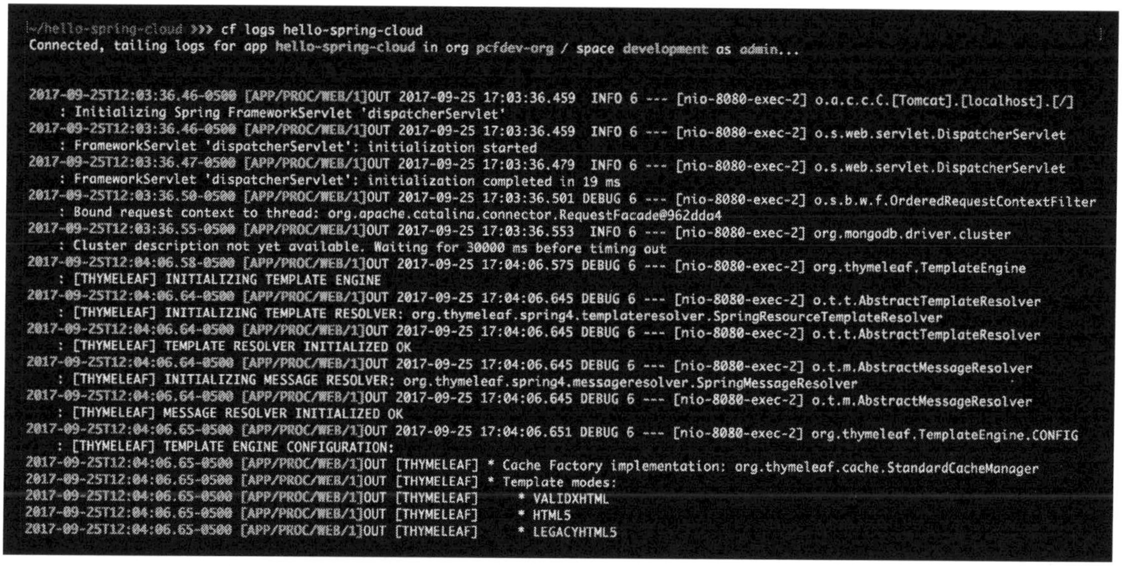

Figure 16: Entering the hello-spring-cloud application on our browser causes the logging output some activity

Figure 16 shows the result of entering our application through the web browser. It outputs a number of event logs to show that the application is running. This logging sits and waits indefinitely and outputs the logs to the users screen. To exit and return back to the prompt, enter *Ctrl + C*.

Managing your application

You've already learned how to view our applications and view its health and status. But, we'd like to perform more functions, such as the ability to run certain maintenance tasks, change routes, scaling of the application, or to delete an application.

Scaling your application

As you already saw in the App Manager, there are two scaling options. The first is to scale vertically and the second is to scale horizontally. Scaling vertically allows us to set all application instances with a defined memory and disk space capacity. Scaling horizontally, on the other hand, allows us to set the number of simultaneous applications that will run at once. Generally, scaling horizontally is desired to maximize the usage of compute resource and management of traffic load for a given application. Scaling vertically, on the other hand, would be used in situations where there is an known increase in use of compute resources on a per application instance basis. For example, larger buffering of incoming datasets.

The CLI scaling command usage is `cf scale <APP_NAME> [-i <instance_count>] [-k <disk_capacity>] [-m <memory_limit>]`. Notice that only the application name is a required input to this command. The other options for instance count, disk capacity, and memory limit are optional and can be input in any combination:

```
[~ >>> cf scale hello-spring-cloud
Showing current scale of app hello-spring-cloud in org pcfdev-org / space development as admin...
OK

memory: 512M
disk: 512M
instances: 2
~ >>>
```

Figure 17: Running the cf scale with hello-spring-cloud as the only argument will display the application's current scaled settings

Running the command `cf scale hello-spring-cloud` will yield an output that displays the current scaling settings for the `hello-spring-cloud` application. Let's now scale our application to have 1 instance, 256 Megabytes of memory, and 256 Megabytes of disk capacity. We run the command `cf scale hello-spring-cloud -i 1 -k 256M -m 256M`. The M's signify Megabytes. We can also input G for Gigabyte:

```
~ >>> cf scale hello-spring-cloud -i 1 -k 256M -m 256M

This will cause the app to restart. Are you sure you want to scale hello-spring-cloud?> yes

Scaling app hello-spring-cloud in org pcfdev-org / space development as admin...
OK
Stopping app hello-spring-cloud in org pcfdev-org / space development as admin...
OK

Starting app hello-spring-cloud in org pcfdev-org / space development as admin...

0 of 1 instances running, 1 starting
0 of 1 instances running, 1 starting
0 of 1 instances running, 1 starting
1 of 1 instances running

App started


OK

App hello-spring-cloud was started using this command `CALCULATED_MEMORY=$($PWD/.java-buildpack/open_jdk_jre/bin/java-buildpack-memory-calc
ulator-2.0.2_RELEASE -memorySizes=metaspace:64m..,stack:228k.. -memoryWeights=heap:65,metaspace:10,native:15,stack:10 -memoryInitials=heap:
100%,metaspace:100% -stackThreads=300 -totMemory=$MEMORY_LIMIT) && JAVA_OPTS="-Djava.io.tmpdir=$TMPDIR -XX:OnOutOfMemoryError=$PWD/.java-bu
ildpack/open_jdk_jre/bin/killjava.sh $CALCULATED_MEMORY -Djavax.net.ssl.trustStore=$PWD/.java-buildpack/container_certificate_trust_store/t
ruststore.jks -Djavax.net.ssl.trustStorePassword=java-buildpack-trust-store-password" && SERVER_PORT=$PORT eval exec $PWD/.java-buildpack/o
pen_jdk_jre/bin/java $JAVA_OPTS -cp $PWD/. org.springframework.boot.loader.JarLauncher`

Showing health and status for app hello-spring-cloud in org pcfdev-org / space development as admin...
OK

requested state: started
instances: 1/1
usage: 256M x 1 instances
urls: hello-spring-cloud-calisthenical-padeye.local.pcfdev.io
last uploaded: Mon Sep 25 16:12:39 UTC 2017
stack: cflinuxfs2
buildpack: container-certificate-trust-store=2.0.0_RELEASE java-buildpack=v3.13-offline-https://github.com/cloudfoundry/java-buildpack.git#
03b493f java-main open-jdk-like-jre=1.8.0_121 open-jdk-like-memory-calculator=2.0.2_RELEASE spring-auto-reconfiguration=1.10...

     state     since                          cpu    memory          disk            details
#0   running   2017-09-25 10:50:33 PM  0.3%   303.6M of 256M   157M of 256M
~ >>>
```

Figure 18: Scaling of the hello-spring-cloud application with 256 Megabytes of memory and disk capacity and horizontally to 1 instance

Upon executing the cf scale parameter as seen in *Figure 18,* you will be prompted to confirm the scaling operation. We are prompted because we decided to scale vertically. Remember that scaling vertically is a destructive process and will require restaging and restarting of the application. If you are only scaling horizontally, this will not require existing application instances to stop.

By now, you may have realized in *Figure 18* that the memory usage had exceeded the actual memory limit that we had set (303.6 M out of 256 M)! This is likely temporary, due to the initial startup of the application. However, this is still a sign of danger of reducing memory limits too much on a running application and the need for more analysis into application memory requirements. When the disk or memory limit is reached, the application instance will be forced to shut down. Cloud Foundry will send the application a SIGTERM signal to notify it of this impending event and that it has 10 seconds to perform its cleanup if it has not crashed yet. After 10 seconds, the application will be forcibly shut down. When there are too many restarts that occur consecutively, that is, flapping, the application will begin staggering the retries so that some leeway is provided to cater for the scenario where any services or system need time to recover before the application is brought up again.

Application tasks

Applications tasks are simply applications or script that is run separately from the main application and its instances. The main application is considered a long-running process, while application tasks are short-lived processes. In doing so, this enables administrative/maintenance tasks to run for the application, that is, *Principal 10: Administrative Processes*. Some tasks include database migrations and batch jobs. Note that the task is only run once in a container for a given application. There is no option to choose which container, as it creates a new container with the application files and runs the intended command.

In the simplest form, we can run Linux script commands on a Linux based cell. Do take note that running tasks manually is generally not of a recommended approach, since it introduces a change that may not be part of a CI/CD process. Nonetheless, the output result of these tasks is collected in the logs, which can be viewed after. The run task command is `cf run-task <APP_NAME> <COMMAND> [--name <TASK_NAME>]`. Here, the command is some existing command/application/script on the application instance and `TASK_NAME` is an optional argument that allows the task to be named. Naming the task will allow us to easily find the task output in the logs. Let's try out the simplest task of directory listing the container content. Run the command `cf run-task hello-spring-cloud "ls -al" --name my-ls`. This will queue the directory listing task to be run in a new container. Note that this may take some time, depending on the task that is being run:

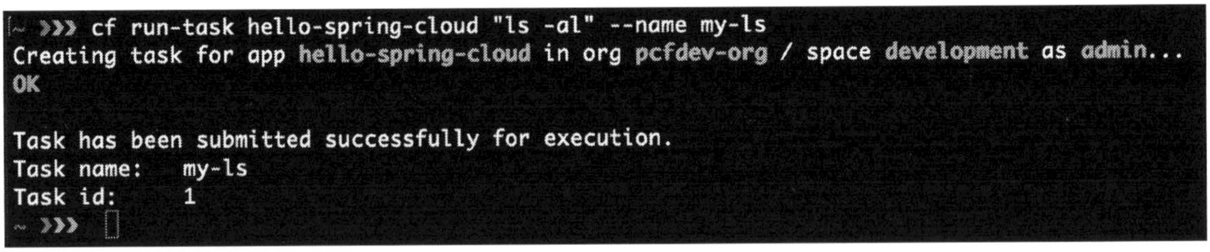

```
[~ >>> cf run-task hello-spring-cloud "ls -al" --name my-ls
Creating task for app hello-spring-cloud in org pcfdev-org / space development as admin...
OK

Task has been submitted successfully for execution.
Task name:   my-ls
Task id:     1
~ >>> []
```

Figure 19: The result of running the cf run-task. The task is queued for execution

Directory listing should be a fast operation. Let's view the result. Run the command `cf logs hello-spring-cloud --recent | grep "my-ls"`. This command will output the most recent logs and only return those that contain the name `my-ls`, as we will see in *Figure 20*. Note the creation and destruction of the container that runs the task.

 The `cf logs hello-spring-cloud --recent | grep "my-ls"` will use `grep`. For other operating systems that do not have grep, for example, Windows, you can either download a `grep` tool, use `FINDSTR` in command prompt or `Select-String` in PowerShell. Alternatively, just call `cf logs hello-spring-cloud --recent` on its own to display all of the log results and find the task output, which is usually at the end of the output.

```
~ >>> cf logs hello-spring-cloud --recent | grep "my-ls"
2017-09-26T00:45:30.59-0500 [APP/TASK/my-ls/0]OUT Creating container
2017-09-26T00:45:30.86-0500 [APP/TASK/my-ls/0]OUT Successfully created container
2017-09-26T00:45:33.39-0500 [APP/TASK/my-ls/0]OUT total 24
2017-09-26T00:45:33.39-0500 [APP/TASK/my-ls/0]OUT drwxr-xr-x 6 vcap root 4096 Sep 26 05:44 .
2017-09-26T00:45:33.39-0500 [APP/TASK/my-ls/0]OUT drwx------ 7 vcap vcap 4096 Sep 26 05:44 ..
2017-09-26T00:45:33.39-0500 [APP/TASK/my-ls/0]OUT drwxr-xr-x 5 vcap vcap 4096 Sep 26 05:44 .java-buildpack
2017-09-26T00:45:33.39-0500 [APP/TASK/my-ls/0]OUT drwxr-xr-x 4 vcap vcap 4096 Sep 26 05:44 BOOT-INF
2017-09-26T00:45:33.39-0500 [APP/TASK/my-ls/0]OUT drwxr-xr-x 3 vcap vcap 4096 Sep 26 05:44 META-INF
2017-09-26T00:45:33.39-0500 [APP/TASK/my-ls/0]OUT drwxr-xr-x 3 vcap vcap 4096 Sep 26 05:44 org
2017-09-26T00:45:33.39-0500 [APP/TASK/my-ls/0]OUT Exit status 0
2017-09-26T00:45:33.41-0500 [APP/TASK/my-ls/0]OUT Destroying container
2017-09-26T00:45:33.92-0500 [APP/TASK/my-ls/0]OUT Successfully destroyed container
~ >>>
```

Figure 20: The output result of the my-ls run-task

Routes and domains

A route serves to enable an addressable (URL) access to an application. A route consists of a hostname and a domain. A hostname is, by default, represented by the application name and the domain is an address that is assigned to an Org. With Routes and domains, it is possible to cleanly separate applications and organize them into Orgs, so that applications of a given domain exist together. We'll also explore other types of routes and domains and also how to map and unmap them later in this chapter.

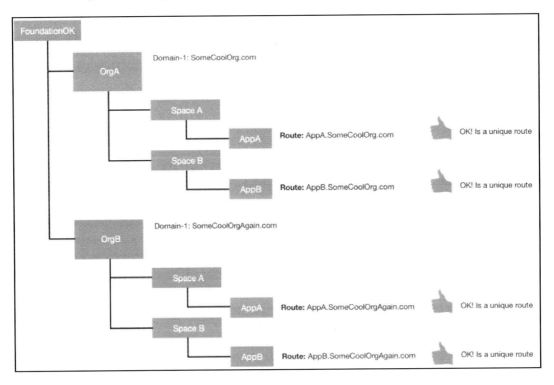

Figure 21: An example of a valid route and domain. Routes must always be unique

It is also possible to have the same domain across Orgs, but it is not possible to have the same route between Orgs. A visual layout of this structure can be seen in *Figure 22.*

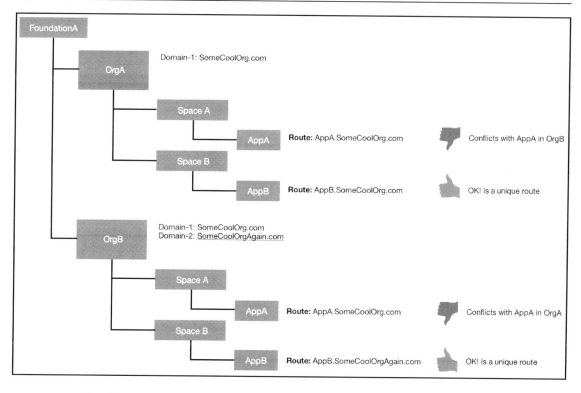

Figure 22: An example of failing case of routes and domain. Routes must be unique but domains can be shared across different Orgs

Domains, HTTP domains, and TCP domains

Domains have some differences in terminology from the conventional domain. Other than that, domains are unique and must be resolved by a DNS server; in Cloud Foundry, a domain can be a *shared domain* or it can be a *private domain*. A *shared domain* is one where a domain is available to all users across all Orgs. A *private domain*, on the other hand, is custom and privately registered. They can also be shared among Orgs, but permissions must be given to specific members of an Org to map their applications routes to use these domains. Another difference between a *shared domain* and *private domain* is that a *shared domain* can be configured to work with either HTTP and TCP, whereas, a *private domain*, can only work with HTTP/HTTPS protocols only.

Domains that work in the HTTP Protocol are called HTTP Domains, while domains that work in TCP are called TCP domains. Due to the nature of TCP being layer 4 on the OSI stack and protocol agnostic, there must be use of a TCP router group that defines a range of ports that are reserved for TCP Routes. We'll look at defining TCP Routes later. In general, a use case of TCP routes is for regulatory requirements that demand the termination of **Transport Layer Security (TLS)** to be close to the application so that the decryption of packets are not performed before reaching the application, but rather, by the application.

Viewing and managing HTTP shared domains

To view the available domains for an Org, run the command `cf domains`:

```
~ >>> cf domains
Getting domains in org pcfdev-org as admin...
name                  status    type
local.pcfdev.io       shared
tcp.local.pcfdev.io   shared    tcp
~ >>>
```

Figure 23: The output of cf domains, shows the domains currently in the Org

To create a new shared domain, we run the command `cf create-shared-domain <domain_name>`. Let's create a new shared HTTP domain called `my-shared-domain.coolorg.com`:

```
~ >>> cf create-shared-domain my-shared-domain.coolorg.com
Creating shared domain my-shared-domain.coolorg.com as admin...
OK
~ >>> cf domains
Getting domains in org pcfdev-org as admin...
name                          status    type
local.pcfdev.io               shared
tcp.local.pcfdev.io           shared    tcp
my-shared-domain.coolorg.com  shared
~ >>>
```

Figure 24: The result of creating the shared HTTP domain my-shared-domain.coolorg.com and running cf domains to get the list of currently available domains for our Org

To delete the shared HTTP domain, we can execute the command `cf delete-shared-domain my-shared-domain.coolorg.com`. You will be prompted to confirm the deletion of the shared domain. This is important because once the domain is removed, it cannot be recovered and applications will lose their respective routes:

```
~ >>> cf delete-shared-domain my-shared-domain.coolorg.com
Deleting domain my-shared-domain.coolorg.com as admin...

This domain is shared across all orgs.
Deleting it will remove all associated routes, and will make any app with this domain unreachable.
Are you sure you want to delete the domain my-shared-domain.coolorg.com? > yes
OK
~ >>> cf domains
Getting domains in org pcfdev-org as admin...
name                  status    type
local.pcfdev.io       shared
tcp.local.pcfdev.io   shared    tcp
~ >>>
```

Figure 25: The result of deleting the HTTP shared domain my-shared-domain.coolorg.com

Viewing and managing TCP shared domains

As we had mentioned earlier, a *shared domain* can work in either HTTP or in TCP. The previous steps showed how to create an HTTP shared domain. We will now explore the creation of TCP shared domains.

The creation of TCP shared domains follow the same path as the HTTP shared domains; the exception here is the requirement for a router-group in the command, that is, `cf create-shared-domain <TCP_DOMAIN_NAME> --router-group <GROUP NAME>`. To retrieve the list of router groups, we can do so through the command `cf router-groups`. The *Figure 26* performs this step and shows the result of creating a TCP domain:

```
~ >>> cf router-groups
Getting router groups as admin ...

name          type
default-tcp   tcp
~ >>> cf create-shared-domain tcp.my-shared-domain.coolorg.com --router-group default-tcp
Creating shared domain tcp.my-shared-domain.coolorg.com as admin...
OK
~ >>> cf domains
Getting domains in org pcfdev-org as admin...
name                               status    type
local.pcfdev.io                    shared
tcp.local.pcfdev.io                shared    tcp
tcp.my-shared-domain.coolorg.com   shared    tcp
~ >>>
```

Figure 26: The result of creating a TCP shared domain tcp.my-shared-domain.coolorg.com

Viewing and managing HTTP private domains

Until now, we've discussed *shared domains*. There remains one more type of domain that we shall look at and that is the *private domain*. It is important to remember that Cloud Foundry currently only supports HTTP private domains and not TCP. Creation of private domains also follows a similar command pattern to shared domains, except it requires an Org name to be associated with and the private domain name. The command is `cf create-domain <ORG_NAME> <PRIVATE_DOMAIN_NAME>`. Let's create a private domain along with a private sub-domain. First, we run the command `cf create-domain pcfdev-org my-private-domain.com` followed by `cf create-domain mycorner.pcfdev-org my-private-domain.com`:

```
~ >>> cf create-domain pcfdev-org my-private-domain.com
Creating domain my-private-domain.com for org pcfdev-org as admin...
OK
~ >>> cf create-domain pcfdev-org mycorner.my-private-domain.com
Creating domain mycorner.my-private-domain.com for org pcfdev-org as admin...
OK
~ >>> cf domains
Getting domains in org pcfdev-org as admin...
name                                status    type
local.pcfdev.io                     shared
tcp.local.pcfdev.io                 shared    tcp
tcp.my-shared-domain.coolorg.com    shared    tcp
my-private-domain.com               owned
mycorner.my-private-domain.com      owned
~ >>>
```

Figure 27: Creation of the private domain my-private-domain.com and its subdomain mycorner.my-private-domain.com. These private domains are created for the pcfdev-org

Notice how we can create a sub-domain for the private domain. We can also create a private sub-domain of a shared domain; however, we cannot create a shared sub-domain for a private domain. To differentiate between *shared* and *private domains*, the status output in `cf domains` show shared or owned, respectively.

To enable a private domain to be used with another Org, say `OrgB`, we execute the command `cf share-private-domain OrgB my-private-domain.com`:

```
[~ >>> cf share-private-domain OrgB my-private-domain.com
Sharing domain my-private-domain.com with org OrgB as admin...
OK
[~ >>> cf login -o OrgB -s development
API endpoint: https://api.local.pcfdev.io

Email> admin

Password>
Authenticating...
OK

Targeted org OrgB

Targeted space development


API endpoint:   https://api.local.pcfdev.io (API version: 2.82.0)
User:           admin
Org:            OrgB
Space:          development
[~ >>> cf domains
Getting domains in org OrgB as admin...
name                                status      type
local.pcfdev.io                     shared
tcp.local.pcfdev.io                 shared      tcp
tcp.my-shared-domain.coolorg.com    shared      tcp
localA.pcfdev.io                    owned
pcfdev-mac.io                       owned
my-private-domain.com               owned
~ >>> █
```

Figure 28: The result of sharing a private domain with OrgB. We logged into OrgB in order to see the domains available to OrgB

Note in *Figure 28*, that even if we shared the parent private domain, the private sub-domain was not shared. Similarly to unshare the use of a private domain, run `cf unshare-private-domain OrgB my-private-domain.com`. *Figure 29* shows the result of unsharing the private domain:

```
[~ >>> cf unshare-private-domain OrgB my-private-domain.com
Unsharing domain my-private-domain.com from org OrgB as admin...
OK
[~ >>> cf domains
Getting domains in org OrgB as admin...
name                                status      type
local.pcfdev.io                     shared
tcp.local.pcfdev.io                 shared      tcp
tcp.my-shared-domain.coolorg.com    shared      tcp
localA.pcfdev.io                    owned
pcfdev-mac.io                       owned
~ >>> █
```

Figure 29: The result of unsharing a private domain with OrgB

Routes, HTTP routes, and TCP routes

A route is an address at which applications can be accessed from. The two main types of routes are HTTP routes, which are those created in HTTP domains, and TCP routes, which are those created in TCP domains.

The difference here, aside from the domain types, is that HTTP routes communicate on port `80` and `443` and cannot reserve any other ports. In contrast to TCP routes, which do not support hostname and paths and has a single use port, that, once reserved, cannot be used again for another different route. A key aspect of HTTP routes in Cloud Foundry is that incoming requests will reach the `GoRouter`, after a load balancer, that maps specific HTTP routes to applications. If there are multiple instances of the application, the `GoRouter` allocates the traffic to each application instance in a round-robin fashion to balance the load. TCP routes, on the other hand, are based on the concept of port mapping where incoming TCP requests on a given port are mapped to an application through a TCP router, after a load balancer.

Before we go further, ensure that you have logged back into the `pcfdev-org` and development space. To list all routes for current Org and Space that you are logged into, run the command `cf routes`. The following figure shows this result:

Figure 30: Listing all the routes for the pcfdev-org in the development space

Creating HTTP routes

To create an HTTP route, run the command `cf create-route <space_name> <domain_name> [--hostname <host_name>] [--path <path_name>]`. The route creation requires the input of which space we wish to assign the route to and also the routes' domain. Optional to this command are the hostname and pathname, which describes a constructed URL address of the format `<hostname_name.domain_name>/<path_name>`. As we delve further into routes, you'll learn what and how these are used.

Running the `cf create-route` command without the optional hostname and path will only work for *private domains*. Note that a *private domain* must be defined first before you can create a route to the *private domain*. We can create the private domain using the `cf create-domain` command, which we had covered in the previous section, *Viewing and managing HTTP Private Domains*:

```
~ >>> cf create-route development my-private-domain.com
Creating route my-private-domain.com for org pcfdev-org / space development as admin...
OK
~ >>>
```

Figure 31: Creating an HTTP private route, my-private-domain.com in the pcfdev-org and development space

Creating HTTP routes with the hostname option

Let's first create a route with the hostname, `superRoute`, for our *development* space at the domain `local.pcfdev.io`:

```
~ >>> cf create-route development local.pcfdev.io --hostname "superRoute"
Creating route superRoute.local.pcfdev.io for org pcfdev-org / space development as admin...
OK
~ >>>
```

Figure 32: Creating the HTTP route superRoute.local.pcfdev.io

From the preceding figure, you will notice that we create a route named `superRoute` without requiring an application called `superRoute`. This is in contrary to the general case where the application name serves as the hostname. This has some very important use cases, one of which is blue-green deployments, which we'll discuss later in this book in `Chapter 11`, *Continuous Integration and Continuous Deployment*, under the section of *Zero downtime deployments*.

Creating HTTP Routes with a Wildcard hostname

Using the hostname option, it is possible to create a wildcard route:

```
~ >>> cf create-route development local.pcfdev.io --hostname "*"
Creating route *.local.pcfdev.io for org pcfdev-org / space development as admin...
OK
~ >>>
```

Figure 33: Creation of an HTTP wildcard route

A wildcard route means any requests with a route that has any hostname entered by the user will be forwarded to the specified domain, for example, `local.pcfdev.io`, as is in the preceding figure.

Creating HTTP context path routing

In the previous sections, we visited the concepts of creating HTTP routes. In this section, we'll look at HTTP context path routing. Using the `cf create-route` with the `--path` option enables us to create a path for a given route for any application:

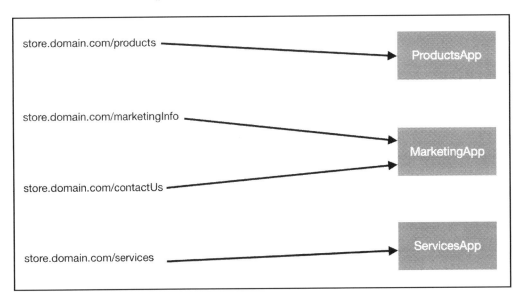

Figure 34: An example of context path routing. Each identical route has a path that routes requests to an application

Context path routing enables us to map applications on the basis of a path for a given route, as we can see in the preceding figure. For one of the earlier paths, we can create a context path route by the command `cf create-route development domain.com --hostname store --path products`. This is extremely useful in architectures for an application, whereby there is a clear separation of responsibilities. This enables a move towards a microservice-like pattern if done properly.

> As of writing, context path routing is not yet supported in ASP.NET on Cloud Foundry. This requires configuration of the Hosted Web Core, located within the HWC buildpack. However, work is underway for this feature.

Let's now do a sample application to show the context path routing in action. We will modify the `hello-spring-cloud-services` application so that its home page displays `Hello Services`. We will then create context paths, by mapping the path `/home` to `hello-spring-cloud` and `/services` to `hello-spring-cloud-services`. Thereafter, we shall deploy them to Cloud Foundry. Before we begin, however, we will need to modify the route mapping code so that the `HomeController` can route any incoming requests to the appropriate controller code.

1. **Modify the hello-spring-cloud application HomeController to take in any route**:
    1. Open the source file located in `hello-spring-cloud/src/main/java/helloworld/HomeController.java` with your favorite editor.
    2. Replace `@RequestMapping("/")` with `@RequestMapping("/*")`.
    3. Navigate to the source `root` directory, that is, `hello-spring-cloud`, and run `mvn clean package`.

2. **Update the hello-spring-cloud context route**: Navigate to the `hello-spring-cloud` directory and use your favorite editor to edit the `manifest.yml` file. Follow these steps:
    1. Rename the name of the application to `hello-spring-cloud-home`.
    2. Remove the line host: `hello-spring-cloud-${random-word}` line.
    3. Add the route `hello-spring-cloud-context-path.local.pcfdev.io/home` as a route to the application.

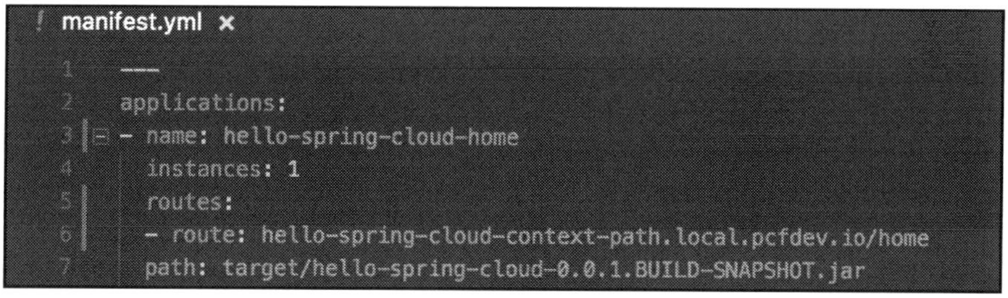

Figure 35: Adding context path routing into the manifest using the route hello-spring-cloud-context-path.local.pcfdev.io/home

3. **Deploy the hello-spring-cloud application to CF**: Run `cf push`.
4. **Create a copy of the hello-spring-cloud application and name it hello-spring-cloud-services**: Navigate to the `root` directory of where your `hello-spring-cloud` application directory is held and run the command `cp -rf hello-spring-cloud hello-spring-cloud-services`.

5. **Update the hello-spring-cloud-services context route**: Navigate to the `hello-spring-cloud-services` directory and use your favorite editor to edit the `manifest.yml` file.

```yaml
 manifest.yml  ✕

 1     ---
 2     applications:
 3     - name: hello-spring-cloud-services
 4       instances: 1
 5       routes:
 6       - route: hello-spring-cloud-context-path.local.pcfdev.io/services
 7         path: target/hello-spring-cloud-0.0.1.BUILD-SNAPSHOT.jar
```

Figure 36: Adding context path routing into the manifest using the route hello-spring-cloud-context-path.local.pcfdev.io/services

6. **Change the front HTML page of hello-spring-cloud-services to output Hello Services**:

   1. Open the source file located in `hello-spring-cloud-services/src/main/java/resources/templates/home.html` with your favorite editor.
   2. Replace `Spring Cloud Demo Application` with `Hello Services`.
   3. Navigate to the source `root` directory, that is, `hello-spring-cloud-services`, and run `mvn clean package`.

```html
 home.html  ✕
 1   <!DOCTYPE HTML>
 2   <html xmlns:th="http://www.thymeleaf.org">
 3   <head>
 4       <title>Getting Started: Serving Web Content</title>
 5       <meta http-equiv="Content-Type" content="text/html; charset=UTF-8" />
 6       <link rel="stylesheet" href="http://netdna.bootstrapcdn.com/bootstrap/3.1.1/css/bootstrap.min.css"/>
 7   </head>
 8   <body>
 9       <div class="container">
10           <div class="jumbotron">
11               <h1>Hello Services</h1>
12               <p>A <a href="http://github.com/cloudfoundry-samples/hello-spring-cloud">Spring application</a>
13                   that uses <a href="https://cloud.spring.io/spring-cloud-connectors/">Spring Cloud Connectors</a> to con
14                   cloud services and get information about cloud environment</p>
15           </div>
```

Figure 37: Updating the home.html document in hello-spring-cloud-services

7. **Deploy the hello-spring-cloud-services application to CF**: Run `cf push`.

8. Now, open up a browser and go
to `http://hello-spring-cloud-context-path.local.pcfdev.io/home`
and `http://hello-spring-cloud-context-path.local.pcfdev.io/serv`
`ices`. You will see the following screens:

Spring Cloud Demo Application

A Spring application that uses Spring Cloud Connectors to connect to cloud services and get information about cloud environment

Cloud Services

Service Connector Type	Connection address
org.apache.tomcat.jdbc.pool.DataSource	\<bad url> h2:mem:testdb;DB_CLOSE_DELAY=-1;DB_CLOSE_ON_EXIT=FALSE
org.springframework.data.mongodb.core.SimpleMongoDbFactory	\<invalid address> Mongo{options=MongoClientOptions{description='null', applicationName='null', readPreference=primary, writeConcern=WriteConcern{w=null, wTimeout=null ms, fsync=null, journal=null, readConcern=com.mongodb.ReadConcern@0, codecRegistry=org.bson.codecs.configuration.ProvidersCodecRegistry@740dba66, commandListeners=[], clusterListeners=[], serverListeners=[], serverMonitorListeners=[], minConnectionsPerHost=0, maxConnectionsPerHost=100, threadsAllowedToBlockForConnectionMultiplier=5, serverSelectionTimeout=30000, maxWaitTime=120000, maxConnectionIdleTime=0, maxConnectionLifeTime=0, connectTimeout=10000, socketTimeout=0, socketKeepAlive=false, sslEnabled=false, sslInvalidHostNamesAllowed=false, alwaysUseMBeans=false, heartbeatFrequency=10000, minHeartbeatFrequency=500, heartbeatConnectTimeout=20000, heartbeatSocketTimeout=20000, localThreshold=15, requiredReplicaSetName='null', dbDecoderFactory=com.mongodb.DefaultDBDecoder$1@18a70c4f,

Figure 38: Output of the hello-spring-cloud-home application at http://hello-spring-cloud-context-path.local.pcfdev.io/home

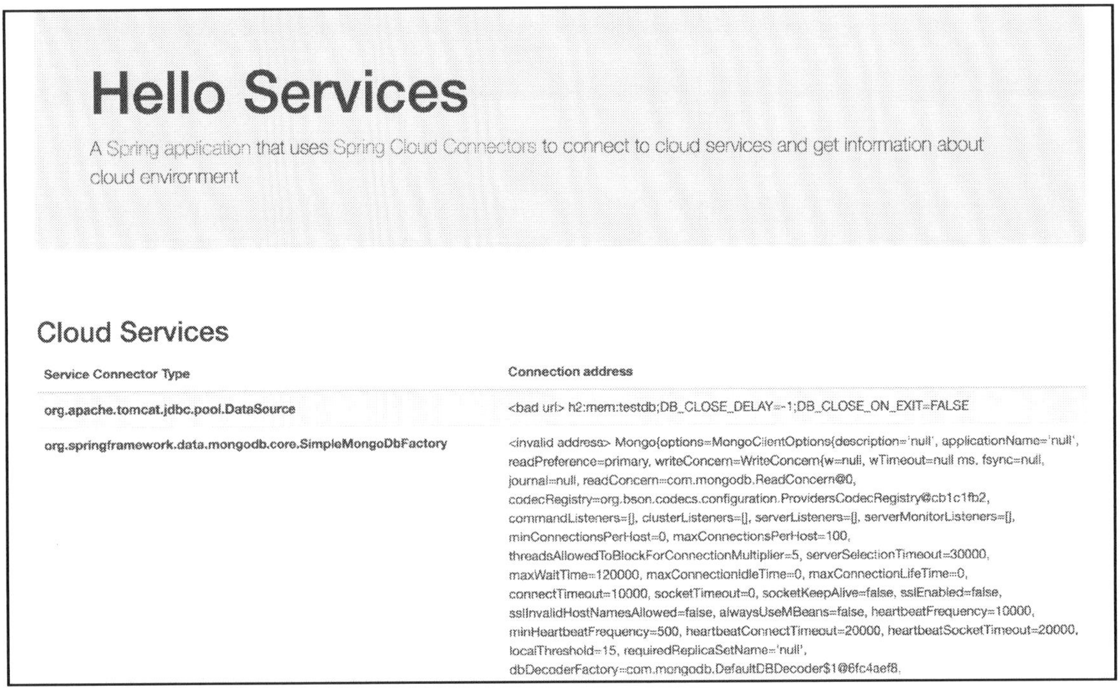

Figure 39: Output of the hello-spring-cloud-services application at http://hello-spring-cloud-context-path.local.pcfdev.io/services

Congratulations! You have implemented a simple application with context path routing.

Creating TCP routes

We created HTTP routes; now, we can turn our attention to TCP routes, which are dependent on ports. The command to run is `cf create-route <space_name> <domain_name> (--port <port_number> | --random-port)`. This is almost identical to the HTTP Route creation, but it must take in either a `--port` or a `--random-port` option. Use the `--random-port` option, if your application can bind to any assigned port number. Otherwise, use `--port` if it is tied to a fixed port number.

Managing routes

In the preceding sections, you've learned how to create routes. Aside from the context path routing, aside from the context path routing, we've only created them, but have not mapped them to an application.

To map an HTTP route to an application run the command: `cf map-route <app_name> <domain_name> [--hostname <host_name>] [--path <path_name>]` or for TCP routes `cf map-route <app_name> <domain_name> (--port <port_number> | --random_port)`.

Notice that the arguments of `cf map-route` are almost identical to `cf create-route`. The only difference is that map-route takes in an application name, while create-route takes in a space name. The `cf map-route` will create a route and map the route to an application in one command. The `cf create-route` will create a route and store it in a space for later use.

To unmap a route, the commands are almost identical the map-route command. For HTTP Routes `cf unmap-route <app_name> <domain_name> [--hostname <host_name>] [--path <path_name>]` or for TCP routes `cf unmap-route <app_name> <domain_name> --port <port_number>`. The only difference between the mapping and unmapping route is that unmapping TCP route only takes in a port number. To unmap the exact route will, of course, require the known and same parameters to invert the process. That is, to unmap the `foo.domain.com/product`, we will need to input foo as the hostname and the product as the path.

Finally, a very useful command to use is `cf check-route`. This command will search the foundation to see whether an input route already exists. The command to run this is `cf check-route <hostname> <domain> [--path <path_name>]`. This will return a result to advise whether the route is taken or not.

Deleting your application

If there is ever a need to delete an application, this can be done so by running the command `cf delete [-r][-f] <APP_NAME>`. The `-f` parameter forces the deletion of the application without prompting you, as it would when there is no force parameter specified. The `-r` also deletes routes that are mapped to this application. By default, deleting applications without the `-r` option means that the mapped routes will be retained. Note that delete is a destructive process and irreversible (aside from re-deploying), therefore, use this with caution!

```
~ >>> cf delete hello-spring-cloud

Really delete the app hello-spring-cloud?> yes
Deleting app hello-spring-cloud in org pcfdev-org / space development as admin...
OK
~ >>>
```

Figure 40: The result of deleting the hello-spring-cloud application without forced deletion. You will be prompted to confirm the deletion before it commences

Monitoring and managing applications using Apps Manager

Monitoring and managing applications can also be done through a web-based graphical user interface, called the App Manager. This is a good alternative for users that are not comfortable with using command line interfaces or simply do not have the cf CLI on hand.

Before we begin, first log into Apps Manager on PCF Dev with the admin credentials. Navigate to the `pcfdev-org` and into the *development* space:

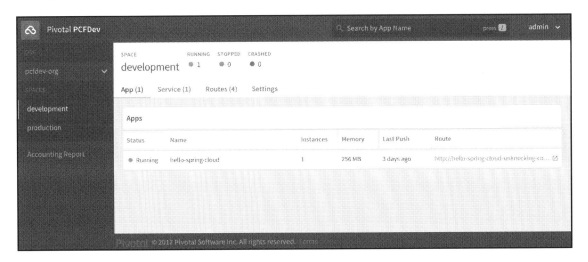

Figure 41: The current applications deployed the pcf dev-org in the development space

The preceding figure shows the first page after navigating to the *development* page. The current application, `hello-spring-cloud`, is deployed in the *development* space of the `pcfdev-org`. We can see on the screen here the application status, its name, the number of application instances running, the maximum memory size of the instance, the last push date, and the URL route.

Click on the application name `hello-spring-cloud` and this will bring us to an overview page of the application, as in the figure here:

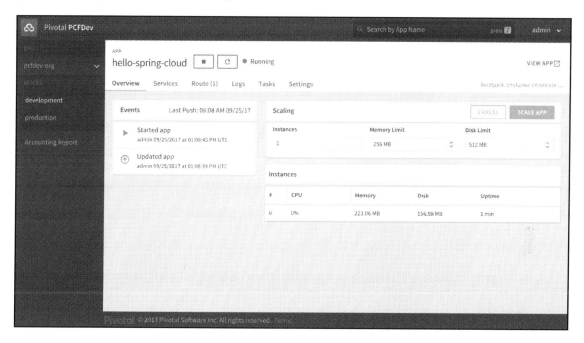

Figure 42: The overview page of the hello-spring-cloud application on Apps Manager

The details page of the `hello-spring-cloud` application has a number of features. This page shows a historical list of events, such as application stated, ended, updated, or crashed. This page also shows information of each application instance, in the box, Instances, with the labeled #0, its memory, disk space, and the uptime. These are some critical pieces of information to enable you to monitor the application and its status. Above, are the scaling options. The options are Instances, memory limit, and disk limit--each with their own control box to adjust the value. The Instances scaling option allows the user to manually select the number of instances they wish to spawn. The memory limit and disk limit scaling options scale each application instance, vertically.

Let's try changing the number of instances to two and the memory limit to 512 Megabytes using the control boxes above. Note that the scaling level depends on the amount of memory and disk space you have on your machine! After changing the values, click on the **SCALE APP** button:

Figure 43: Scale App confirmation prompt dialog

You will be prompted to confirm your changes as shown in the preceding figure. Click on the **SCALE APP** button to proceed with the scaling. The scaling will proceed to create two application instances with 512 Megabytes of memory per instance. This may take a few seconds to complete:

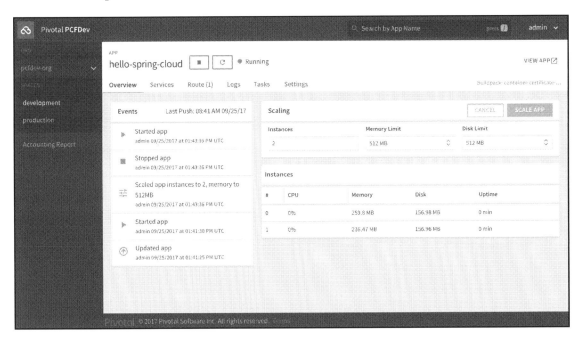

Figure 44: The result of scaling the application to 2 instances with 512 Megabytes per instance

Scaling the application vertically will stop all current applications, regardless of whether it is in the middle of servicing some transaction. So, beware when doing this in a running environment.

Figure 45: The Services tab of the hello-spring-cloud application

The **Services** tab will show the services bound to this application. To bind an instantiated service, click on the **BIND A SERVICE** button. Currently, there is the `my-database-service` MySQL service bound to this application, as we expected:

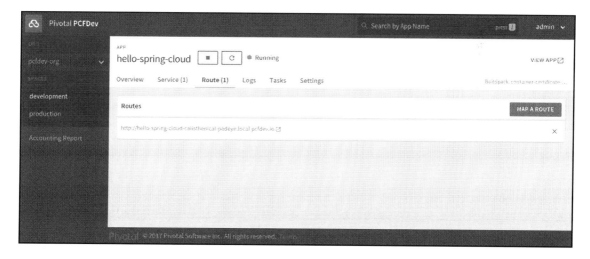

Figure 46: The Route tab of the hello-spring-cloud application

The **Route** tab will show the current routes set for this application. You can map a new additional route by clicking on the **MAP A ROUTE** button.

Figure 47: The Logs tab of the hello-spring-cloud application

The **Logs** tab will show the output of the application logs. This output is the result of the application outputting text to `stdout` and `stderr`. Press the play symbol button to enable continuous output of the logs. You can repeatedly press this button to get an immediate refresh of the output. Note that the logs are the result of outputting directly from an internal temporary ring buffer and is therefore limited and will disappear. Your platform should be configured to be outputting the log to a log management service, such as *Splunk* or *ELK:*

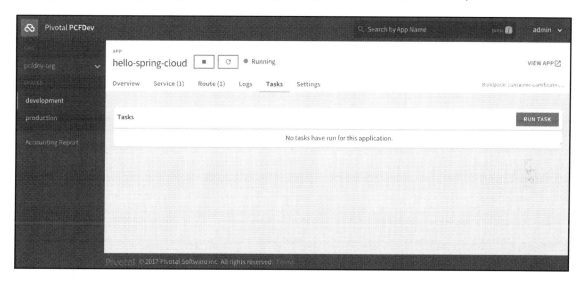

Figure 48: The Tasks tab of the hello-spring-cloud application

The **Tasks** tab allows the setting up of administrative/maintenance tasks, such as database migration. Click on the **RUN TASK** button to set a task to run for the application:

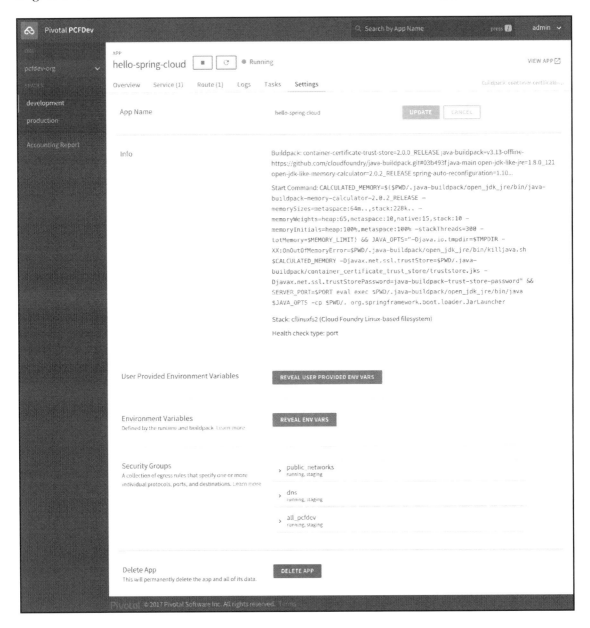

Figure 49: The Settings tab of the hello-spring-cloud application

The **Settings** tab enables some administrative control of the application. This page allows you to change the name of the application on Cloud Foundry, view the current build pack information, view the user provided environment variables and system environment variables, and view application security groups and delete the application.

Application Performance Monitoring (APM)

We've looked at the logging and basic monitoring capabilities provided by Cloud Foundry, but what if we wish to have a profiled measurement of an application's performance? The APM provides a means to this through the collection and aggregation of certain data emitted from applications. We won't go through in detail on APM here due to a large number of services available at `https://pivotal.io/platform/pcf-marketplace/monitoring-metrics-and-logging` that could be integrating into your application. In essence, APMs assist developers in monitoring their application and potentially providing valuable performance indicators for applications that may require more resources at different times of a day, or when the application itself has a bug that is consuming too many resources.

Methods of integration of these APM services varies is all highly dependent on your organization on which APM service they will adopt. For example, PCF metrics will require the installation of the PCF Metrics tile by your organization's platform operators, which would give performance insights into all applications on the platform. Application Dynamics (AppD), on the other hand, will require an installed platform tile, supported buildpacks with the AppD agent, an AppD controller, and applications to instantiate and bind to the AppD service. In this way, applications are registered, their metrics collected and aggregated and can be viewed on an AppD dashboard.

Summary

In this chapter, we deployed the first application onto Cloud Foundry. Thereafter, we visited the concepts of managing and monitoring your applications through the cf CLI and through Apps Manager. In particular, to manage our applications, we can scale it, manage routes, perform administrative tasks using cf tasks, and delete our applications. To monitor our applications, we can view the application logs by either tailing it to view the output of your applications in real-time or just view the last snapshot of what had recently occurred. In the next chapter, we'll look into building microservices.

7
Microservices and Worker Applications

A traditional monolithic application is developed as one big application and then deployed as a whole. One of the drawbacks of monolithic applications is that, if one of the modules in the application stops working, then it takes down the entire application, causing significant downtime, which is not desirable. Additionally, the application teams are not agile in releasing new features, making new features available with a release in four to six months.

To be able to release features faster and more effectively, companies started investing in technology and encouraging developers to design applications using Microservices Architecture.

Microservices Architecture is not a new concept and it's getting more attention due to the evolution of new frameworks and design patterns.

In this chapter, we will discuss the Microservices Architecture in the context of Cloud Foundry. In Chapter 5, *Architecting and Building Apps for the Cloud*, you learned about the 15-factor app-guiding principles, and we will use a few of those principles to build a simple worker application.

The Netflix OSS libraries, such as Eureka, Hystrix, and Config Server can be used to build resiliency into the microservices. We will discuss these patterns and will incorporate them into our worker application.

What are microservices?

Some applications are easier to build and maintain when they are broken down into smaller services that work together. Each service is developed independently, and it has its own lifecycle. An application is made up of multiple such services. *A microservice is a modular service that can be developed and deployed independently.*

A microservices architecture is an approach to develop an application that is composed of smaller services. Each service runs in its own process and communicates with other processes over the network using HTTP/HTTPS, Messaging, WebSockets, or any TCP protocol. Each microservice implements a specific end-to-end domain or business capability within a bounded context, and each service is developed autonomously and deployed independently. A microservice should own its related domain data model and domain logic (sovereignty and decentralized data management), based on different data storage technologies (Caching, SQL, and NoSQL) and different programming languages. A microservice architecture provides long-term agility.

A developer should not worry about the size or the number of lines of code that go into developing that service. The primary focus should be to create a loosely coupled service that can be developed, deployed, and scaled independently. When identifying and designing a microservices, avoid creating direct dependencies on other microservices.

The microservices can scale out independently. With a single monolithic application, you must scale it out as a unit, but with a microservice architecture, you can instead scale out specific microservices. This way, the services that need more processing power or network bandwidth to support the demand can then be scaled horizontally. That means cost savings because you need less hardware.

Microservices architecture enables continuous integration and continuous delivery of the application, which in turn accelerates delivery of new features into the application. This architecture allows us to run and test the individual microservice in isolation, and allows us to enhance them autonomously while maintaining clear contracts between them. When enhancing the features in a microservice, you should not change the contracts or interfaces, and you can continue to enhance the internal implementation of the microservice. Modifying the interface would create breaking changes for other dependent microservices.

To successfully release a microservices-based system into production using Pivotal Cloud Foundry, the following aspects should be considered:

- Rapid application delivery, usually with different teams focusing on different microservices
- Monitoring and health checks of the services by the platform
- Auto-scaling of microservices
- Zero downtime deployment of microservices using CI/CD strategies
- No additional tickets required for creating a new set of virtual machines to enable deployment of these microservices

Worker applications

In `Chapter 6`, *Deploying Apps to Cloud Foundry*, you learned how to build and deploy a simple web application into Cloud Foundry on PCF Dev. Once the application was pushed onto PCF Dev, the platform created a route to the application that could then be used by the users to communicate with the various endpoints exposed by the application. In this section, we will talk about the applications that have no route, but that run in the background, performing a task. *A worker application is basically a process, lower level than a web application, that maps naturally to many so-called back-office jobs.*

These applications generally have no API endpoints, and can be treated as the jobs that are run every night, to keep various systems in sync. A worker application can be written in any language and be deployed into Cloud Foundry.

Fortune teller worker application

We will now build a Spring Boot application that will run every five seconds and output a random fortune. Let's call this application `fortune-teller`.

This application is a **Spring Boot** (`https://spring.io/guides/gs/spring-boot/`) application. You can use the IDE of your choice for this exercise.

We will begin by creating a class called `FortuneCookieGenerator.java`. This class will be responsible for generating random fortunes using the words list. The length of the fortune will be limited by the `fortuneLength` attribute. The contents of the `FortuneCookieGenerator.java` are as follows:

```
package cf.developers;
import java.util.Random;
import org.springframework.beans.factory.annotation.Value;
import org.springframework.stereotype.Component;
@Component
public class FortuneCookieGenerator {
@Value("${words}")
    private String[] words;

    @Value("${length}")
    private int fortuneLength;

    public void generate() {
        Random random = new Random();

        int wordsInSentence = 0;
        StringBuilder randomSentenceStringBuilder = new
StringBuilder();

        while(fortuneLength != wordsInSentence) {
            int pos = random.nextInt(words.length);
            String word = words[pos];
            randomSentenceStringBuilder.append(word).append(" ");
            wordsInSentence++;
    }

        System.out.println(randomSentenceStringBuilder.toString());
        }
    }
```

A few points to note here:

- The `@Component` annotation defines this class to be considered as a candidate for auto-detection when using annotation-based configuration and classpath scanning.
- We are injecting the values for *words* and `fortuneLength`. The values are being read from the `application.properties` under the `src/main/resources` director of the project.
- We are using `System.out.println()` to write the fortune to the console out. This information will be available to us when we look at the application logs.

Now that we have the business logic ready, we can construct the main class and call it `FortuneTellerApplication.java`. This class will be responsible for starting an embedded `tomcat` container. The annotation `@EnableScheduling` enables the `spring-scheduled` task execution capability, and the `@Scheduled` annotation marks the method as a scheduled task.

The contents of `FortuneTellerApplication.java` are as follows:

```
package cf.developers;
import org.springframework.beans.factory.annotation.Autowired;
import org.springframework.boot.SpringApplication;
import
org.springframework.boot.autoconfigure.SpringBootApplication;
import org.springframework.scheduling.annotation.EnableScheduling;
import org.springframework.scheduling.annotation.Scheduled;
@SpringBootApplication
@EnableScheduling
public class FortuneTellerApplication {
@Autowired
FortuneCookieGenerator fortuneCookieGenerator;
    public static void main(String[] args) {
        SpringApplication.run(FortuneTellerApplication.class,
args);
    }

  @Scheduled(cron = "${cron.schedule}")
    private void generateFortune() {
        fortuneCookieGenerator.generate();
}
}
```

The maven `pom.xml` defines the `spring-boot-starter-parent`, which has a list of all of the latest versions and their dependencies defined. This is managed by the Spring Boot team. The `spring-boot-starter` dependency is smart enough to manage all the dependencies on the open source libraries that this application needs. The contents of `pom.xml` are as follows:

```
<?xml version="1.0" encoding="UTF-8"?><project
xmlns="http://maven.apache.org/POM/4.0.0"
xmlns:xsi="http://www.w3.org/2001/XMLSchema-instance"
xsi:schemaLocation="http://maven.apache.org/POM/4.0.0
http://maven.apache.org/xsd/maven-4.0.0.xsd">
<modelVersion>4.0.0</modelVersion>
<groupId>cf.developers</groupId>
<artifactId>fortune-teller</artifactId>
<version>0.0.1-SNAPSHOT</version>
```

```
<packaging>jar</packaging>
<name>fortune-teller</name><description>CF For Developers - Fortune
Teller Worker Application</description>
<parent>
<groupId>org.springframework.boot</groupId>
        <artifactId>spring-boot-starter-parent</artifactId>
        <version>1.5.7.RELEASE</version>
        <relativePath/> <!-- lookup parent from repository -
-></parent>
<properties>
<project.build.sourceEncoding>UTF-8</project.build.sourceEncoding>
<project.reporting.outputEncoding>UTF-8</project.reporting.outputEn
coding>
        <java.version>1.8</java.version>
</properties>
<dependencies>
<dependency>
            <groupId>org.springframework.boot</groupId>
        <artifactId>spring-boot-
starter</artifactId>\</dependency>
<dependency>
<groupId>org.springframework.boot</groupId>
        <artifactId>spring-boot-starter-test</artifactId>
        <scope>test</scope>
        </dependency>
</dependencies>
<build>
<plugins>
        <plugin>
            <groupId>org.springframework.boot</groupId>
            <artifactId>spring-boot-maven-
plugin</artifactId></plugin>
</plugins>
</build>
</project>
```

The `application.properties` file is read by the Spring Boot application. During application startup, the `@Value` annotations are resolved by looking into the system's environment followed by other property files. The `application.properties` can also be customized per the Spring profiles, for example, `application-dev.properties` or `application-prod.properties`, where `dev` and `prod` are the Spring profiles. The contents of `application.properties` are as follows:

```
words=...
length=6
cron.schedule=*/5 * * * *
```

Building and deploying the fortune teller application to PCF Dev

To build and deploy the fortune teller application to PCF Dev, let's start with cloning the GitHub repository and building the code:

- Clone the source code from: `https://github.com/Cloud-Foundry-For-Developers/chapter-7`
- Switch to the `chapter-7/fortune-teller` directory and execute `mvn clean install`

We will need an Org and a Space to deploy our applications. So, we should create an Org first and then a Space. To create an Org, execute `cf create-org cloudfoundry-for-developers`:

```
[~/D/w/fortune-teller >>> cf create-org cloudfoundry-for-developers
Creating org cloudfoundry-for-developers as admin...
OK

Assigning role OrgManager to user admin in org cloudfoundry-for-developers ...
OK

TIP: Use 'cf target -o "cloudfoundry-for-developers"' to target new org
~/D/w/fortune-teller >>>
```

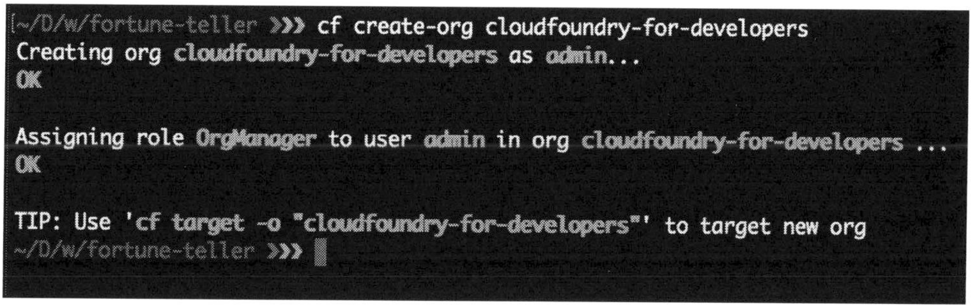

Figure 1: Create an Org on PCF Dev

Next, create a Space by executing `cf create-space -o cloudfoundry-for-developers development`:

```
~/D/w/fortune-teller >>> cf create-space -o cloudfoundry-for-developers development    ⚡ 1 master
Creating space development in org cloudfoundry-for-developers as admin...
OK
Assigning role RoleSpaceManager to user admin in org cloudfoundry-for-developers / space developm
ent as admin...
OK
Assigning role RoleSpaceDeveloper to user admin in org cloudfoundry-for-developers / space develo
pment as admin...
OK

TIP: Use 'cf target -o "cloudfoundry-for-developers" -s "development"' to target new space
~/D/w/fortune-teller >>>                                                                    master
```

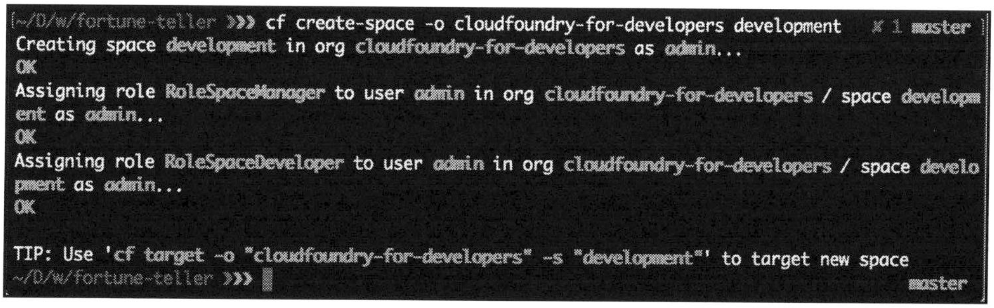

Figure 2: Create a Space in the Org created earlier on PCF Dev

Now, let's target to the Org and Space that we created in the previous section, by executing `cf target -o "cloudfoundry-for-developers" -s "development"`:

```
[~/D/w/fortune-teller >>> cf target -o "cloudfoundry-for-developers" -s "development"
api endpoint:   https://api.local.pcfdev.io
api version:    2.82.0
user:           admin
org:            cloudfoundry-for-developers
space:          development
```

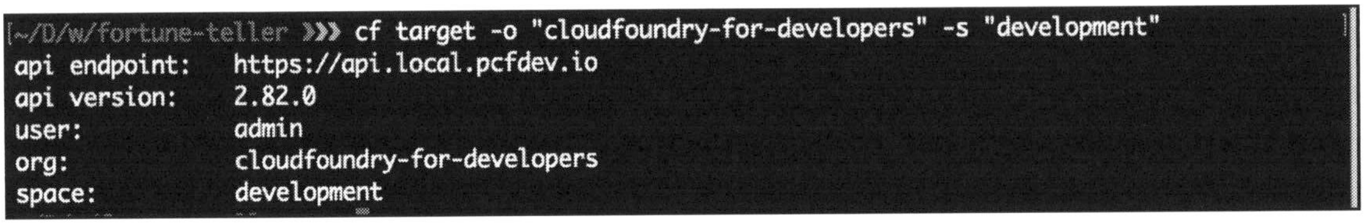

Figure 3: Target to the Org and Space on PCF Dev using the cf CLI

Now that we have the compiled code and an Org/Space available on PCF Dev, we will push this application. Run the `cf push fortune-teller -p target/fortune-teller-0.0.1-SNAPSHOT.jar --no-route --health-check-type=process` from the `fortune-teller` directory:

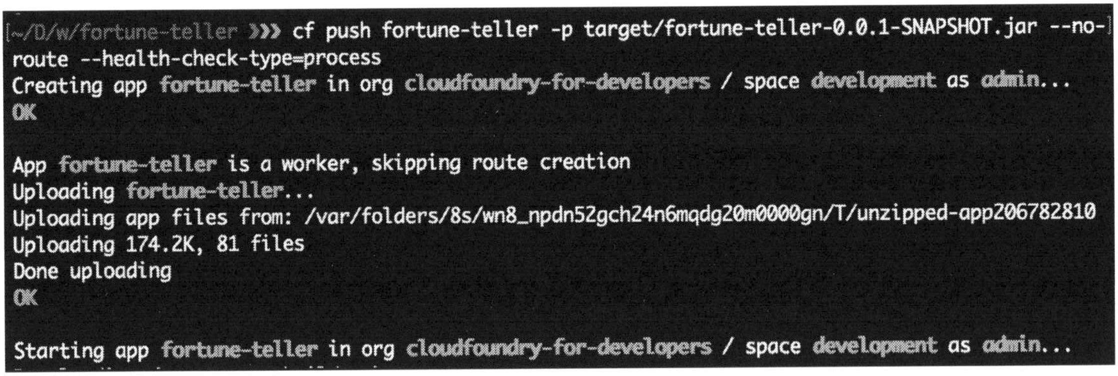

```
[~/D/w/fortune-teller >>> cf push fortune-teller -p target/fortune-teller-0.0.1-SNAPSHOT.jar --no-
route --health-check-type=process
Creating app fortune-teller in org cloudfoundry-for-developers / space development as admin...
OK

App fortune-teller is a worker, skipping route creation
Uploading fortune-teller...
Uploading app files from: /var/folders/8s/wn8_npdn52gch24n6mqdg20m0000gn/T/unzipped-app206782810
Uploading 174.2K, 81 files
Done uploading
OK

Starting app fortune-teller in org cloudfoundry-for-developers / space development as admin...
```

Figure 4: Deploy fortune-teller application on PCF Dev

After the application has started successfully, you should see the stats of the application in the output on the terminal:

```
Showing health and status for app fortune-teller in org cloudfoundry-for-developers / space devel
opment as admin...
OK

requested state: started
instances: 1/1
usage: 256M x 1 instances
urls:
last uploaded: Thu Sep 28 14:55:21 UTC 2017
stack: cflinuxfs2
buildpack: container-certificate-trust-store=2.0.0_RELEASE java-buildpack=v3.13-offline-https://g
ithub.com/cloudfoundry/java-buildpack.git#03b493f java-main open-jdk-like-jre=1.8.0_121 open-jdk-
like-memory-calculator=2.0.2_RELEASE spring-auto-reconfiguration=1.10...

     state     since                 cpu     memory          disk            details
#0   running   2017-09-28 09:55:42 AM  0.0%   93.5M of 256M   128.9M of 512M
```

Figure 5: Output from the cf CLI after the fortune-teller application has started successfully

Now, let's look at the logs for this application, and verify whether the fortune is being generated to the console output. This is done by executing `cf logs fortune-teller`:

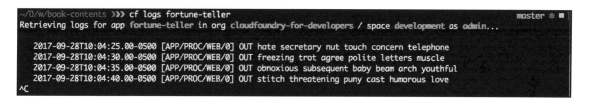

Figure 6: Using cf CLI to view the fortune-teller application logs

The same information is available in the Apps Manager PCF Dev. If you log in to your PCF Dev Apps Manager and select the `fortune-teller` application running in the `cloudfoundry-for-developers` Org and development Space, you can select **Logs** and view the output generated by the application:

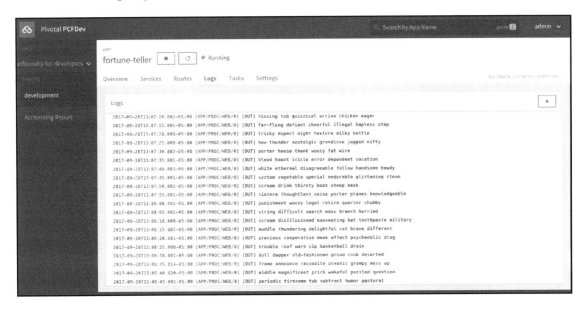

Figure 7: Using Apps Manager on PCF Dev to view the fortune-teller application logs

There are some key takeaways here:

- When the application is pushed, we specify `--no-route` to tell Cloud Foundry not to create a route for the application as this is a worker application.
- Next, we specify `--health-check-type=process` and this instructs Cloud Foundry to monitor the worker application as a background process.
- When the application is pushed, the **Logs** output **App fortune-teller is a worker, skipping route creation**. This confirms that Cloud Foundry will skip route creation for this application.
- The default memory assigned to the Spring Boot application is **256 MB**.
- The application was deployed with the `java_buildpack` detected, as this buildpack has the required runtime to support this application. You will learn more about buildpacks in later chapters.

Application resiliency

Every application should have some resiliency built into it. There could be number of issues that could occur in an application that's comprised of multiple microservices.

In this section, we will talk about the resiliency provided by the application. We will also discuss some known design patterns that can help us solve the issues listed in the preceding section.

Resiliency provided by Cloud Foundry

Before we talk about building resiliency into the application, let's talk about what Cloud Foundry provides out-of-the-box to make the applications resilient to **Platform as a Service (PaaS)** outages:

- Cloud Foundry has a built-in mechanism to monitor applications. When an application is pushed into Cloud Foundry, then the number of instances requested during the deployment defines the desired state for an application. If the application is scaled manually, then the new number of instances override the desired state. Internal to Cloud Foundry, there are components that monitor the running application instances for all applications, and compare them with the desired state. If there are any discrepancies found, then Cloud Foundry resurrects the missing application instances.
- For an application to be highly available in Cloud Foundry, there should be a minimum of two instances deployed at any point in time. So, if one of the application instances goes down for any reason, then the other application instance will be serving the requests, while the other one is being resurrected by Cloud Foundry. This provides a better experience to the end user. At any given time, the requests are evenly distributed between all of the running application instances.

Building resiliency into microservices

Just as the platform provides some resiliency, the application should also build some logic to handle failures. There could be scenarios when the application, that is composed of multiple microservices, could fail due to unavailability of one or more microservices. There are many possible reasons for the application to fail as a whole:

- Since the microservices communicate with one another over the network, there are high chances of failures due to network latency or network outages.

- Once the network connections are restored, generally, the applications need to be recycled, in order to restore the connections with the downstream applications.
- An outage of one service generally takes down the entire application.
- Change management causes some outages, too. Any new microservice rollout could fail due to either configuration changes or a bad build.

To address some of the design concerns listed earlier, Netflix built a few **Common Runtime Services and Libraries** (`https://netflix.github.io/`), such as Eureka, Hystrix, Ribbon, and Turbine. Since those were made Open Source Software by Netflix, the Spring team built a Spring Cloud project that wraps all of these libraries and provides a convenient way to create business logic using them. The project can be found on the Spring Cloud website: `http://projects.spring.io/spring-cloud/`.

Per the Spring Cloud documentation, Spring Cloud (`http://cloud.spring.io/spring-cloud-static/spring-cloud.html`) provides tools for developers to quickly build some of the common patterns in distributed systems (for example, configuration management, service discovery, circuit breakers, intelligent routing, micro-proxy, control bus, one-time tokens, global locks, leadership election, distributed sessions, and cluster state). Coordination of distributed systems leads to boilerplate patterns; by using Spring Cloud, developers can quickly stand up services and applications that implement those patterns. They will work well in any distributed environment, including the developer's own laptop, bare metal data centers, and managed platforms such as Cloud Foundry.

Using the Config Server for managing application configuration

Spring Cloud Config provides server and client-side support for externalized configuration in a distributed system. With the Config Server, you have a central place to manage external properties for applications across all environments. The default implementation of the server storage backend uses Git.

The Spring Cloud Config Server helps in change management and allows developers to maintain the application configuration in a centralized location:

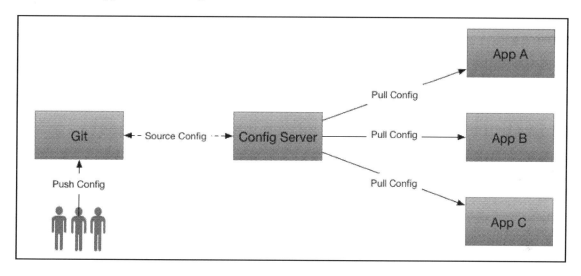

Figure 8: Config Server workflow

The workflow involved in storing and fetching the application configuration from the source control like Git or SVN is:

1. The developers commit the configuration files into a source control, such as Git or SVN.
2. The Config Server application is configured to fetch the configuration from Git. The setup involves passing in the source control connection details, repo name, label, and authentication details.
3. The application then pulls the configuration from the Config Server by specifying the `spring.application.name` in the `bootstrap.yml` file.

To better understand the process, let's modify our `fortune-teller` application to use the PCF Spring Config Server service to fetch the application configuration from Git.

Begin by adding the `spring-cloud-services-starter-config-client` dependency in our `pom.xml`. We need this library, as this application will be a client for the Config Server instance that we will be creating in later steps:

```
<dependency>
    <groupId>io.pivotal.spring.cloud</groupId>
    <artifactId>spring-cloud-services-starter-config-client</artifactId>
</dependency>
```

We also need to add the following dependency in the `dependencyManagement` section in the `pom.xml`:

```
<dependencyManagement>
    <dependencies>
      <dependency>
        <groupId>org.springframework.cloud</groupId>
        <artifactId>spring-cloud-dependencies</artifactId>
        <version>${spring-cloud.version}</version>
        <type>pom</type>
        <scope>import</scope>
      </dependency>
      <dependency>
        <groupId>io.pivotal.spring.cloud</groupId>
        <artifactId>spring-cloud-services-dependencies</artifactId>
        <version>${spring-cloud-services.version}</version>
        <type>pom</type>
        <scope>import</scope>
      </dependency>
    </dependencies>
  </dependencyManagement>
```

Next, we need to create a file with the name `bootstrap.yml` under the `src/main/resources` directory. During the application startup, the `bootstrap.yml` is read first, and the runtime supplies the name of the application to the Config Server. The Config Server then tries to find the properties for the requested application name and profile in GitHub. So, let's paste the following contents into the `bootstrap.yml`:

```
---
spring:
application:
name: fortune-teller
```

We will now remove the words and length parameters from `application.properties`. We want to get a new set of values for these two parameters from the Config hosted on Git:

```
cron.schedule=*/5 * * * *
```

Finally, let's update `FortuneCookieGenerator.java` to include the `@RefreshScope` annotation. Place this annotation right above the `@Component` annotation. Beans annotated this way can be refreshed at runtime, and any components that are using them will get a new instance on the next method call, fully initialized and injected with all dependencies:

```
@RefreshScope
@Component
public class FortuneCookieGenerator {
    ...
    ...
    ...
}
```

The complete code is available at: `https://github.com/Cloud-Foundry-For-Developers/chapter-7/tree/master/fortune-teller-with-config-server`.

Let's now deploy the application onto PCF Dev. To do this, we will first need to ensure that the code builds. Execute `mvn clean install` from the `chapter-7/fortune-teller-with-config-server` directory.

Now, using the cf CLI, we will create an instance of Config Server in PCF Dev. Before that, let's list all the services available in the marketplace. To list all of the services, run `cf marketplace`:

Figure 9: Listing available services in PCF Dev

We are interested in the service with the description `Config Server for Spring Cloud Applications`.

To create an instance of `Config Server`, we need to execute `cf create-service -c '{"Git": { "uri": "https://github.com/Cloud-Foundry-For-Developers/chapter-7", "label": "master", "searchPaths" : "application-configuration" } }' p-config-server standard config-server`. In this command, we are performing two tasks: one, creating an instance of the `Config Server`, and two, we are specifying the Git configuration for the `Config Server` to retrieve the application properties:

```
[~/D/w/c/fortune-teller-with-config-server >>> cf create-service -c '{"git": { "uri": "https://github.com/Cloud-Foundry-F]
or-Developers/chapter-6", "label": "master", "searchPaths" : "application-configuration" } }' p-config-server standard c
onfig-server
Creating service instance config-server in org cloudfoundry-for-developers / space development as admin...
OK

Create in progress. Use 'cf services' or 'cf service config-server' to check operation status.
```

Figure 10: Creating an instance of config-server service offered in the PCF Dev marketplace using cf CLI

To verify whether the service instance we created in the previous step completed successfully, we can use the help text from the generated output to query for the service instance creation. This is done by executing `cf service config-server`. If the status is `create succeeded`, then it indicates that the service creation is complete:

```
[~/D/w/c/fortune-teller-with-config-server >>> cf service config-server                                     master ]

Service instance: config-server
Service: p-config-server
Bound apps:
Tags:
Plan: standard
Description: Config Server for Spring Cloud Applications
Documentation url: http://docs.pivotal.io/spring-cloud-services/
Dashboard: https://spring-cloud-broker.local.pcfdev.io/dashboard/p-config-server/bc0e2f37-3ca9-4ec1-af17-9702a375855e

Last Operation
Status: create succeeded
Message:
Started: 2017-09-29T06:29:56Z
Updated: 2017-09-29T06:30:59Z
```

Figure 11: Querying for the successful service instance creation

Log in to the **Apps Manager** and in the **development** Space, select **Service | Config Server** and then click the **Manage** button:

Figure 12: Viewing the config-server service instance using Apps Manager on PCF Dev

If the specified Git repository configuration is correct, then you should see the message **Config server is online**:

Figure 13: Checking the config-server service instance dashboard using Apps Manager on PCF Dev

At this time, we can push the updated application onto PCF Dev and instruct Cloud Foundry not to start the application. This is done to avoid the application deployment from failing, as the required parameters, **words** and **length**, have not yet been supplied. We will bind the application to the `Config Server` instance that we created after the application has been pushed into Cloud Foundry. So, execute `cf push fortune-teller -p target/fortune-teller-with-config-server-0.0.1-SNAPSHOT.jar --no-route --health-check-type=process --no-start`:

```
[~/D/w/c/fortune-teller-with-config-server >>> cf push fortune-teller -p target/fortune-teller-with-config-server-0.0.1-S]
NAPSHOT.jar --no-route --health-check-type=process --no-start
Updating app fortune-teller in org cloudfoundry-for-developers / space development as admin...
OK

App fortune-teller is a worker, skipping route creation
Uploading fortune-teller...
Uploading app files from: /var/folders/8s/wn8_npdn52gch24n6mqdg20m0000gn/T/unzipped-app806096377
Uploading 484.7K, 96 files
Done uploading
OK
```

Figure 14: Pushing the fortune-teller application into PCF Dev using cf CLI

Now that we have pushed the application bits into PCF Dev, we will bind the application `fortune-teller` to the `Config Server` instance `fortune-teller-config-server-instance`. This is done by executing `cf bind-service fortune-teller config-server`. By doing this, we are creating a dependency between the application and the `Config Server` service:

```
[~/D/w/c/fortune-teller-with-config-server >>> cf bind-service fortune-teller config-server              master ]
 Binding service config-server to app fortune-teller in org cloudfoundry-for-developers / space development as admin...
 OK
 TIP: Use 'cf restage fortune-teller' to ensure your env variable changes take effect
 ~/D/w/c/fortune-teller-with-config-server >>>                                                            master
```

Figure 15: Bind fortune-teller application to the Config Server service instance using cf CLI

At this point, we can start the application. Once we start the application, it will communicate with the `Config Server` to pull down the application properties from Git. To do this, run `cf start fortune-teller`:

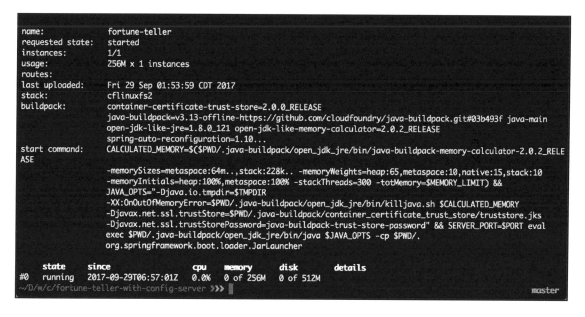

Figure 16: Start the fortune-teller application after the Config Server service instance has been bound to the application

Once the application is running, the output on the terminal will show that the application has started and provide all of the stats about the application:

```
name:              fortune-teller
requested state:   started
instances:         1/1
usage:             256M x 1 instances
routes:
last uploaded:     Fri 29 Sep 01:53:59 CDT 2017
stack:             cflinuxfs2
buildpack:         container-certificate-trust-store=2.0.0_RELEASE
                   java-buildpack=v3.13-offline-https://github.com/cloudfoundry/java-buildpack.git#03b493f java-main
                   open-jdk-like-jre=1.8.0_121 open-jdk-like-memory-calculator=2.0.2_RELEASE
                   spring-auto-reconfiguration=1.10...
start command:     CALCULATED_MEMORY=$($PWD/.java-buildpack/open_jdk_jre/bin/java-buildpack-memory-calculator-2.0.2_RELE
ASE
                   -memorySizes=metaspace:64m..,stack:228k.. -memoryWeights=heap:65,metaspace:10,native:15,stack:10
                   -memoryInitials=heap:100%,metaspace:100% -stackThreads=300 -totMemory=$MEMORY_LIMIT) &&
                   JAVA_OPTS="-Djava.io.tmpdir=$TMPDIR
                   -XX:OnOutOfMemoryError=$PWD/.java-buildpack/open_jdk_jre/bin/killjava.sh $CALCULATED_MEMORY
                   -Djavax.net.ssl.trustStore=$PWD/.java-buildpack/container_certificate_trust_store/truststore.jks
                   -Djavax.net.ssl.trustStorePassword=java-buildpack-trust-store-password" && SERVER_PORT=$PORT eval
                   exec $PWD/.java-buildpack/open_jdk_jre/bin/java $JAVA_OPTS -cp $PWD/.
                   org.springframework.boot.loader.JarLauncher

     state     since                  cpu     memory       disk        details
#0   running   2017-09-29T06:57:01Z   0.0%    0 of 256M    0 of 512M
~/D/w/c/fortune-teller-with-config-server >>>                                              master
```

Figure 17: Status of the fortune-teller application after the application has started successfully

We can now look at the logs for this new application and see some new fortunes getting generated. The words list is defined in the configuration that is on Git. To look at the logs, run `cf logs fortune-teller`:

```
[~/D/w/c/fortune-teller-with-config-server >>> cf logs fortune-teller                                    master ]
Retrieving logs for app fortune-teller in org cloudfoundry-for-developers / space development as admin...

   2017-09-29T02:00:55.00-0500 [APP/PROC/WEB/0] OUT brocaded prestigious waucht effortlessness telex
   2017-09-29T02:01:00.00-0500 [APP/PROC/WEB/0] OUT interhabitation copulation painstakingness pelorus pentasyllable
   2017-09-29T02:01:05.00-0500 [APP/PROC/WEB/0] OUT prestigious mitzi unmurmuring pentasyllable pentasyllable
   2017-09-29T02:01:10.00-0500 [APP/PROC/WEB/0] OUT unassuring misallying unstinted penlite convictional
   2017-09-29T02:01:15.00-0500 [APP/PROC/WEB/0] OUT reprosecuting gobo convictional auricularly rhumbatron
   2017-09-29T02:01:20.00-0500 [APP/PROC/WEB/0] OUT ectosteal arimathea tsuga ectosteal unassuring
   2017-09-29T02:01:25.00-0500 [APP/PROC/WEB/0] OUT puttied puttied brocaded fitful brocaded
   2017-09-29T02:01:30.00-0500 [APP/PROC/WEB/0] OUT pilaf austrian aromatise fisticuff cabling
   2017-09-29T02:01:35.00-0500 [APP/PROC/WEB/0] OUT telex makings painstakingness biconcave xanthophyllous
   2017-09-29T02:01:40.00-0500 [APP/PROC/WEB/0] OUT flab unstinted phototherapist menseless cabling
   2017-09-29T02:01:45.00-0500 [APP/PROC/WEB/0] OUT effortlessness pelorus boer tsuga gobo
```

Figure 18: View the fortune-teller application logs when configured with config-server service instance

Congratulations! The application now has a central location to host its properties. The release of this microservice should be simple and less error-prone. If there is an incorrect configuration in the source control, then the user can revert the changes in the source control and have the config updated on the application without restarting the application. For more details on how to use the actuator endpoints to pull the latest configuration changes without restarting the application, refer to the **Spring Cloud Config Server** documentation at: `https://spring.io/guides/gs/centralized-configuration/`.

Service Registry for application registration and discovery

Service Registry in Cloud Foundry provides applications with an implementation of the Service Discovery pattern, one of the key tenets of a microservice-based architecture. Service Registry is based on Eureka (`https://github.com/Netflix/eureka`), Netflix's Service Discovery server and client.

To manually configure each client of a service or adopt some form of access convention can be difficult and prove to be fragile in production. Instead, the applications can use the Service Registry to dynamically discover and call registered services:

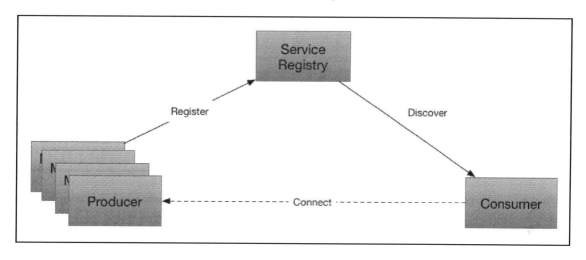

Figure 19: Service Registry workflow

Here, on startup, the producer registers itself by supplying metadata about itself, such as the host and port information. The Service Registry expects a regular heartbeat message from each service instance. If an application instance begins to consistently fail to send the heartbeat, the Service Registry will remove that application instance from its registry. The consumer gets the information about the producer from the Service Registry, and then uses that metadata to invoke the producer.

With this dynamic service discovery pattern, it makes it easier to build and manage microservices. Also, the dependent service information is not directly hardcoded into the application properties, making it less error-prone. If there are multiple application instances of the producer application, the consumer need not worry about implementing any special load-balancing techniques, as load-balancing logic is handled internally by the Ribbon Client, which is already bundled with the application.

Now, let's modify the application that has the `Config Server` service instance bound to it, to now use the Service Registry service to fetch the random sentences from the `fortune-teller-api` application.

Before we tweak the fortune-teller application, let's push the `fortune-teller-api` application. To do this, switch to the `chapter-7/fortune-teller-api` directory and run `mvn clean install`.

Push the `fortune-teller-api` application into PCF Dev, by executing `cf push fortune-teller-api -p target/fortune-teller-api-0.0.1-SNAPSHOT.jar --no-start`. We will start this application after creating the `Service Registry` instance:

```
[~/D/w/c/fortune-teller-api >>> cf push fortune-teller-api -p target/fortune-teller-api-0.0.1-SNAPSHOT.jar --no-start          ]
Creating app fortune-teller-api in org cloudfoundry-for-developers / space development as admin...
OK

Creating route fortune-teller-api.local.pcfdev.io...
OK

Binding fortune-teller-api.local.pcfdev.io to fortune-teller-api...
OK

Uploading fortune-teller-api...
Uploading app files from: /var/folders/8s/wn8_npdn52gch24n6mqdg20m0000gn/T/unzipped-app236503645
Uploading 800.6K, 114 files
Done uploading
OK
```

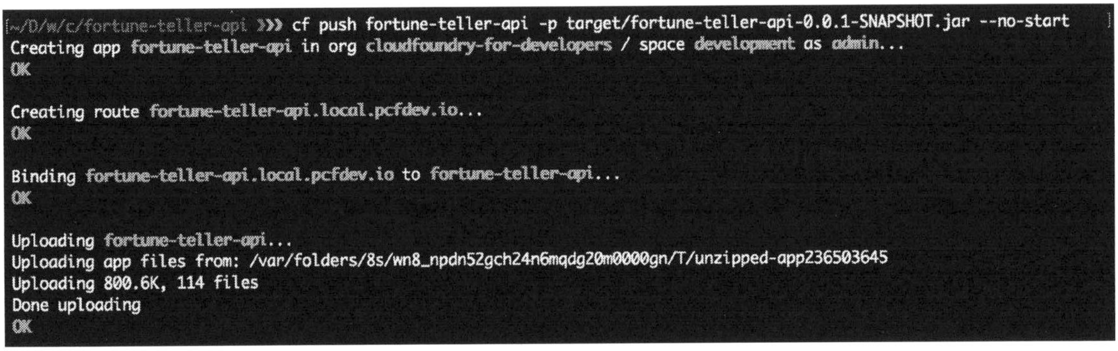

Figure 20: Push fortune-teller-api application

To create the `Service Registry` instance from the PCF Dev marketplace, we execute `cf create-service p-service-registry standard service-registry`, where `p-service-registry` is the `Service Registry` name, `standard` is the name of the plan, and `service-registry` is the instance name that we will use to bind to the application:

```
[~/D/w/c/fortune-teller-api >>> cf create-service p-service-registry standard service-registry                    master ]
Creating service instance service-registry in org cloudfoundry-for-developers / space development as admin...
OK

Create in progress. Use 'cf services' or 'cf service service-registry' to check operation status.
```

Figure 21: Create service-registry service instance

Validate if the `service-registry` service instance creation was a success by executing `cf service service-registry` and validating if the status is `create succeeded`:

```
[~/D/w/c/fortune-teller-api >>> cf service service-registry                    × 130 master

Service instance: service-registry
Service: p-service-registry
Bound apps:
Tags:
Plan: standard
Description: Service Registry for Spring Cloud Applications
Documentation url: http://docs.pivotal.io/spring-cloud-services/
Dashboard: https://spring-cloud-broker.local.pcfdev.io/dashboard/p-service-registry/dce2c83d-e32a-4380-847c-8c370e243625

Last Operation
Status: create succeeded
Message:
Started: 2017-09-29T08:02:55Z
Updated: 2017-09-29T08:04:59Z
```

Figure 22: Validate if service-registry service instance creation is successful

We should bind the `fortune-teller-api` application to the `service-registry` service instance. To do this, execute `cf bind-service fortune-teller-api service-registry`:

```
[~/D/w/c/fortune-teller-api >>> cf bind-service fortune-teller-api service-registry           master
Binding service service-registry to app fortune-teller-api in org cloudfoundry-for-developers / space development as adm
in...
OK
TIP: Use 'cf restage fortune-teller-api' to ensure your env variable changes take effect
```

Figure 23: Bind fortune-teller-api application to the service-registry service instance

Finally, start the `fortune-teller-api` application, by executing `cf start fortune-teller-api`:

```
[~/D/w/c/fortune-teller-api >>> cf start fortune-teller-api                              master
Starting app fortune-teller-api in org cloudfoundry-for-developers / space development as admin...

Staging app and tracing logs...
    Downloading dotnet-core_buildpack...
    Downloading python_buildpack...
    Downloading php_buildpack...
    Downloading java_buildpack...
    Downloading ruby_buildpack...
    Downloaded dotnet-core_buildpack
    Downloading nodejs_buildpack...
    Downloaded php_buildpack
    Downloaded java_buildpack
    Downloading go_buildpack...
    Downloading staticfile_buildpack...
```

Figure 24: Start the fortune-teller-api application after binding to the service-registry service instance

Check if the application is in the *running* state by looking at the output generated by the preceding `cf push` command:

```
Waiting for app to start...

name:             fortune-teller-api
requested state:  started
instances:        1/1
usage:            256M x 1 instances
routes:           fortune-teller-api.local.pcfdev.io
last uploaded:    Fri 29 Sep 02:59:29 CDT 2017
stack:            cflinuxfs2
buildpack:        container-certificate-trust-store=2.0.0_RELEASE
                  java-buildpack=v3.13-offline-https://github.com/cloudfoundry/java-buildpack.git#03b493f java-main
                  open-jdk-like-jre=1.8.0_121 open-jdk-like-memory-calculator=2.0.2_RELEASE
                  spring-auto-reconfiguration=1.10...
start command:    CALCULATED_MEMORY=$($PWD/.java-buildpack/open_jdk_jre/bin/java-buildpack-memory-calculator-2.0.2_RELE
ASE
                  -memorySizes=metaspace:64m..,stack:228k.. -memoryWeights=heap:65,metaspace:10,native:15,stack:10
                  -memoryInitials=heap:100%,metaspace:100% -stackThreads=300 -totMemory=$MEMORY_LIMIT) &&
                  JAVA_OPTS="-Djava.io.tmpdir=$TMPDIR
                  -XX:OnOutOfMemoryError=$PWD/.java-buildpack/open_jdk_jre/bin/killjava.sh $CALCULATED_MEMORY
                  -Djavax.net.ssl.trustStore=$PWD/.java-buildpack/container_certificate_trust_store/truststore.jks
                  -Djavax.net.ssl.trustStorePassword=java-buildpack-trust-store-password" && SERVER_PORT=$PORT eval
                  exec $PWD/.java-buildpack/open_jdk_jre/bin/java $JAVA_OPTS -cp $PWD/.
                  org.springframework.boot.loader.JarLauncher

     state     since                   cpu      memory            disk              details
#0   running   2017-09-29T08:10:32Z    156.2%   230.9M of 256M    162.7M of 512M
~/D/w/c/fortune-teller-api >>>                                                        master
```

Figure 25: Status of the fortune-teller-api application after binding to the service-registry service instance

If the application has started successfully, then the `Service Registry` instance dashboard should list the `fortune-teller-api` application, under the `Registered Apps` section. To verify this information, log in to the **Apps Manager**, select **cloudfoundry-for-developers** Org, under that select **development** Space, and then click on the **Services** tab:

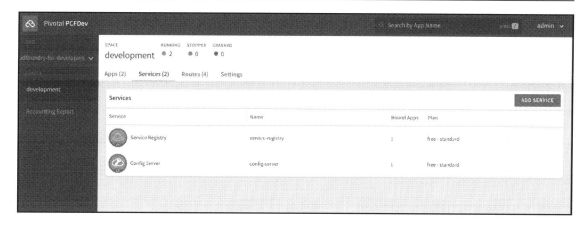

Figure 26: Viewing services bound to the fortune-teller-api application using the App Manager

Next, click on the **Service Registry** that has the name `service-registry`:

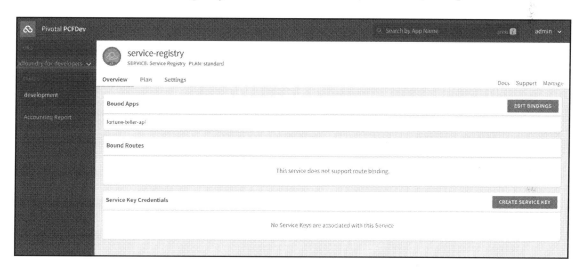

Figure 27: View the service-registry service instance using the App Manager

The `Service Registry` instance dashboard should list the `fortune-teller-api`:

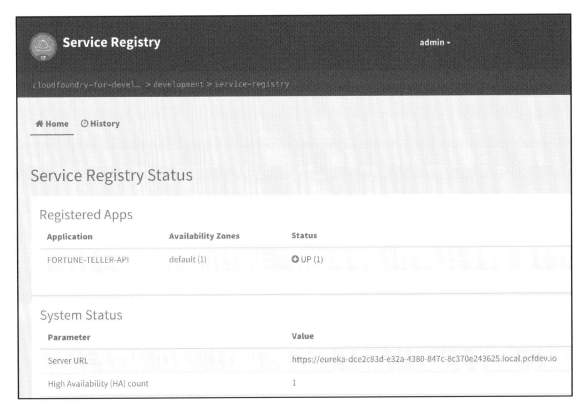

Figure 28: View the service-registry service instance dashboard using the Apps Manager

Now, let's focus our attention on the `fortune-teller` application. Switch to the `chapter-7/fortune-teller-with-config-server-and-service-registry` directory and edit the `pom.xml` file to include the `spring-cloud-services-starter-service-registry` jar. This starter project will pull in all of the dependencies required by the application to consume the `Service Registry` service, when it is bound to it:

```
<dependency>
  <groupId>io.pivotal.spring.cloud</groupId>
  <artifactId>spring-cloud-services-starter-service-
registry</artifactId></dependency>
<dependencyManagement>
  <dependencies>
    <dependency>
      <groupId>org.springframework.cloud</groupId>
```

```
        <artifactId>spring-cloud-dependencies</artifactId>
        <version>${spring-cloud.version}</version>
        <type>pom</type>
        <scope>import</scope>
      </dependency>
      <dependency>
        <groupId>io.pivotal.spring.cloud</groupId>
        <artifactId>spring-cloud-services-dependencies</artifactId>
        <version>${spring-cloud-services.version}</version>
        <type>pom</type>
        <scope>import</scope>
      </dependency>
    </dependencies>
  </dependencyManagement>
```

Once we have the dependencies defined, we need to update the `bootstrap.yml`. Since this is a worker application, it does not have a route. So, we need to tell the Eureka client to use the IP address instead of the default, which is hostname. If this configuration is missed, then the application will not register successfully with the `Service Registry` service instance. So, add the following to the `bootstrap.yml`:

```
eureka:
  instance:
    prefer-ip-address: true
```

We will need to add the `@EnableDiscoveryClient` in `FortuneTellerApplication.java`. This annotation tells the application to register itself with the `Service Registry` using the IP address of the application:

```
@SpringBootApplication
@EnableScheduling
@EnableDiscoveryClient
public class FortuneTellerApplication {
@Autowired
FortuneCookieGenerator fortuneCookieGenerator;
....
....
}
```

In the `FortuneTellerApplication.java`, we will need to define the `RestTemplate` bean and annotate it with `@LoadBalanced`. The annotation marks the `RestTemplate` bean to be configured to use a `LoadBalancerClient`, which is provided by the `Ribbon Client`:

```
@Bean
@LoadBalanced
```

```
public RestTemplate restTemplate() {
return new RestTemplate();
}
```

In the `FortuneCookieGenerator.java`, we will update the `generate` method to invoke the `generate` method of the `fortune-teller-api` application so it will generate a random set of words. Here, we will specify the URI to be `//fortune-teller-api/generator` and pass in the length as a parameter. The `RestTemplate` will resolve the URI by getting the information of `fortune-teller-api` from the `Service Registry`:

```
public void generate() {
URI uri = UriComponentsBuilder.fromUriString("//fortune-teller-api/generator")
.queryParam("length", fortuneLength).build().toUri();
String sentence = restTemplate.getForObject(uri, String.class);
System.out.println(sentence);
}
```

At this time, we can compile the code by executing `mvn clean install` from the `chapter-7/fortune-teller-with-config-server-and-service-registry` directory.

Once the code is compiled, we can push the new bits by executing `cf push fortune-teller -p target/fortune-teller-with-config-server-and-service-registry-0.0.1-SNAPSHOT.jar --no-route --health-check-type=process --no-start`. We specify the `--no-start` option, as we still need to bind the `fortune-teller` application to the `Service Registry` service instance that we had created when we pushed the `fortune-teller-api` application:

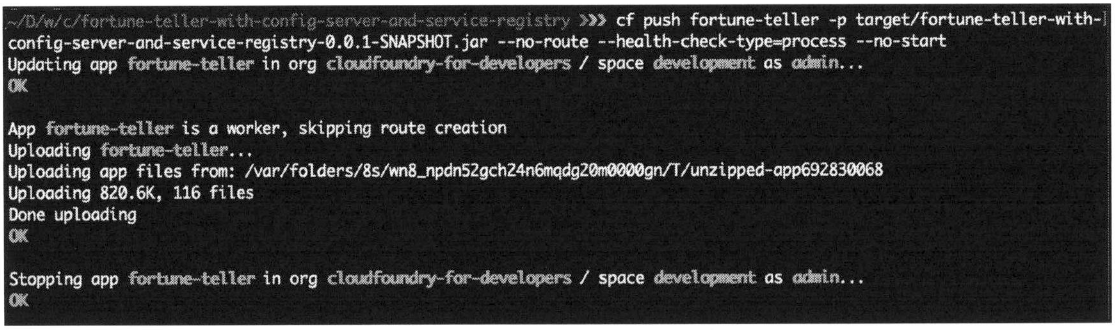

Figure 29: Push the updated fortune-teller application onto PCF Dev

We will bind the `fortune-teller` application to the `Service Registry` service, by executing `cf bind-service fortune-teller service-registry`:

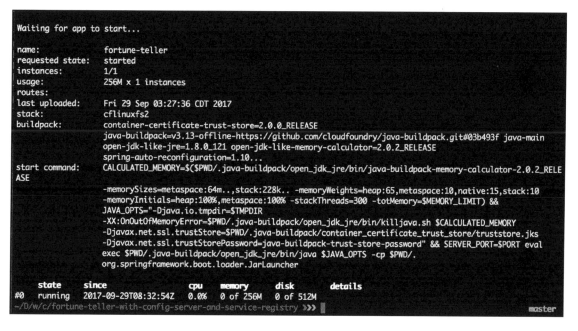

Figure 30: Bind the fortune-teller application with the Service-Registry service instance

We can now start the `fortune-teller` application by executing `cf start fortune-teller`, and validate the application status:

Figure 31: Output of the fortune-teller application after it has started successfully

Finally, we can validate the `fortune-teller` application logs. This time, the fortune is being generated by the `fortune-teller-api` application, and not by the `fortune-teller` application. Let's take a look at the logs by running `cf logs fortune-teller`:

```
 2017-09-29T03:33:25.54-0500 [APP/PROC/WEB/0] OUT },Server stats: [[Server:fortune-teller-api.local.pcfdev.io:8625854a
-069a-40ec-7dce-b6c3;   Zone:local.pcfdev.io;   Total Requests:0;        Successive connection failure:0;        Total bl
ackout seconds:0;       Last connection made:Thu Jan 01 00:00:00 UTC 1970;      First connection made: Thu Jan 01 00:00:
00 UTC 1970;     Active Connections:0;   total failure count in last (1000) msecs:0;      average resp time:0.0;  90 perce
ntile resp time:0.0;    95 percentile resp time:0.0;     min resp time:0.0;      max resp time:0.0;      stddev resp time
:0.0]
 2017-09-29T03:33:25.54-0500 [APP/PROC/WEB/0] OUT ]}ServerList:org.springframework.cloud.netflix.ribbon.eureka.DomainE
xtractingServerList@75353605
 2017-09-29T03:33:26.06-0500 [APP/PROC/WEB/0] OUT ARROM AVIDE GATHO ATCHE CLUSE
 2017-09-29T03:33:26.51-0500 [APP/PROC/WEB/0] OUT 2017-09-29 08:33:26.510  INFO 5 --- [erListUpdater-0] c.netflix.conf
ig.ChainedDynamicProperty  : Flipping property: fortune-teller-api.ribbon.ActiveConnectionsLimit to use NEXT property: n
iws.loadbalancer.availabilityFilteringRule.activeConnectionsLimit = 2147483647
 2017-09-29T03:33:30.01-0500 [APP/PROC/WEB/0] OUT HURAL CLUDE SAMAN LEVIT ASIVE
 2017-09-29T03:33:35.01-0500 [APP/PROC/WEB/0] OUT EQUIR ELOWN UPOIN EMPOL YEDED
 2017-09-29T03:33:40.02-0500 [APP/PROC/WEB/0] OUT PROCE CIELL PREAT SPANK LITIR
 2017-09-29T03:33:45.02-0500 [APP/PROC/WEB/0] OUT TWOUN FRART YOUSS BODUR OPEDE
 2017-09-29T03:33:50.01-0500 [APP/PROC/WEB/0] OUT CURCE ABOTE WRITA SKINA NERIT
 2017-09-29T03:33:55.01-0500 [APP/PROC/WEB/0] OUT OFFIN CEPET TRODY NANGE FLOWS
```

Figure 32: Logs output of the fortune-teller application

It is that simple to use the `Service Registry` service to discover other microservices. This pattern makes the configuration simple and easy to manage.

One issue that still exists in this application is that when the `fortune-teller-api` application is stopped, then the `fortune-teller` application will stop generating any random sentences, and generates exceptions in the logs.

Stop the `fortune-teller-api` application by executing `cf stop fortune-teller-api`:

```
~/D/w/c/fortune-teller-with-config-server-and-service-registry >>> cf stop fortune-teller-api                    ✗ 1 master
Stopping app fortune-teller-api in org cloudfoundry-for-developers / space development as admin...
OK
```

Figure 33: Stopping the fortune-teller-api application

In the `fortune-teller` application logs, we will see a bunch of exceptions:

```
Retrieving logs for app fortune-teller in org cloudfoundry-for-developers / space development as admin...

    2017-09-29T03:40:45.01-0500 [APP/PROC/WEB/0] OUT TABLE VEDED EQUIR VESTA GENSE
    2017-09-29T03:40:50.01-0500 [APP/PROC/WEB/0] OUT AWARY DUSIT HOLLE YOUGH RUCED
    2017-09-29T03:40:55.02-0500 [APP/PROC/WEB/0] OUT     at org.springframework.aop.framework.ReflectiveMethodInvocation.
proceed(ReflectiveMethodInvocation.java:157) ~[spring-aop-4.3.11.RELEASE.jar!/:4.3.11.RELEASE]
    2017-09-29T03:40:55.02-0500 [APP/PROC/WEB/0] OUT     at org.springframework.scheduling.support.ScheduledMethodRunnabl
e.run(ScheduledMethodRunnable.java:65) ~[spring-context-4.3.11.RELEASE.jar!/:4.3.11.RELEASE]
    2017-09-29T03:40:55.02-0500 [APP/PROC/WEB/0] OUT     at java.util.concurrent.Executors$RunnableAdapter.call(Executors
.java:511) [na:1.8.0_121]
    2017-09-29T03:40:55.02-0500 [APP/PROC/WEB/0] OUT     at java.lang.Thread.run(Thread.java:745) [na:1.8.0_121]
    2017-09-29T03:40:55.02-0500 [APP/PROC/WEB/0] OUT     at cf.developers.FortuneCookieGenerator$$FastClassBySpringCGLIB$
$e8442d48.invoke(<generated>) ~[classes/:na]
    2017-09-29T03:40:55.02-0500 [APP/PROC/WEB/0] OUT     at org.springframework.cglib.proxy.MethodProxy.invoke(MethodProx
y.java:204) ~[spring-core-4.3.11.RELEASE.jar!/:4.3.11.RELEASE]
    2017-09-29T03:40:55.02-0500 [APP/PROC/WEB/0] OUT     at cf.developers.FortuneTellerApplication.generateFortune(Fortun
eTellerApplication.java:33) ~[classes/:na]
    2017-09-29T03:40:55.02-0500 [APP/PROC/WEB/0] OUT 2017-09-29 08:40:55.024 ERROR 5 --- [pool-7-thread-1] o.s.s.s.TaskUt
```

Figure 34: Errors listed in the fortune-teller application after stopping the fortune-teller-api application

This is not desired, and we still want the `fortune-teller` application to fall back to its own sentence-generating logic if the `fortune-teller-api` application goes down for any reason. We will fix this issue using the **circuit breaker pattern**, which is discussed in the next section.

Circuit breakers and dashboard

To limit the duration of operations, we can use timeouts. Timeouts can prevent hanging operations and keep the system responsive. However, using static, fine-tuned timeouts in microservices communication is an anti-pattern; we are in a highly dynamic environment where it's almost impossible to come up with the right timing limitations that work well in every case.

Circuit breakers insulate a service from its dependencies by preventing remote calls when a dependency is determined to be unhealthy, just as electrical circuit breakers protect homes from burning down due to excessive use of power. Circuit breakers are implemented as state machines:

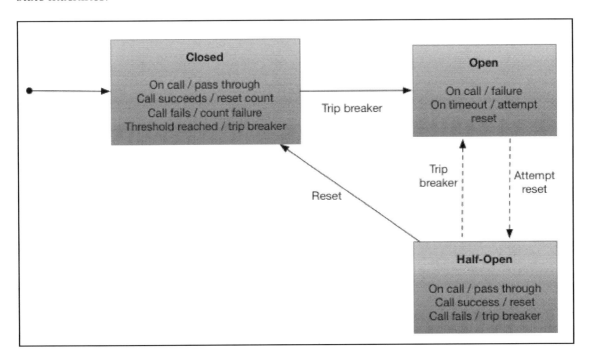

Figure 35: Circuit breaker workflow

In the closed state, all calls are simply passed through to the dependency. If any of these calls fail, the failure is counted. When the failure count reaches a specified threshold within a specified time period, the circuit trips into the open state. In the open state, calls always fail immediately. After a predetermined period of time, the circuit transitions into a *half-open* state. In this state, calls are again attempted to the remote dependency. Successful calls transition the circuit breaker back into the closed state, while failed calls return the circuit breaker to the open state.

Bulkhead is used in the industry to partition a ship into sections, so that sections can be sealed off if there is a hull breach. In the software development, it's used to partition a service, to avoid the entire application from failing. Building partitions into the microservice is one of the ways to avoid any application outages.

Netflix has produced a very powerful library for fault tolerance in Hystrix that employs these patterns and more. Hystrix allows code to be wrapped in `HystrixCommand` objects in order to wrap that code in a circuit breaker.

We will now modify the `fortune-teller` application to include the circuit breaker pattern, to prevent the application from going down when the `fortune-teller-api` application is unavailable for various reasons.

We need to add the `spring-cloud-services-starter-circuit-breaker` library dependency in the `pom.xml` to include the `CircuitBreaker` functionality in the `fortune-teller` application:

```
<dependency>
<groupId>io.pivotal.spring.cloud</groupId>
<artifactId>spring-cloud-services-starter-circuit-
breaker</artifactId></dependency>
```

We need to add the `@EnableCircuitBreaker` annotation in `FortuneTellerApplication.java`, to enable a `CircuitBreaker` implementation:

```
@SpringBootApplication
@EnableScheduling
@EnableCircuitBreaker
@EnableDiscoveryClient
public class FortuneTellerApplication {
@Autowired
FortuneCookieGenerator fortuneCookieGenerator;
...
...
}
```

We need to modify the `FortuneCookieGenerator.java` to include the `@HystrixCommand` annotation over the methods that depend on other microservices. This annotation allows us to define a `fallbackMethod`, which is invoked whenever the downstream system is unavailable. Let's look at how we implement this in our class. We will first add the `@HystrixCommand` annotation over the `generate` method, and then we will write an additional method and call it `defaultGenerate`, which will be called when the `fortune-teller-api` application is not available:

```
@HystrixCommand(fallbackMethod = "defaultGenerate")
public void generate() {
URI uri = UriComponentsBuilder.fromUriString("//fortune-teller-
api/generator")
 .queryParam("length", fortuneLength).build().toUri();
 String sentence = restTemplate.getForObject(uri, String.class);
```

```
  System.out.println(sentence);
 }
 public void defaultGenerate() {
  Random random = new Random();
  int wordsInSentence = 0;
  StringBuilder randomSentenceStringBuilder = new StringBuilder();
  while (fortuneLength != wordsInSentence) {
  int pos = random.nextInt(words.length);
  String word = words[pos];
  randomSentenceStringBuilder.append(word).append(" ");
  wordsInSentence++;
 }
  System.out.println(randomSentenceStringBuilder.toString());
 }
```

So, when there is a failure in the generate method, the `defaultGenerate` method gets invoked. This happens until the `fortune-teller-api` application comes back online, and then the `generate` function will resume its normal operations.

Let's now compile the code. So, switch to `chapter-7/fortune-teller-with-config-server-and-service-registry-and-hystrix`, and execute `mvn clean install`.

Since we need the circuit breaker service, we need to create the service instance of the circuit breaker dashboard for Spring Cloud applications from the marketplace. This is done by executing `cf create-service p-circuit-breaker-dashboard standard circuit-breaker`, where `p-circuit-breaker-dashboard` is the service name of the circuit breaker service, `standard` is the plan available for this service, and `circuit-breaker` is the instance name that we will use to bind to the application:

```
[~/D/w/c/fortune-teller-with-config-server-and-service-registry-and-hystrix >>> cf create-service p-circuit-breaker-dashb]
oard standard circuit-breaker
Creating service instance circuit-breaker in org cloudfoundry-for-developers / space development as admin...
OK

Create in progress. Use 'cf services' or 'cf service circuit-breaker' to check operation status.
```

Figure 36: Create the circuit-breaker service instance using cf CLI

We will now push the updated `fortune-teller` application onto PCF Dev, by executing `cf push fortune-teller -p target/fortune-teller-with-config-server-and-service-registry-and-hystrix-0.0.1-SNAPSHOT.jar --no-route --health-check-type=process --no-start`:

```
~/D/w/c/fortune-teller-with-config-server-and-service-registry-and-hystrix >>> cf push fortune-teller -p target/fortune-
teller-with-config-server-and-service-registry-and-hystrix-0.0.1-SNAPSHOT.jar --no-route --health-check-type=process --n
o-start
Updating app fortune-teller in org cloudfoundry-for-developers / space development as admin...
OK

App fortune-teller is a worker, skipping route creation
Uploading fortune-teller...
Uploading app files from: /var/folders/8s/wn8_npdn52gch24n6mqdg20m0000gn/T/unzipped-app329679622
Uploading 1.1M, 135 files
Done uploading
OK

Stopping app fortune-teller in org cloudfoundry-for-developers / space development as admin...
OK
```

Figure 37: Push the updated fortune-teller application onto PCF Dev

Let's validate whether the `circuit-breaker` service creation is complete by executing `cf service circuit-breaker`:

```
[~/D/w/c/fortune-teller-with-config-server-and-service-registry-and-hystrix >>> cf service circuit-breaker          master ]

Service instance: circuit-breaker
Service: p-circuit-breaker-dashboard
Bound apps:
Tags:
Plan: standard
Description: Circuit Breaker Dashboard for Spring Cloud Applications
Documentation url: http://docs.pivotal.io/spring-cloud-services/
Dashboard: https://spring-cloud-broker.local.pcfdev.io/dashboard/p-circuit-breaker-dashboard/310d780d-e6c0-4981-9781-95c
62c998db8

Last Operation
Status: create succeeded
Message:
Started: 2017-09-29T10:08:20Z
Updated: 2017-09-29T10:10:25Z
```

Figure 38: Validate if the circuit-breaker service instance creation is successful

If the service instance creation is a success, then we can bind the `fortune-teller` application to this newly-created service. This is done by executing `cf bind-service fortune-teller circuit-breaker`:

```
~/D/w/c/fortune-teller-with-config-server-and-service-registry-and-hystrix >>> cf bind-service fortune-teller circuit-br
eaker
Binding service circuit-breaker to app fortune-teller in org cloudfoundry-for-developers / space development as admin...
OK
TIP: Use 'cf restage fortune-teller' to ensure your env variable changes take effect
```

Figure 39: Bind the fortune-teller application to the circuit-breaker service instance

Now, we can start the `fortune-teller` application, and also the `fortune-teller-api` application, if it's not already running. This is done by executing `cf start fortune-teller` and `cf start fortune-teller-api`, accordingly.

> If the application fails to start due to out of memory errors, then run `cf scale fortune-teller -m` 1024M.

Once the `fortune-teller` application has started, let's take a look at the logs, by executing `cf logs fortune-teller`:

```
   2017-09-29T05:21:51.00-0500 [APP/PROC/WEB/0] OUT },Server stats: [[Server:fortune-teller-api.local.pcfdev.io:76da608d
-6d5b-412e-5b92-4f1c;   Zone:local.pcfdev.io;   Total Requests:0;      Successive connection failure:0;       Total bl
ackout seconds:0;        Last connection made:Thu Jan 01 00:00:00 UTC 1970;       First connection made: Thu Jan 01 00:00:
00 UTC 1970;    Active Connections:0;   total failure count in last (1000) msecs:0;     average resp time:0.0;  90 perce
ntile resp time:0.0;     95 percentile resp time:0.0;      min resp time:0.0;      max resp time:0.0;       stddev resp time
:0.0]
   2017-09-29T05:21:51.00-0500 [APP/PROC/WEB/0] OUT ]}ServerList:org.springframework.cloud.netflix.ribbon.eureka.DomainE
xtractingServerList@5dd3c9ef
   2017-09-29T05:21:51.19-0500 [APP/PROC/WEB/0] OUT ISTRA DAYEA ALSOM LOODY DELTH
   2017-09-29T05:21:51.95-0500 [APP/PROC/WEB/0] OUT 2017-09-29 10:21:51.955  INFO 6 --- [erListUpdater-0] c.netflix.conf
ig.ChainedDynamicProperty : Flipping property: fortune-teller-api.ribbon.ActiveConnectionsLimit to use NEXT property: n
iws.loadbalancer.availabilityFilteringRule.activeConnectionsLimit = 2147483647
   2017-09-29T05:21:55.02-0500 [APP/PROC/WEB/0] OUT RABIT OUSID BLIGH AFTEE TONOT
   2017-09-29T05:22:00.01-0500 [APP/PROC/WEB/0] OUT VELTE HIRSO APEAL CRASS HATEE
   2017-09-29T05:22:05.01-0500 [APP/PROC/WEB/0] OUT EXPED ECIER THIGH OPECH ENDET
   2017-09-29T05:22:10.12-0500 [APP/PROC/WEB/0] OUT QUEST NALIF GUEND GROVE MAINT
   2017-09-29T05:22:15.02-0500 [APP/PROC/WEB/0] OUT NONOR GANTA KNOTH MUNGE ROBLE
   2017-09-29T05:22:20.01-0500 [APP/PROC/WEB/0] OUT NELOW SMATH IDEST PHESS MUNTA
```

Figure 40: View the fortune-teller application logs using cf CLI

Let's simulate a failure by stopping the `fortune-teller-api` application. To do this, execute `cf stop fortune-teller-api`.

Now, if we continue to look at the `fortune-teller` application logs, we will not see the previous errors that we saw in the last section. This time, the sentences are generated using the words that the application retrieved from Git, through the `Config Server` service instance:

```
^C
|~/D/w/book-contents >>> cf logs fortune-teller                                    x 130 master ■
Retrieving logs for app fortune-teller in org cloudfoundry-for-developers / space development as admin...

   2017-09-29T05:24:25.01-0500 [APP/PROC/WEB/0] OUT WRIER AUSEE HUSIT AMOUP BINUM
   2017-09-29T05:24:30.01-0500 [APP/PROC/WEB/0] OUT VANGS NARGE FOLED BEGAR EQUAL
   2017-09-29T05:24:35.03-0500 [APP/PROC/WEB/0] OUT reassimilate quill omnivore sham postpone
   2017-09-29T05:24:40.01-0500 [APP/PROC/WEB/0] OUT xanthophyllous omnivore tartarian trismic turniplike
   2017-09-29T05:24:45.00-0500 [APP/PROC/WEB/0] OUT remigial aromatise countrywomen austrian hims
   2017-09-29T05:24:50.01-0500 [APP/PROC/WEB/0] OUT nonleguminous pentasyllable penlite reassimilate waucht
^C
```

Figure 41: View the fortune-teller application logs when the fortune-teller-api is unavailable

We can also look at the Hystrix dashboard, by logging in to **Apps Manager**, selecting our working Org and Space, and clicking on the **Services** tab:

Figure 42: View the services bound to the fortune-teller application using Apps Manager

Select the **circuit-breaker** service and click on the **Manage** button. It will open a new tab and take you to the Hystrix Dashboard:

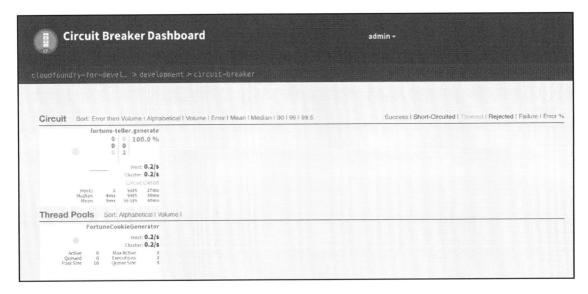

Figure 43: View the circuit-breaker service instance dashboard using Apps Manager

To cause the circuit to open, modify the `generate` method in the `fortune-teller` application to increase the number of calls.

If we now start the `fortune-teller-api` application again, the failures will reduce to zero, and the sentences will be generated by the `fortune-teller-api` application. So, start the application and look at the `fortune-teller` logs to see if the circuit is closed again. Start the `fortune-teller-api` by executing `cf start fortune-teller-api`, and keep tailing the logs :

```
2017-09-29T05:35:50.02-0500 [APP/PROC/WEB/0] OUT seamanship kain radiobiology effortlessness menseless
2017-09-29T05:35:55.00-0500 [APP/PROC/WEB/0] OUT cavilled unassuring thriftiest mor waucht
2017-09-29T05:36:00.00-0500 [APP/PROC/WEB/0] OUT hyenoid unheeded wabasha puttied postpone
2017-09-29T05:36:05.00-0500 [APP/PROC/WEB/0] OUT solacing coadunate columellate klootchman saragossa
2017-09-29T05:36:10.01-0500 [APP/PROC/WEB/0] OUT klootchman postpone penlite significative phototherapist
2017-09-29T05:36:15.00-0500 [APP/PROC/WEB/0] OUT hyenoid remigial menseless illaudable boer
2017-09-29T05:36:20.00-0500 [APP/PROC/WEB/0] OUT hyenoid dinka penlite institutes brocaded
2017-09-29T05:36:25.28-0500 [APP/PROC/WEB/0] OUT ADIDE MRSTE IMMER ADMIT EACHE
2017-09-29T05:36:30.02-0500 [APP/PROC/WEB/0] OUT WRIAN TWEVE HEITY FULTE SMAKE
2017-09-29T05:36:35.02-0500 [APP/PROC/WEB/0] OUT ASHOP ESCRA HOTEL PULLS DOMEN
```

Figure 44: View the fortune-teller application logs after the fortune-teller-api is reachable

Now when we refresh the Hystrix dashboard, we can see there are no failures, and that the applications are running as desired:

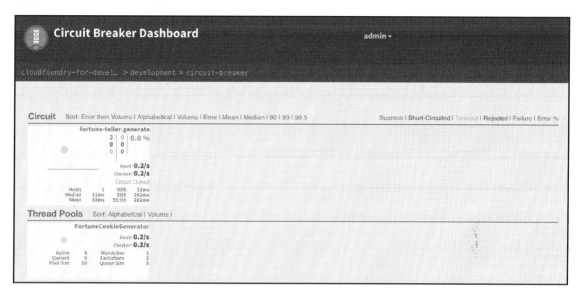

Figure 45: View the circuit-breaker dashboard after the connection with fortune-teller-api application has been restored

This concludes our discussion on the Circuit Breaker and Hystrix dashboards. Now we know how to use the Spring Cloud Services provided by Pivotal Cloud Foundry to make our applications more resilient.

References

- Matt Stine, *Migrating to Cloud-Native Application Architectures*, O'Reilly, 1st Ed., ISBN: 978-1-491-92679-6, Feb. 2015
- Sourabh Sharma, *Mastering Microservices with Java*, Packt Publishing, ISBN: 9781785285172, June 2016

Summary

In this chapter, we discussed what microservices are. We also talked about worker applications and implemented and deployed an application onto PCF Dev.

We discussed how to instruct Cloud Foundry to not create routes for the worker application using the `--no-route` option during the application push and the various health check types that Cloud Foundry uses to monitor an application. In our worker example, we used `--health-check-type=process`.

We learned about the resiliency that the Cloud Foundry platform provides, and discussed how the application can be made to be resilient using the `Config Server`, `Service Registry`, and Hystrix dashboard services provided by the Pivotal Cloud Foundry platform.

8
Services and Service Brokers

So far in this book, we have learned how to view the available services, create an instance of a service, and bind it to our applications for use. This chapter focuses on deeper concepts of services and how to author services and publish them on the marketplace so that they can be consumed by other applications. The key concepts that you will learn in this chapter are:

- Binding services to applications
- User-provided services
- What is a service broker?
- Creating and deploying custom service brokers
- Route services
- Service integration strategies

Services on Cloud Foundry

Services bring value to development teams and organizations by abstracting the stateful nature of these services from applications and decoupling the upgrade path from applications in a true microservices-like pattern.

Let's briefly revisit the simplest steps for creating a service and binding it to our application:

1. The developer finds the details of the service that they wish to use via the marketplace by calling `cf marketplace`. The marketplace is simply a listing of all of the services that can be provisioned on your foundation for your Org and/or Space. These services can be free of charge or have associated subscription costs. We covered most of this in `Chapter 6`, *Deploying Apps to Cloud Foundry*. We'll go into detail later in this chapter about how we can publish our own services on the marketplace.

2. Next, the developer creates an instance of the service through the `cf create-service <SERVICE_NAME> <PLAN> <INSTANCE_NAME> [-c <JSON_PARAMETERS>]` command.

3. Once the service instance is available, the developer binds it to their application via the `cf bind-service <APP_NAME> <INSTANCE_NAME>` command. Alternatively, they may specify this in a CF push manifest to perform the binding when deploying the application.

This is a great way for provisioning and binding to new services on Cloud Foundry, but what if the service resource is already provisioned and resides outside of Cloud Foundry? One approach to resolve this is to expose the connection strings and credentials as external configuration for a particular application. If there are other applications that need to use this service, they will need to also include the additional external configuration on their own. As you can probably imagine, this potentially leads to a great level of maintenance. That is, should any of the configuration or credentials change, all application configuration must change as well. Two approaches can be considered to avoid this. The first is through a user-provided service and the second is through service brokers.

User-provided services are those that don't appear in the marketplace and exist as service instances, once created, with custom credential and configuration fields. These services are then consumed like any other services in the marketplace, with the exception that they are restricted to the scope of the space where they are created. Therefore, the application must also be in the same space. Thereafter, an application must also be able to read the user-provided service configuration from the VCAP_SERVICES environment variable.

The second approach, through service brokers, enables services to be published in the marketplace and enable any application that has access to the service broker to consume the available published services in the marketplace. Service brokers are essentially an API that Cloud Foundry exposes that enables the management of services through the marketplace.

Another type of service that will be discussed in this chapter is route services. Route services are those that work on/transform all incoming requests to an application. First off, however, we shall explore in depth how services are consumed by applications.

Service binding of applications

Whenever a service is bound to an application (or to multiple applications), the key step it performs is to inject the service's configuration and credentials into an application. This information can be found in an application's environment variables, within VCAP_SERVICES. The VCAP_SERVICES is a JSON object that contains an array of information pertaining to bound services for that application. This is on the contrary to its sister JSON object, VCAP_APPLICATION, that holds information pertaining to the configuration of the application itself, such as its URL, memory limits, and disk capacity. We can view an application's environment variable through the cf env <APP_NAME> command.

If we clone a fresh copy of the `hello-spring-cloud` application from `https://github.com/Cloud-Foundry-For-Developers/hello-spring-cloud.git` and deploy it onto Cloud Foundry, we can perform a `cf env hello-spring-cloud`:

```
~/W/B/C/hello-spring-cloud >>> cf env hello-spring-cloud
Getting env variables for app hello-spring-cloud in org pcfdev-org / space development as admin...
OK

System-Provided:


{
 "VCAP_APPLICATION": {
  "application_id": "9ba402ce-4f37-4d9b-b719-495cb1b29d54",
  "application_name": "hello-spring-cloud",
  "application_uris": [
   "hello-spring-cloud-overground-bongo.local.pcfdev.io",
   "hello-spring-cloud-radical-nonapproachabness.local.pcfdev.io"
  ],
  "application_version": "a73d36c5-61e1-44d3-b51d-df8f5ead7ea7",
  "cf_api": "http://api.local.pcfdev.io",
  "limits": {
   "disk": 512,
   "fds": 16384,
   "mem": 256
  },
  "name": "hello-spring-cloud",
  "space_id": "cba855d5-9728-42af-a77a-6189742f7140",
  "space_name": "development",
  "uris": [
   "hello-spring-cloud-overground-bongo.local.pcfdev.io",
   "hello-spring-cloud-radical-nonapproachabness.local.pcfdev.io"
  ],
  "users": null,
  "version": "a73d36c5-61e1-44d3-b51d-df8f5ead7ea7"
 }
}

No user-defined env variables have been set

No running env variables have been set

No staging env variables have been set

~/W/B/C/hello-spring-cloud >>> 
```

Figure 1: Getting the environment variables of a fresh copy of hello-spring-cloud application without any bounded services

Figure 1 shows the environment variables of `hello-spring-cloud`. Notice that there's only `VCAP_APPLICATION` and that `VCAP_SERVICES` is not visible. This is because we have not bound any services to our fresh copy of the `hello-spring-cloud` application. If not done so already, instantiate a MySQL database service (`p-mysql`) named `my-database-`

service and bind the service instance to `hello-spring-cloud`. Run `cf env hello-spring-cloud` again. Note that you will need to perform a `cf restart hello-spring-cloud` if you wish to see the output in a browser:

```
~/W/B/C/hello-spring-cloud >>> cf env hello-spring-cloud
Getting env variables for app hello-spring-cloud in org pcfdev-org / space development as admin...
OK

System-Provided:
{
 "VCAP_SERVICES": {
  "p-mysql": [
   {
    "credentials": {
     "hostname": "mysql-broker.local.pcfdev.io",
     "jdbcUrl": "jdbc:mysql://mysql-broker.local.pcfdev.io:3306/cf_f590661d_93f3_4741_b0ab_5a781914edce?user=R8cNWvNSLMrw2e1A\u0026password=oJqWMD0bQ8NZixFw",
     "name": "cf_f590661d_93f3_4741_b0ab_5a781914edce",
     "password": "oJqWMD0bQ8NZixFw",
     "port": 3306,
     "uri": "mysql://R8cNWvNSLMrw2e1A:oJqWMD0bQ8NZixFw@mysql-broker.local.pcfdev.io:3306/cf_f590661d_93f3_4741_b0ab_5a781914edce?reconnect=true",
     "username": "R8cNWvNSLMrw2e1A"
    },
    "label": "p-mysql",
    "name": "my-database-service",
    "plan": "1gb",
    "provider": null,
    "syslog_drain_url": null,
    "tags": [
     "mysql"
    ],
    "volume_mounts": []
   }
  ]
 }
}

{
 "VCAP_APPLICATION": {
  "application_id": "9ba402ce-4f37-4d9b-b719-495cb1b29d54",
  "application_name": "hello-spring-cloud",
  "application_uris": [
   "hello-spring-cloud-overground-bongo.local.pcfdev.io",
   "hello-spring-cloud-radical-nonapproachabness.local.pcfdev.io"
  ],
  "application_version": "a73d36c5-61e1-44d3-b51d-df8f5ead7ea7",
  "cf_api": "http://api.local.pcfdev.io",
  "limits": {
   "disk": 512,
   "fds": 16384,
   "mem": 256
  },
  "name": "hello-spring-cloud",
  "space_id": "cba855d5-9728-42af-a77a-6189742f7140",
  "space_name": "development",
  "uris": [
   "hello-spring-cloud-overground-bongo.local.pcfdev.io",
   "hello-spring-cloud-radical-nonapproachabness.local.pcfdev.io"
  ],
  "users": null,
  "version": "a73d36c5-61e1-44d3-b51d-df8f5ead7ea7"
 }
}

No user-defined env variables have been set

No running env variables have been set

No staging env variables have been set

~/W/B/C/hello-spring-cloud >>>
```

Figure 2: Getting the environment variables of a fresh copy of the hello-spring-cloud application with a MySQL bounded services

Figure 2 now shows the VCAP_SERVICES JSON object. It currently shows a single MySQL service bound to the hello-spring-cloud application. The pieces of information that we see injected are the service broker name, service plan, tags, and most importantly, service configuration information such as connection strings and randomly generated credentials.

For our application to make use of this service, it needs only to read in the host details and credentials and form the connection string or use the jdbcUrl entry, if it is supported, and instantiate a database access driver to interact with the resource. To generalize our implementation, our application code would only need to look for key information such as the tag or the start of the URI scheme, that is, mysql://, to know what type of database driver class we need to instantiate. This is essentially how the spring-cloud-connector for Cloud Foundry works. It utilizes the tag name and URI scheme to form a connection string to be used with the correct database drivers.

OK, so how do I exactly get the VCAP_SERVICES JSON out in my app? It is highly recommended that existing libraries such as Spring Cloud Connector and Steeltoe are used to access the environment variables. However, if one requires a custom access, the solution is going to be dependent on the language that is used. The following provided is a pseudo-code, plus a Java code snippet example of interacting with the p-mysql credentials. Do remember however that this code will only work when an application has been deployed on Cloud Foundry and is bound to a service. If you attempt to run the code locally, it will fail because there is no VCAP_SERVICES environment variable. Therefore, if you do use this code, ensure your code has the correct handling for local testing or if there are no services bound to your application. Alternatively, to test your code locally, you could mock the VCAP_SERVICES environment variables on your local machine before running your application:

```
/* pseudo-code for access VCAP_SERVICES and do something with
the credentials - using p-mysql as an example */

VCAP_SERVICES_jsonString =
get_environment_variable("VCAP_SERVICES")

VCAP_SERVICES_json =
JSONReader_ParseToJSON(VCAP_SERVICES_jsonString)

mysqlCredentials = VCAP_SERVICES_json["p-
mysql"][0]["credentials"]
```

```
/* Java code snippet for access VCAP_SERVICES and do something
with the credentials - using p-mysql as an example */

try
{
    JSONObject vcap_services = new
JSONObject(System.getenv("VCAP_SERVICES"));

    JSONObject p_mysql_credentials = vcap_services
                            .getJSONArray("p-mysql")
                            .getJSONObject(0)
                            .getJSONObject("credentials"));

}
catch(JSONException exception)
{
    System.out.println(exception.getMessage());
    System.out.println(exception.getStackTrace());
}
```

User-provided services

So far, we understand how to instantiate a new service from the marketplace and we understand how applications work with bound services through the VCAP_SERVICES JSON object in the application environment variable. We will now visit user-provided services. With user-provided services, a developer is given the freedom to define a service instance that has custom service configuration data fields that their application will read in order to identify and connect to the resource. This is the simplest and least amount of work required to get started with connecting to a service that is external to your Cloud Foundry platform; however, be aware that user-provided services, once they are created, are service instances and are scoped within a space in Cloud Foundry. An application in another space will not see the user-provided service instance.

The command to create a user-provided service is `cf create-user-provided-service <INSTANCE_NAME> [-p <CREDENTIALS>]`. The `<INSTANCE_NAME>` is the name of the service instance that will be created and `<CREDENTIALS>` are the fields that are injected into an application's `VCAP_SERVICES` environment variable. The `<CREDENTIALS>` can be either a string of field names, that is, `"hostUrl, username, password, extraInfo"`, or it can be an actual JSON string with corresponding values, that is, `'{"hostUrl": "www.service.com", "username": "dave", "password": "blah", "extraInfo": "This is a user-provided service"}'`. If we use the string of field names, the cf CLI will interactively ask us to input the values for each field and generate the JSON object for us. Let's create a user-provided service now with a JSON object string as the input. Run the following command:

```
cf create-user-provided-service my-user-service -p  '{"hostUrl":
"www.service.com", "username": "dave", "password":"blah", "extraInfo":
"This is a user-provided service"}'
```

 In Windows, we need to escape the double quotes within the JSON object string, that is, `cf create-user-provided-service my-user-service -p  '{\"hostUrl\": \"www.service.com\", \"username\": \"dave\", \"password\":\"blah\", \"extraInfo\": \"This is a user-provided service\"}'`.

```
~/W/8/C/hello-spring-cloud >>> cf create-user-provided-service my-user-service -p  '{"hostUrl": "www.service.com", "username": "dave", "password":"blah", "extraInfo":
"This is a user-provided service"}'
Creating user provided service my-user-service in org pcfdev-org / space development as admin...
OK
~/W/8/C/hello-spring-cloud >>> cf services
Getting services in org pcfdev-org / space development as admin...
OK

name                service        plan   bound apps                                  last operation
my-database-service p-mysql        1gb    hello-spring-cloud, hello-spring-cloud-home  update succeeded
my-user-service     user-provided
~/W/8/C/hello-spring-cloud >>>
```

Figure 3: Creating a user-provided service with our own defined fields

We can now bind the user-provided service, using the `cf bind-service hello-spring-cloud my-user-service` command. Let's bind the service to the `hello-spring-cloud` application and observe what happens:

```
~/W/E/C/hello-spring-cloud >>> cf bind-service hello-spring-cloud my-user-service
Binding service my-user-service to app hello-spring-cloud in org pcfdev-org / space development as admin...
OK
TIP: Use 'cf restage hello-spring-cloud' to ensure your env variable changes take effect
~/W/E/C/hello-spring-cloud >>> cf env hello-spring-cloud
Getting env variables for app hello-spring-cloud in org pcfdev-org / space development as admin...
OK

System-Provided:
{
 "VCAP_SERVICES": {
  "p-mysql": [
   {
    "credentials": {
     "hostname": "mysql-broker.local.pcfdev.io",
     "jdbcUrl": "jdbc:mysql://mysql-broker.local.pcfdev.io:3306/cf_f590661d_93f3_4741_b0ab_5a781914edce?user=R8cNWvNSLMrwZe1A\u0026password=oJqMMD0bQ8NZixFw",
     "name": "cf_f590661d_93f3_4741_b0ab_5a781914edce",
     "password": "oJqMMD0bQ8NZixFw",
     "port": 3306,
     "uri": "mysql://R8cNWvNSLMrwZe1A:oJqMMD0bQ8NZixFw@mysql-broker.local.pcfdev.io:3306/cf_f590661d_93f3_4741_b0ab_5a781914edce?reconnect=true",
     "username": "R8cNWvNSLMrwZe1A"
    },
    "label": "p-mysql",
    "name": "my-database-service",
    "plan": "1gb",
    "provider": null,
    "syslog_drain_url": null,
    "tags": [
     "mysql"
    ],
    "volume_mounts": []
   }
  ],
  "user-provided": [
   {
    "credentials": {
     "extraInfo": "This is a user-provided service",
     "hostUrl": "www.service.com",
     "password": "blah",
     "username": "dave"
    },
    "label": "user-provided",
    "name": "my-user-service",
    "syslog_drain_url": "",
    "tags": [],
    "volume_mounts": []
   }
  ]
 }
}

{
 "VCAP_APPLICATION": {
  "application_id": "9ba402ce-4f37-4d9b-b719-495cb1b29d54",
  "application_name": "hello-spring-cloud",
  "application_uris": [
   "hello-spring-cloud-overground-bongo.local.pcfdev.io",
   "hello-spring-cloud-radical-nonapproachabness.local.pcfdev.io"
  ],
  "application_version": "a73d36c5-61e1-44d3-b51d-df8f5ead7ea7",
  "cf_api": "http://api.local.pcfdev.io",
  "limits": {
   "disk": 512,
   "fds": 16384,
   "mem": 256
  },
  "name": "hello-spring-cloud",
  "space_id": "cba855d5-9728-42af-a77a-618974f7140",
  "space_name": "development",
  "uris": [
   "hello-spring-cloud-overground-bongo.local.pcfdev.io",
   "hello-spring-cloud-radical-nonapproachabness.local.pcfdev.io"
  ],
  "users": null,
  "version": "a73d36c5-61e1-44d3-b51d-df8f5ead7ea7"
 }
}

No user-defined env variables have been set

No running env variables have been set

No staging env variables have been set

~/W/E/C/hello-spring-cloud >>>
```

Figure 4: Binding of hello-spring-cloud application to a user-provided service and the environment variables of the application thereafter

Figure 4 shows the result of binding an application to the user-provided service created previously. What we see in the `VCAP_SERVICES` JSON object is a new entry called `user-provided`, containing the fields input when we ran the `create-user-provided-service` command.

To update the fields and the value of our user-provided service, we can execute the `cf update-user-provided-service <INSTANCE_NAME> [-p <CREDENTIALS>]` command. Be aware when running the `update` command, all fields in `<CREDENTIALS>` must be typed again, even if the field has no changes, otherwise, they will be overwritten with the new fields in the string.

Finally, to delete a user-provided service, simply call `cf delete-service <INSTANCE_NAME>` and confirm the deletion. However, be aware that the service instance needs to be unbound from all applications first before it can be deleted.

Using user-provided services is a first-level approach to services. It is simple and requires the least amount of work to get some external service available to your applications. However, you may find that the user-provided service cannot be used with applications that are located in a different space. One way is to create the user-provided service at every space, but this will run into maintenance issues in the future. To overcome the space limitation, we can look into creating our own custom service brokers. With custom service brokers, we are able to publish the availability of external services at an Org or Space scope. Conveniently, if you wish to perform a quick test, there is a fixed service broker at: `https://github.com/cloudfoundry-community/worlds-simplest-service-broker`. This implementation is similar to a user-provided service, except that it is geared towards publishing a single external service via a service broker. This would enable you to span the service, as required, to multiple Orgs and Spaces. However, eventually, it is best to develop your own service broker that best suits your organization to publish all of the external services in your organization as needed. We will provide a template and the steps to deploy this template in the next section.

Service brokers

By now, you may be thinking, how can one get their service published in the marketplace and how does it all work together? The key component to this is through a service broker. A service broker is responsible for most, if not all, aspects of the life cycle of services in the marketplace. They are responsible for publishing the services and plans offered, performing service provisioning when requested, binding applications to service instances and, potentially, vice-versa when unbinding and deprovisioning. Service brokers are deployed within an Org and be configured to be a restricted space. An implementation of a service broker is an application that implements the service broker API.

Structure of services on a service broker

Before we proceed further, let's discuss the structure of services on a service broker. A service broker publishes a list of services that it offers. For every service that is published, there must be at least one associated plan for that corresponding service. A service plan is simply a variant of the service that is offered. For example, there may be a plan that is free of charge but with limited disk capacity, and there may be another plan that has a higher disk capacity but has a cost associated with it. Thus, that is why when instantiating a service through `cf create-service`, it is necessary to specify the service name, the desired service plan, and an instance name that your applications can refer to.

With this in mind, if your organization has a number of services hosted externally to Cloud Foundry, you could create a single service broker that consolidates all of the externally available services and publishes them to be securely usable by your developers. It is securely usable because your service broker would be able to bind applications with the credentials without requiring developers to know and store them. Thereafter, you would be able to limit the access to services and the service plan to certain Orgs.

Although you may be able to create a service broker with chargeable service plans, be mindful of how this works in your organization. First, understand usage patterns and their implications before proceeding with a charging approach. The most important part of services is that they should be enabling and encouraging uptake. Be agile and adapt as necessary thereafter.

The Open Service Broker API

The **Open Service Broker API** (**OSB API**) is an open standard that describes the way in which a platform's marketplace interacts with service brokers through HTTP. Such platform support includes Cloud Foundry, Heroku, Kubernetes, and OpenShift. The standard describes a RESTful protocol used to communicate between a platform and a service broker. Therefore, the implementation of specific endpoints must be fulfilled in order for a service broker to operate with a platform. As we described earlier, the key operations are service catalog management, provisioning, binding, updating, unbinding, and deprovisioning. There is also an additional operation, last operation status, used for asynchronous service operations. Each operation corresponds to a specific RESTful endpoint, which we describe in the following figure. However, aside from the endpoints, there also exists a standardized description of the HTTP response/request protocol, that can be found at: `https://github.com/openservicebrokerapi/servicebroker`. The following figure describes these REST endpoints, as of version 2.13 of the OSB API.

Operation	Endpoint
Catalog	`GET /v2/catalog`

Provision	`PUT /v2/service_instances/{instance_id}?accepts_incomplete=<bool>`
	• `{instance_id}` is a globally unique ID used for later operations such as binding and updating.
	Parameters:
	• `accepts_incomplete` is an optional input parameter describing if the marketplace and its client application supports asynchronous operations.
	  ○ `default behavior`: This is false if `accepts_incomplete` is not included
	  ○ `true`: This is an asynchronous operation by the platform and will operate with asynchronous response codes from the broker
	  ○ `false`: This is the only synchronous operation supported by the platform and will operate with synchronous response codes from the broker

Binding	`PUT /v2/service_instances/{instance_id}/service_bindings/{binding_id}` • `{instance_id}` is a globally unique ID. This should match the previous ID that was used for provisioning. • `{binding_id}` is a globally unique ID that will be used later for unbinding.

Update	`PATCH /v2/service_instances/{instance_id}?accepts_incomplete=<bool>`
	• `{instance_id}` is a globally unique ID. This should match the previous ID that was used for provisioning.
	Parameters:
	• `accepts_incomplete` is an optional input parameter describing if the marketplace and its client application support asynchronous operations.
	  ○ `default behavior`: This is false if `accepts_incomplete` is not included
	  ○ `true`: This is an asynchronous operation supported by the platform and will operate with asynchronous response codes from the broker
	  ○ `false`: This is the only synchronous operation supported by the platform and will operate with synchronous response codes from the broker

Unbind	`DELETE /v2/service_instances/{instance_id}/service_bindings/{binding_id}?service_id=<string>&plan_id=<string>` • `{instance_id}` is a globally unique ID. This should match the previous ID that was used for provisioning. • `{binding_id}` is a globally unique ID that was used for binding of a service instance, with a corresponding `{instance_id}` that was used for provisioning. **Parameters:** • `service_id` is a mandatory input parameter and must not be empty. This describes the ID of the service from the catalog • `plan_id` is a mandatory input parameter and must not be empty. This describes the ID of the plan from the catalog

Deprovision	`DELETE /v2/service_instances/{instance_id}?accepts_incomplete=<bool>&service_id=<string>&plan_id=<string>`
	• `{instance_id}` is a globally unique ID. This should match the previous ID that was used for provisioning.
	Parameters:
	• `accepts_incomplete` is an optional input parameter describing if the marketplace and its client application supports asynchronous operations.
	  ○ `default behavior`: This is false if `accepts_incomplete` is not included
	  ○ `true`: This is an asynchronous operation supported by the platform and will operate with asynchronous response codes from the broker
	  ○ `false`: This is the only synchronous operation supported by the platform and will operate with synchronous response codes from the broker
	• `service_id` is a mandatory input parameter and must not be empty. This describes the ID of the service from the catalog.
	• `plan_id` is a mandatory input parameter and must not be empty. This describes the ID of the plan from the catalog.

Last operation status	`GET /v2/service_instances/{instance_id}/last_operation?operation=<string>&service_id=<string>&plan_id=<string>` • `{instance_id}` is a globally unique ID. This should match the previous ID that was used for provisioning. **Parameters:** • `operation`: This is an optional input parameter describing the asynchronous operation that was last performed being either provision, update, or deprovision • `service_id`: This is an optional input parameter and must not be empty. This describes the ID of the service from the catalog • `plan_id`: This is an optional input parameter and must not be empty. This describes the ID of the plan from the catalog

Let's look at a sequence diagram of how they are used and interact with CF and a resource server in a typical scenario:

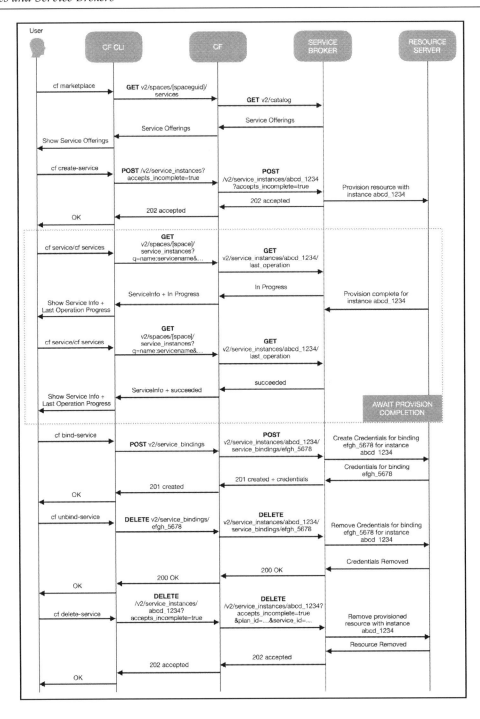

Figure 5: A sequence diagram showing a typical use-case of the broker interaction with the Cloud Foundry and a user initiating the operations. We assume in this figure that the instance ID is abcd_1234 and the binding ID is efgh_5678. Note that by default, the interaction of service creation between Cloud Foundry and the service broker is asynchronous. The interaction between the service broker and the resource server is only an example and can be implemented in a way that a resource server and broker permits.

Figure 5 shows a sequence diagram of events when a user makes a cf CLI command call in relation to services and the corresponding service broker. In a real scenario, commands such as `cf marketplace` would provide an output of the services available from all of the registered service brokers on a platform. Further, an implementation may vary between service brokers. For example, not all services are required to be bound to an application, they simply need to be provisioned to provide some service on the platform. In that instance, bind and unbind may not need to be implemented and we only need the `bindable` field in the catalog to be set to *false*. This field is specified in the HTTP response body of the catalog endpoint.

It is good practice to ensure that a service broker application code never maintains state. This ensures clean implementation and lessens the burden of requiring extra code to maintain state in various scenarios.

HTTP request and response structure

While we don't list all of the HTTP request and response content here, we'll describe its general structure. The full specification of the HTTP request and response structures for each endpoint can be found in the OSB API Standard. An HTTP request is one that is sent from a Cloud Foundry platform to a service broker and an HTTP response, is, on the contrary, sent from the service broker to a Cloud Foundry platform:

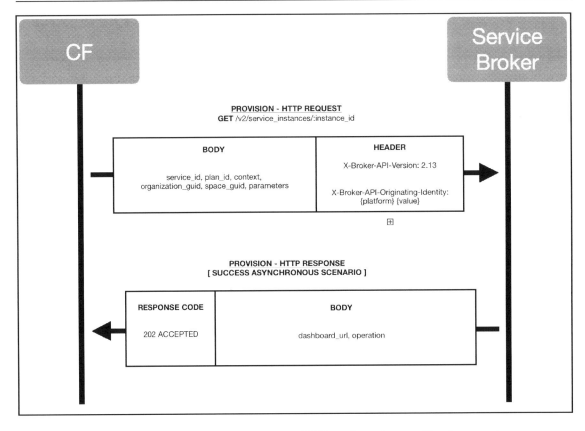

Figure 6: A success scenario for the Provision, showing the content of HTTP request/response for a successful asynchronous request.

Figure 6 shows a successful HTTP request/response with an asynchronous provisioning operation. A different response code would be output if some other operation had occurred. For example, 200 OK is outputted, if there was a request to provision a service but the service was already created with the same parameters. Further, the HTTP request header contains `X-Broker-API-Originating-Identity`, which is an optional header parameter. All other operations follow the aforementioned HTTP protocol but with different request/response contents.

Asynchronous and synchronous operations

Asynchronous operations, for the OSB API, represent a way in which long-running operations such as provision, deprovision, and update are non-blocking. The result is that an incomplete response is returned, usually with the response code 202 Accepted. This allows the platform to complete the request operation and provide some timely feedback that would allow a user to perform other functions. Contrast this to a synchronous operation; the platform would be blocked waiting for a response and the user would have to wait for the completion before they can do something else. On certain requests, the `allow_incomplete=true` query string is provided along with a request to an endpoint to signify that the platform is available to accept asynchronous operations. This means that the service broker must also support asynchronous operations. Should the service broker not support `allow_incomplete=true`, it ignores this parameter and performs its operations synchronously. However, should the service broker not support synchronous operations and `allow_incomplete=false`, or it is not included as a parameter, the service broker will fail and return a response code 422 Unprocessable Entity. This means that the platform must support asynchronous operations in order to work with the service broker. On Cloud Foundry, asynchronous operations are supported and the `allow_incomplete=true` parameter is always included with each supporting operation endpoint when using the cf CLI.

Authentication

It is possible to deploy and utilize service brokers that communicate insecurely with Cloud Foundry without any authentication. However, it is recommended by the OSB API that communications between the broker and CF be secured with TLS and authentication. If authentication is implemented, HTTP basic authentication must be used to authenticate communications between CF and the broker. With a Java application, Spring Boot security can be used to help achieve this.

Custom service brokers on Cloud Foundry

In general, there are a few known ways of deploying a service broker on Cloud Foundry. The key message to remember is that Cloud Foundry only requires an implementation of the service broker application that follows the OSB API. This means, for example, that it is possible to implement a service broker in an existing service application and simply expose the OSB API endpoints.

Some alternative ways are:

- The service broker is packaged along with the services and deployed by BOSH alongside CF
- The service broker is deployed by BOSH, but the services are optionally provisioned, if needs be, and maintained externally to CF
- The service broker is deployed on CF with services either provisioned by some external resource server or they already exist external to CF
- The service broker and services are run and maintained outside of CF

An important factor to remember is that a service broker can only be registered once per foundation. This is controlled by the service IDs provided by the broker, the service broker name, and the route to the broker. Therefore, it is important to map out the visibility of these services and where the service broker should be deployed first. The scope of the service broker available can be restricted to any number of organizations, a particular space, and down to a particular plan. By default, upon registering a broker to CF, the services are disabled for all organizations and all spaces.

Deploying and registering custom service brokers on Cloud Foundry

We'll use a service broker sample application for this section. The service broker sample application is a template application containing all defined RESTful endpoints that will assist in developing other service broker applications. The template application is located at `https://github.com/Cloud-Foundry-For-Developers/chapter-10.git`, which you can use to template your own service broker in the future. The template Java source code is structured so that the `Controller` package holds the service broker controller with the OSB API endpoints and the `Models` package contains data structures that correlate with the request and response body objects. From a developer's point of view, they need only to add their own implementation code into the service broker controller, while returning a reply using the appropriate model data structures and HTTP status response codes specified by the OSB API:

```
public ResponseEntity<String> catalog(
        @RequestHeader(value="X-Broker-API-Version") String osbVersion
    )
{
    log.info("Performing Catalog:");
    log.info("OsbVersion is " + osbVersion);

    // Create a dummy service
    Services services = new Services(
        new Service[]{
            new Service(/* service id = */"acb56d7c-XXXX-XXXX-XXXX-feb140a59a66",
                    /* name = */"My-Service",
                    /* description = */"MyService Plan",
                    /* tags= */new String[]{"cloudfoundryfordevelopers","dummy"},
                    /* requires = */new String[]{},
                    /* bindable = */true,
                    /* metadata = */new Metadata("My-Service", "www.image.com", "some dummy service", "www.docs.com", "www.support.com"),
                    /* plans = */new Plan[] {
                                            new Plan("plan1234", "servicePlan", "ServicePlan Description")
                                    },
                    /* dashboard_client = */null,
                    /* updateable = */true
            ),
            new Service(/* service id = */"acb56d7c-XXXX-XXXX-XXXX-feb140a59a67",
                    /* name = */"My-Service2",
                    /* description = */"MyService2 Plan",
                    /* tags= */new String[]{"cloudfoundryfordevelopers","dummy"},
                    /* requires = */new String[]{},
                    /* bindable = */true,
                    /* metadata = */new Metadata("My-Service2", "www.image.com", "some dummy service", "www.docs.com", "www.support.com"),
                    /* plans = */new Plan[] {
                                            new Plan("plan5678", "servicePlanA", "ServicePlan Description"),
                                            new Plan("plan1012", "servicePlanB", "ServicePlan Description")
                                    },
                    /* dashboard_client = */null,
                    /* updateable = */true
            ),
        }
    );

    return new ResponseEntity<String>(gson.toJson(services), HttpStatus.OK);
}
```

Figure 7: A snippet of the code from the service broker sample application. The template shows the mocked data that returns two services for the catalog endpoint

Let's now retrieve and deploy the custom service broker application. Please ensure you are the admin user for this example:

1. Download the ZIP or Git clone from `https://github.com/Cloud-Foundry-For-Developers/chapter-10.git`.

2. Change into the service broker application directory, `ServiceBrokerTemplateApplication`, and run `mvn clean package`.

3. Run the `cf push` command.

After the push completes, we need to register the service broker application with Cloud Foundry through the cf CLI. We do this by running the `cf create-service-broker <BROKER_NAME> <USERNAME> <PASSWORD> <URL_TO_APP> [--space-scoped]` command. Here, `<BROKER_NAME>` is the name of the service broker. This only serves as a label for other CF operations, such as deleting the service broker. Both `<USERNAME>` and `<PASSWORD>` are the credentials required to communicate with the service broker endpoints. This, as previously mentioned, requires HTTP basic authentication. If there is no authentication, these fields must still be entered with any string, but will be ignored by the service broker. The `<URL_TO_APP>` is the HTTP/HTTPS URL to the application. In this instance, it should be the URL provided after pushing the service broker to CF. `--space-scoped` is a parameter that specifies that the service broker is only visible in the current space. For space developers, this is not optional and must be specified. For this example, we'll run the following command:

```
cf create-service-broker my-broker none none
http://service-broker-template.local.pcfdev.io
```

```
~/W/B/C/c/ServiceBrokerTemplateApplication >>> cf create-service-broker my-broker none none http://service-broker-template.local.pcfdev.io
Creating service broker my-broker as admin...
OK
~/W/B/C/c/ServiceBrokerTemplateApplication >>> cf service-brokers
Getting service brokers as admin...

name          url
local-volume  http://localbroker.local.pcfdev.io
my-broker     http://service-broker-template.local.pcfdev.io
p-mysql       http://mysql-broker.local.pcfdev.io
p-rabbitmq    http://rabbitmq-broker.local.pcfdev.io
p-redis       http://redis-broker.local.pcfdev.io
~/W/B/C/c/ServiceBrokerTemplateApplication >>> ▌
```

Figure 8: The result of running cf create-service-broker followed by cf service-brokers shows the newly registered service broker

Figure 8 shows the result of running the `cf create-service-broker` command. We can also run the `cf service-brokers` command to display the currently registered service brokers.

Running the `cf create-service-broker` command causes Cloud Foundry to query the catalog of the service broker to retrieve all of the service offering information. If there are any issues with the returned catalog data, the `create-service-broker` command will fail and return the invalid catalog JSON data to `stdout` for review.

If we run `cf marketplace`, we will find that our service is not listed, as shown in *Figure 9*:

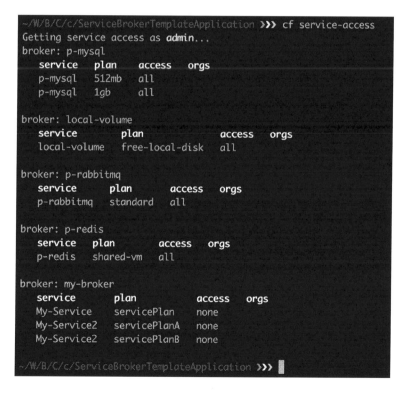

Figure 9: The result of running cf marketplace immediately after registering our service broker

This is due to Cloud Foundry setting the service access to none by default. To verify this, run `cf service-access`:

Figure 10: The result of running cf service-access. Notice there is no access to services provided by the service broker we had just registered

Figure 10 shows that the services provided by the service broker we just registered are set to none. To enable access to our service, we can run the `cf enable-service-access <SERVICE_NAME> [-p plan] [-o org]` command. This command, in essence, enables service access for a particular service from our service broker for a given plan to a given Org. The `<SERVICE_NAME>` parameter is the name of the service from our service broker. `-p` allows our to finely control the availability of plans for a given Org through the `-o` paramater. If `-o` is not specified, it is assumed that access is enabled for all Orgs on the foundation. If `-p` is not specified, it is assumed that all plans for the service are to be enabled. The inverse to this command is the `cf disable-service-access` command with the same parameters, which disables access of a service to an organization. Let's enable all of the services from our broker. Run the `cf enable-service-access My-Service` and `cf enable-service-access My-Service2 -p servicePlanB` commands. Run `cf marketplace` to display the services now available for creation:

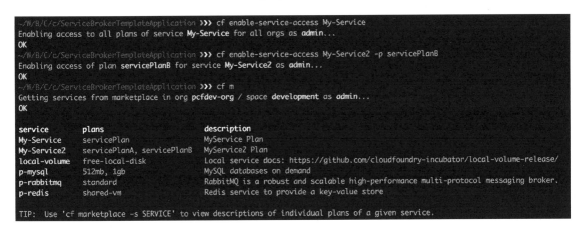

Figure 11: We enabled the two service offerings from our service-broker. We did not, however, enable the access to My-Service2 with servicePlanA

Figure 11 shows the current state of the marketplace. Notice that we did not enable `My-Service2` with *servicePlanA* previously, however, it is still displayed in the marketplace. If we attempt to create a service for *servicePlanA*, the cf CLI will return a failure result advising that there is no permission.

Congratulations! You have deployed and registered a service broker on Cloud Foundry. Try `cf create-service` and `cf bind-service`, followed by `cf env <APP_NAME>`, to see the credentials that are listed in the sample application to be bound to our application.

Figures 12 and *13* show an example of this:

```
@RequestMapping(value = "/v2/service_instances/{instance_id}/service_bindings/{binding_id}", method = RequestMethod.PUT)
public ResponseEntity<Object> binding(
        @RequestHeader(value="X-Broker-API-Version")    String  osbVersion,
        @RequestHeader(value="X-Broker-API-Originating-Identity", required=false)    String originatingIdentity,
        @PathVariable("instance_id")    String instanceId,
        @PathVariable("binding_id")    String bindingId,
        @RequestBody             String requestBody)

{
    log.info("Performing Binding:");
    log.info("OsbVersion is " + osbVersion);
    log.info("OriginatingIdentity is " + originatingIdentity);
    log.info("Instance id is " + instanceId);
    log.info("Binding id  is " + bindingId);
    log.info("Request Body is " + requestBody);

    BindingRequestBody bindingRequestBody = gson.fromJson(requestBody, BindingRequestBody.class);

    log.info(bindingRequestBody);

    // Let's assume we're binding only with credentials
    JsonObject credentialsTest = new JsonObject();
    credentialsTest.addProperty("UserName", "abcd1234567899");
    credentialsTest.addProperty("Password", "oerh.oiwGH3pibhVF");
    credentialsTest.addProperty("Host", "http://my.own.resource");

    Binding binding = new Binding(credentialsTest, null, null, null);
    return new ResponseEntity<>(gson.toJson(binding), HttpStatus.OK);
}
```

Figure 12: Code snippet of the bind-service endpoint. It returns a fixed set of credentials for any incoming bind request.

```
~/W/B/C/c/ServiceBrokerTemplateApplication >>> cf env hello-spring-cloud-home
Getting env variables for app hello-spring-cloud-home in org pcfdev-org / space development as admin...
OK

System-Provided:
{
 "VCAP_SERVICES": {
  "My-Service": [
   {
    "credentials": {
     "Host": "http://my.own.resource",
     "Password": "oerh.oiwGH3pibhVF",
     "UserName": "abcd1234567899"
    },
    "label": "My-Service",
    "name": "mydummyservice",
    "plan": "servicePlan",
    "provider": null,
    "syslog_drain_url": null,
    "tags": [
     "cloudfoundryfordevelopers",
     "dummy"
    ],
    "volume_mounts": []
   }
  ],
```

Figure 13: The environment variables of our application that is bound with My-Service. Notice that the credentials are identical to that in the code in Figure 12

Updating custom service brokers

Should the catalog, or the implementation of any part, change for the service broker application, an update call needs to be run rather than repushing the service broker application to Cloud Foundry. Repushing the application will not enforce the changes to propagate to Cloud Foundry. Calling update will, on the other hand, refresh all the changes. The command to do this is: `cf update-service-broker <BROKER_NAME> <USERNAME> <PASSWORD> <URL_TO_APP>`.

Route services

We've visited the concepts of services, user-provided services, and custom service brokers. What if there was a requirement to provide services to applications on the basis of incoming traffic to that application? That is, provide some processing/analysis and action on incoming request traffic for a given application, before it reaches the application. This is what route services provide. Route services can be instantiated through service brokers in the marketplace or through user-provided route services. We'll explore these in detail in this section. Alternatively, this could be done in a microservice fashion using a service registry to perform container-to-container networking. However, this would not be in the form of a service that is using the service capabilities of Cloud Foundry.

Enabling route services

In order to use route services, the platform operator must update the cf-release manifest with an appropriate passphrase and additional configurations relating to enabling HTTPS and SSL certificates. The passphrase is used by the Gorouter to encrypt header information that is sent to a route service and then to an application. Details of the route service enablement for the Cloud Foundry platform can be found at: `https://docs.cloudfoundry.org/services/route-services.html#architecture-comparison`.

Service broker and service instance implementation requirements

For route services to work with an application, both the service broker and the service instance implementation must fulfill certain requirements. The meaning of service instance implementation refers to the actual route service implementation.

From the service broker's perspective, it must return the route binding information for the following operations:

- **Catalog**: The service catalog must include `requires: ["route_forwarding"]`. Not doing so will prevent service instances from being bound to a route.
- **Binding**: When a user binds a service instance to a route, Cloud Foundry will call the service broker's bind endpoint with a route address in the `bind_resource.route` field. The `bind_resource.route` field is an URL that specifies the route mapped to an application that clients had used to reach the application. In return, the binding process may optionally return `route_service_url` in the HTTP response body. This is a proxy address to signal to Cloud Foundry where it should route its requests. The URL must be an HTTPS scheme in order for this to work. If a service broker does not specify the `route_service_url`, the service broker remains free to update the service that is already in the request path.

From a route service implementation perspective, the requirements are only necessary and applicable when the service broker application sends a `route_service_url` during the aforementioned binding process. During the binding process, when a service broker provides a `route_service_url`, all requests are proxied through to this URL. This occurs because Cloud Foundry detects the presence of `route_service_url` and updates its Gorouter to associate all incoming requests with this URL.

There are three key route service implementation matters to consider:

- **Timeout**: A route service must complete its task within an allotted time specified in the configuration manifest of the Cloud Foundry Gorouter in BOSH. These changes must be performed at the platform level if required. The two key elements are `router.route_service_timeout` and `request_timeout_in_seconds`. The former relates to the time in which a route service must forward a request to an application. This defaults to 60 seconds. The latter represents the response time for all requests, which defaults to 900 seconds.
- **SSL Certificates**: When a route service is in development, the Gorouter on Cloud Foundry forwards self-signed certificates to the service instead of one that is signed by a trusted authority. The route service will need to handle self-signed certificates, in this case, upon completing processing of incoming requests and deciding to forward the request to the URL specified in the `X-CF-Forwarded-Url` header.

- **Request Forwarding**: When the route service has completed its task, it may choose to forward the request to the original requested URL, a different URL, or even reject it on failing scenarios. When a reject occurs, the requests are forwarded back to the original requested URL. Note that when forwarding a request to another URL, it must not be an existing application already bound to a route service. The Cloud Foundry GoRouter will provide three headers in the incoming requests. One is the original requesting URL, and another two are headers used by the Cloud Foundry Gorouter to validate the requests from a route service. These headers in detail are:

  - **X-CF-Forwarded-URL**: This header contains the original requestor's destination URL. A route service is free to forward requests to this URL or to another.

  - **X-CF-Proxy-Signature**: The proxy signature contains encrypted information that is decryptable only by the Cloud Foundry Gorouter. The information is essentially the original requestor URL and a timestamp. The Gorouter has three uses for this header:

    1. Verify that the request to be forwarded matches the original requestor URL.

    2. Verify that a timeout has not occurred. Should a forwarded request URL not match the original requestor URL and the forwarded URL resolves to an application that is also bound to a route service, the request is rejected by the Gorouter.

    3. Prevent recursive delivery of the requests to route services. That is, if the Gorouter sees this header, it will not forward it to a route service again. Therefore, it is critical that a route service does not strip out the **X-CF-Proxy-Signature** and **X-CF-Proxy-Metadata** headers.

  - **X-CF-Proxy-Metadata**: Contains information that assists in the encryption and decryption of the **X-CF-Proxy-Signature**.

 We've mentioned this already, but we'll put it here again as it is common to see this problem; ensure that the **X-CF-Proxy-Signature** and **X-CF-Proxy-Metadata** are **not stripped off**, otherwise a recursive delivery of requests will occur!

Route service deployment strategies

There are three ways to deploy a route service, and they are as a fully brokered route service, a static-brokered route service, and a user-provided route service. They all provide a route service, however, each strategy has its advantages and disadvantages, which we shall list here. The disadvantage common to all deployment strategies is that they all will require extra network hops to reach the application.

Fully-brokered route service

In a fully-brokered route service, all incoming requests to applications are, as usual, sent to the Gorouter through a load balancer, which will detect if there is a route service. As per *Figure 14*, upon detecting the route service, the Gorouter forwards the request to the route service instance attached with the URL forwarding, signature, and metadata headers. The route service instance will complete its task and forward the request back to the destination URL through the load balancer, which will forward the request to the Gorouter. The Gorouter will detect the presence of the Signature and Metadata headers, and so not forward to the route service again, but instead forward to the application:

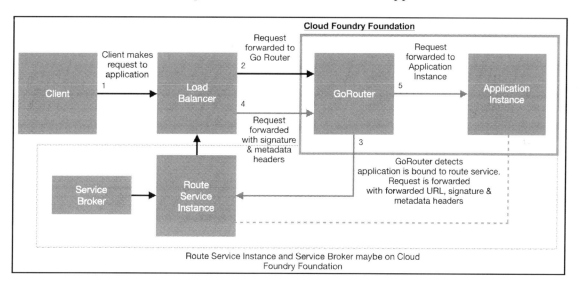

Figure 14: A flow diagram of a fully-brokered route service

Advantages:

- The broker can dynamically update the route service as needed
- Traffic to applications that don't use this route service is unaffected with an extra network hop
- Setup of the route service is performed all on Cloud Foundry and doesn't require external infrastructure

Disadvantages:

- Traffic to applications that do use this route service will need extra network hops

Static-brokered route service

In a static-brokered route service scenario, a route service instance is set up externally to Cloud Foundry prior to a load balancer. Applications on Cloud Foundry would still need to bind to the service so that the service broker can configure the route service to process registered applications and then forward the requests to the load balancer:

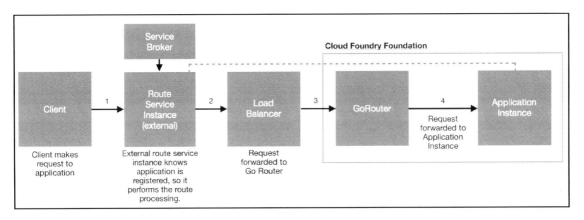

Figure 15: A flow diagram of a static-brokered route service

Advantages:

- The broker can dynamically update the route service as needed
- Traffic to applications that use the route service requires fewer network hops, in comparison to the fully-brokered route service setup

Disadvantages:

- All traffic to applications on Cloud Foundry will be routed to the route service and will need extra network hops
- Operators need to set up the infrastructure outside of Cloud Foundry for this to work

User-provided route service

A user-provided route service enables route services to be associated with an application within a Cloud Foundry space. The user-provided service points to a route service instance that may be on Cloud Foundry or is located externally. This is similar to the fully-brokered solution, the exception being that there is no service broker. This has an advantage in terms of implementation simplicity, in that a service broker does not need to be implemented and that the user-provided service needs only be bound to a route. Of course, as with all user-provided services, these must be managed manually since the service broker is not there to perform the administration and they only exist at a space level from where they are instantiated. In essence, the Gorouter will forward incoming requests to the route service via the user-provided service instance if it detects that an application is bound to that user-provided route service instance. Therefore, firewall consideration for external route services must be set up beforehand:

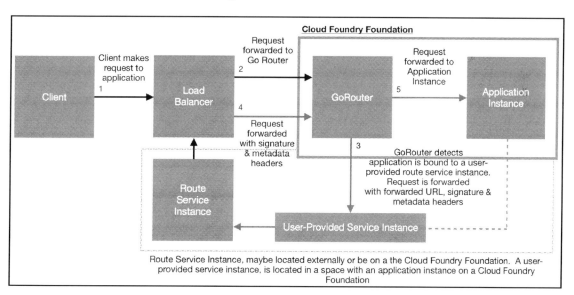

Figure 16: A flow diagram of a user-provided route service

Advantages:

- Simplicity in terms of the least amount of work to get a route service running
- Traffic to applications that don't use this route service is unaffected with an extra network hop
- Setup of the route service is performed all on Cloud Foundry and doesn't require external infrastructure

Disadvantages:

- Traffic to applications that do use this route service will need extra network hops
- For external route services, operators need to set up the access to enable traffic to be accepted from the Cloud Foundry Gorouter
- Management of the route service is a manual process without the service broker

Route service example

We'll use a logging route service example here. The purpose of the logging route service is to simply log all incoming requests to `stdout`. To deploy this example, follow the proceeding steps. The logging route service can be bound to any application. For this example, we'll use the `hello-spring-cloud` sample application from Chapter 6, *Deploying Apps To Cloud Foundry,* which is located at: `https://github.com/Cloud-Foundry-For-Developers/logging-route-service`. Push this application to Cloud Foundry if you have not already done so:

1. Download the logging route service sample application from: `https://github.com/Cloud-Foundry-For-Developers/logging-route-service`.
2. Push this application to Cloud Foundry by running `cf push`. The application is developed in Go. By default, PCF Dev has the Go buildpack.
3. Once the application is pushed successfully, create a user-provided route service using the `-r` parameter: `cf create-user-provided-service logRouteService -r https://log-route-service-application.local.pcfdev.io`. This will allow the binding of services to an application through the route URL.

4. Bind the logging route service application to the `hello-spring-cloud` sample application through the `cf bind-route-service local.pcfdev.io logRouteService --hostname hello-spring-cloud` command.

5. Perform a tailing of the logging route service application through the `cf logs log-route-service-application` command.

6. Run the `hello-spring-cloud` application in a browser through the URL provided after pushing the application. Now, have a look at the tailed logs from our `log-route-service-application`:

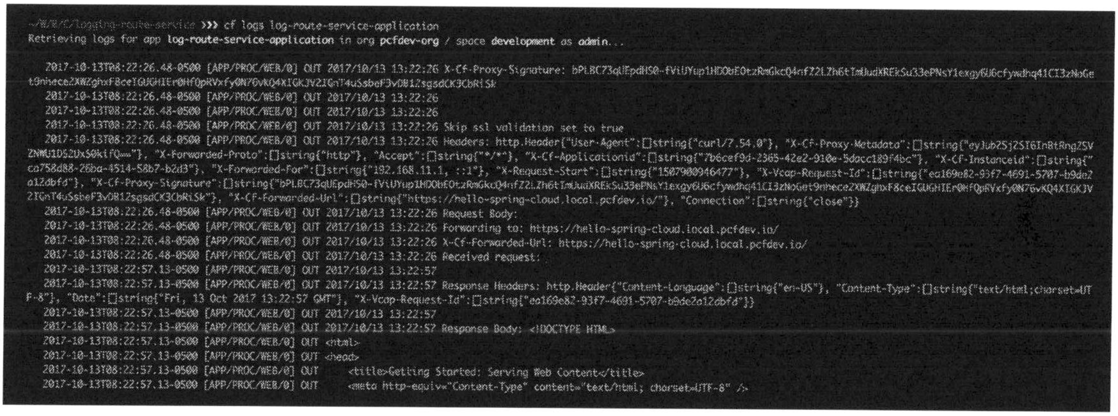

Figure 17: Output of the logging route service, after running the hello-spring-cloud application, to which the route service was bounded to

Service integration strategies

You've learned about user-provided services and service brokers to manage services external to PCF, but which service strategy is best for your organization? This would vary from organization to organization. Unless the answer was known with all service usage data available on hand, the best approach is to be agile and adapt as necessary to minimize the effort to reach your intended goal. Follow a test-driven approach. Start with the simplest solution, learn, and adapt. If there is, at the current time, a manageable number of Orgs or Spaces, say five Spaces, using an external service, a user-provided service approach would be best. Thereafter, if the number of external services increases and spans out to multiple Orgs, a service broker would be a good solution.

The key concept to remember is that so far we've talked about services external to PCF. This means that your organization's platform team would be responsible for managing the service. There are two additional service integration strategies, managed services and on-demand services. These two strategies require service brokers and the development of service tiles. We do not go into the topic of service tiles in this book, as these are managed by your organization's platform team. More details can be found at: `https://docs.`
`pivotal.io/tiledev/index.html`. However, aside from the higher level of implementation complexity and planning for high availability, the real difference is where these services reside and how they are provisioned. At it's simplest, a managed service approach requires an external service to be relocated to Cloud Foundry and run with a fixed number of **virtual machines** (**VMs**) with a fixed amount of allocated resources. This enables Cloud Foundry to monitor and manage these VMs. Thus, if there are any failing VMs, Cloud Foundry would recreate these failing VMs as needed. In an on-demand service scenario, the fixed VMs are not created and allocated beforehand. Instead, the VMs for the service are provisioned on-demand when developers make a call to `cf create-service`.

Summary

In this chapter, we briefly revisited the concepts of services and how they are bound to applications. We then introduced user-provided services, service brokers, and route services. By now, you will be able to implement your own service brokers and route services. We also looked at understanding the different strategies for deploying service brokers and route services. The implications of different approaches to route services were particularly important, as they may affect incoming requests for all of the applications on your Cloud Foundry foundation. Finally, we briefly discussed integration strategies for your services. In the next chapter, we'll look into Buildpacks and how to create your own on Cloud Foundry!

9
Buildpacks

In the `Chapter 6`, *Deploying Apps to Cloud Foundry*, we briefly touched upon buildpacks. We'll dive deeper into buildpacks in this chapter. By the end of the chapter you will be able to understand:

- The big picture about buildpacks and their role in relation to applications on Cloud Foundry
- Common buildpacks
- Consuming and managing buildpacks
- How buildpacks actually work in the background
- Creating buildpacks

Buildpacks on Cloud Foundry

Historically, through the pioneering efforts of Heroku, the management of Ruby (the programming language) dependencies were merged with the base operation system image, called a stack in the Heroku world. On Cloud Foundry, this is called a stemcell. It was later identified that, by separating the Ruby dependencies into a component called Buildpacks, they were able to iterate quickly on the Ruby dependencies relative to the operating system image. In essence, a buildpack is the runtime and framework support for an application.

For most applications that are built on a framework, dependencies and runtime frameworks are usually required to be shipped with the application, or they are installed on the target platform where applications are to be run on. Some examples include the .NET Framework and Java Runtime. Of course, an alternative is to statically compile all dependencies into a single executable binary, if there is an option, but this would usually result in a very large file. With buildpacks, the polyglot feature of Cloud Foundry shines.

In the case of running an application on Cloud Foundry, these dependencies and runtime frameworks need to be included with the application in order for it to run. These are packaged together into a package called a buildpack. However, a buildpack contains a lot more capability than just a runtime framework. As mentioned
previously, a buildpack consists of a set of tools, potential runtime components, and scripts that are programmed to retrieve dependencies required by the application, move the compiled output to some run location, compile the code, and/or configure the application for running in the container. What's really nice about all of this is that the dependencies and packaging are consistent throughout all environments. For the developer, aside from a plethora of development languages to use, it means that they can be sure they are using dependencies and frameworks that are tied to a known version, leading to greater confidence in their code. For the platform team, it is a way of providing a packaged framework and dependency that is always consistent on all foundations, for all development teams. This leads to fewer work problems relating to maintaining different dependencies and runtimes on different foundations.

 For some buildpacks, it is possible to push source code onto Cloud Foundry and allow a buildpack to pull in the tagged dependencies and compile the application into an executable binary. However, this is not recommended. Consider the situation whereby the buildpack runtime framework is version 1 but your local development machine is version 2. This will introduce an environment parity issue and potentially introduce a different application behavior. It is recommended that applications be built with all artifacts included as a package prior to being deployed on Cloud Foundry. This is usually done as part of a CI/CD pipeline. The application that you push is built with a known runtime framework version and tagged with a build version, ensuring environment parity. Of course, in this instance if the buildpack version is older than what was compiled with the application, it is usually noticeable up front, with applications erroring out with required versions of the runtime framework. This is much easier to diagnose and fix.

Common buildpacks on Cloud Foundry

Running the `cf buildpacks` command will show a list of available buildpacks on your foundation. These buildpacks are commonly available on most foundations. This may be configured differently by your platform team depending on your organization's policies:

```
~ >>> cf buildpacks
Getting buildpacks...

buildpack               position   enabled   locked   filename
java_buildpack          1          true      false    java-buildpack-offline-v3.13.zip
ruby_buildpack          2          true      false    ruby_buildpack-cached-v1.6.37.zip
nodejs_buildpack        3          true      false    nodejs_buildpack-cached-v1.5.32.zip
go_buildpack            4          true      false    go_buildpack-cached-v1.8.1.zip
python_buildpack        5          true      false    python_buildpack-cached-v1.5.18.zip
php_buildpack           6          true      false    php_buildpack-cached-v4.3.31.zip
staticfile_buildpack    7          true      false    staticfile_buildpack-cached-v1.4.5.zip
binary_buildpack        8          true      false    binary_buildpack-cached-v1.0.11.zip
dotnet-core_buildpack   9          true      false    dotnet-core_buildpack-cached-v1.0.15.zip
~ >>>
```

Figure 1: Running cf buildpacks will display a list of available buildpacks on your foundation. In this instance, this figure shows the buildpacks available on PCFDev

In *Figure 1*, the list of buildpacks are shown to be installed on PCFDev with some additional information, including position, enabled, locked, and the filename. These pieces of information are related to the order to check and associate a buildpack to an application during deployment, when no buildpack is specified for the application. Enabled signifies whether a buildpack is used on the foundation, locked provides a means to locking a buildpack so that its version remains and does not upgrade in any buildpack upgrade event, and the filename is the source filename of the buildpack.

Generally, changing/setting the order is performed by the platform team and is most useful for strategizing the migration of applications to using new versions of a buildpack. For example, setting version 1 of a buildpack to be at position 5, and putting version 2 of the same buildpack to be at position 6. This would enable production level applications to automatically use the version 1 of the buildpack for a period of time, while development teams test out version 2 of the buildpack. Later, at a given cut-off date, a migration would swap positions of the version 1 and version 2 buildpacks so that all applications would now use the version 2 buildpack. Version 1 may remain on the list for regression tests. This would be all achieved by the platform team's automated upgrade pipelines, which would get the up-to-date buildpacks and promote and update buildpacks defined by some strategy, such as the previously mentioned one.

From *Figure 1*, most of the buildpacks' supported languages are self-explanatory, that is, `dotnet-core_buildpack` for .NET Core applications. There is, of course, additional detailed framework support, that is, Java with Spring; it may be possible to configure buildpacks through environment variables, which you will set through the `cf set-env` command or in your application manifest. A list of common buildpacks, their support information, and configuration are all documented within their respective GitHub pages at `https://docs.cloudfoundry.org/buildpacks`.

There are two special buildpacks that will be discussed here. They are the binary buildpack and the static-file buildpack. The binary buildpack enables any form of webserver, as a binary, to run in a container. There are two requirements that must be adhered to in order for your application to run. The first: your web application must be reading in the **PORT** environment variable that your web service application will bind to receive and send requests or responses. The second: a `startup` command, so that the binary buildpack knows how to start your application. This can be done by including a file named `procfile` at the `root` directory of the application or through a `-c` option on the `cf push` command or manifest:

- `procfile` **file content sample**:

  ```
  web: ./executable-app-binary
  ```

- `-c` **option sample**:

  ```
  cf push -c "./executable-app-binary"
  ```

 If you do not want to read in the **PORT** environment variable in your application, you could create a webserver app that is started up with the PORT as an argument input to your application. For example, `cf push -c "./executable-app-binary  $PORT"`.

The second special buildpack is the static buildpack, which is used to serve static content, such as websites containing HTML files, CSS , and JavaScript. The minimum requirement for this buildpack is to include a file named `Staticfile` with your static content at the `root` directory. The `Staticfile` may be empty and will serve an `index.html` file in the same location as the file. Alternatively, `Staticfile` can contain various configuration parameters, for example, the location of an `index.html` file to be used is in a sub-directory. More details about the `StaticFile` parameters can be found at: `https://docs.cloudfoundry.org/buildpacks/staticfile/#configure-and-push`.

While we have just discussed the common buildpacks and the two special types of buildpacks, this does not mean that you would be limited to only these. One approach is to create or customize buildpacks, and the other is to explore buildpacks that have already been contributed to the Cloud Foundry community at `https://github.com/cloudfoundry-community/cf-docs-contrib/wiki/Buildpacks`.

Consuming and managing buildpacks on Cloud Foundry

 Depending on the policies of your organization, you may not have permission to manage and/or consume external buildpacks. Buildpacks may be administered by your organization's platform team.

Offline versus online buildpacks

You will notice that when you download buildpacks, there is sometimes an option for offline (cached) or online (uncached) versions that are available for downloading. A buildpack is online/uncached when it has remote internet access during the application staging. This enables a buildpack to have a smaller footprint and download the necessary dependencies for the application when needed. However, this presents a security issue when deploying into production environments. Ideally, there should not be any external remote access for a buildpack in those types of environments. Therefore, there are offline/cached buildpacks that contain pre-downloaded dependencies and internal code that prevents remote access. Offline/cached buildpacks are often much larger in size than their online counterparts.

Consuming external buildpacks on Cloud Foundry

By now, we already know how to consume packs installed on Cloud Foundry through the cf CLI. What if we want to use a buildpack that is not installed on our foundation? This can be achieved by specifying an external buildpack location through the -b option with `cf push`.

```
cf push java-app-name -b https://github.com/cloudfoundry/java-buildpack.git
```

For example, the preceding command will push an application named `java-app-name` and force it to download and use the latest buildpack from `https://github.com/cloudfoundry/java-buildpack.git`.

 For Windows applications, you will need to directly specify the ZIP file, that is, `cf push winapp -s windows2012R2 -b https://github.com/cloudfoundry/hwc-buildpack/releases/download/v2.3.11/hwc-buildpack-v2.3.11.zip`.

Adding a new buildpack to Cloud Foundry

However, if there is a need, installing a buildpack will pre-download the buildpack onto your foundation. This is much faster than re-downloading the buildpack for every `cf push`. We install a new buildpack through the `cf create-buildpack <BUILDPACK_NAME> <PATH> <POSITION> [--enable|--disable]` command. `<BUILDPACK_NAME>` is the name of the new buildpack. This will be used in your `cf push` command and manifest. `<PATH>` must contain a path to a buildpack ZIP file, the path may be from a URL or from a local directory. `<POSITION>` represents the order in the buildpack list from which staging will perform the detection test. `--enable` and `--disable` will enable or disable the buildpack from staging, respectively. By default, the new buildpack is enabled. Let's add a new version of our Java buildpack to the foundation. In this instance, we'll add in version 4.6 of the Java buildpack, but place it at position two, since we don't want Java applications using version 4.6 immediately, without some testing. Run the following command:

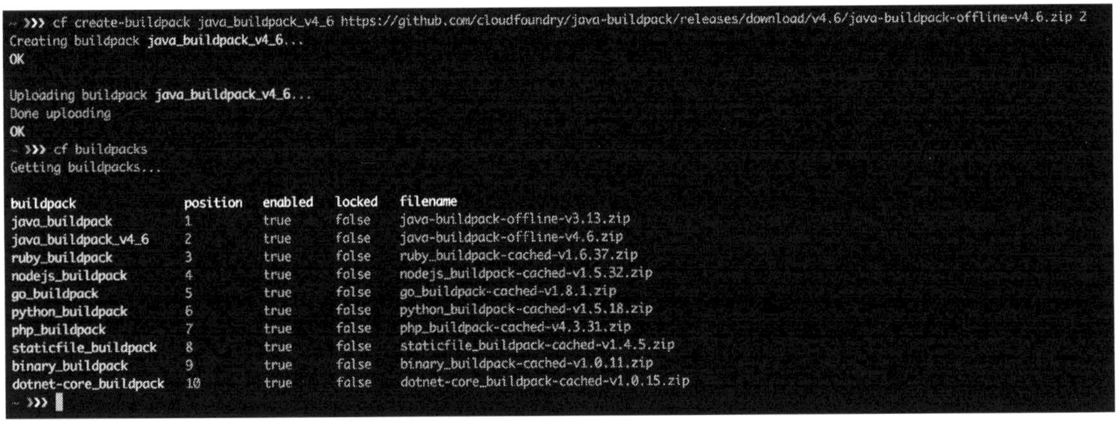

```
cf create-buildpack java_buildpack_v4_6
https://github.com/cloudfoundry/java-buildpack/releases/download/v4.6/java-
buildpack-offline-v4.6.zip 2
```

The preceding command will create a new Java buildpack named `java_buildpack_v4_6` that holds Java buildpack version 4.6 and places it at position number two on our buildpack list:

Figure 2: Creating a new Java buildpack version 4.6 and placing it at position number 2

Updating a buildpack on Cloud Foundry

To update an existing buildpack on our foundation, we can run the `cf update-buildpack <CURRENT_BUILDPACK_NAME> [-p PATH] [-i POSITION] [--enable|--disable] [--lock|--unlock]` command. `<CURRENT_BUILDPACK_NAME>` refers to the current buildpack name found in the buildpacks list. The remaining parameters, `-p PATH`, `-i POSITION`, `--enable/--disable`, and `--lock/--unlock` perform the following, respectively: specify the path to the new ZIP file for the buildpack, the new position–as an integer–for the buildpack, enable/disable the buildpack, and set the lock/unlock state of the buildpack.

However, notice that the preceding command does not rename the buildpack. To rename a buildpack, we can do so through the `cf rename-buildpack <CURRENT_BUILDPACK_NAME> <NEW_BUILDPACK_NAME>` command, which renames it to `<CURRENT_BUILDPACK_NAME> to <NEW_BUILDPACK_NAME>`.

Let's try updating the Go buildpack to version 1.8.11, and renaming our buildpack to the `gogo_buildpack`. We'll run the following commands:

```
cf update-buildpack go_buildpack -p
https://github.com/cloudfoundry/go-buildpack/releases/download/v1.8.11/go-b
uildpack-v1.8.11.zip
```

and,

```
cf rename-buildpack go_buildpack gogo_buildpack
```

```
~ >>> cf update-buildpack go_buildpack -p https://github.com/cloudfoundry/go-buildpack/releases/download/v1.8.11/go-buildpack-v1.8.11.zip
Updating buildpack go_buildpack...
Done uploading
OK
~ >>> cf rename-buildpack go_buildpack gogo_buildpack
Renaming buildpack go_buildpack to gogo_buildpack...
OK
~ >>> cf buildpacks
Getting buildpacks...

buildpack              position   enabled   locked   filename
java_buildpack         1          true      false    java-buildpack-offline-v3.13.zip
java_buildpack_v4_6    2          true      false    java-buildpack-offline-v4.6.zip
ruby_buildpack         3          true      false    ruby_buildpack-cached-v1.6.37.zip
nodejs_buildpack       4          true      false    nodejs_buildpack-cached-v1.5.32.zip
gogo_buildpack         5          true      false    go-buildpack-v1.8.11.zip
python_buildpack       6          true      false    python_buildpack-cached-v1.5.18.zip
php_buildpack          7          true      false    php_buildpack-cached-v4.3.31.zip
staticfile_buildpack   8          true      false    staticfile-buildpack-cached-v1.4.5.zip
binary_buildpack       9          true      false    binary_buildpack-cached-v1.0.11.zip
dotnet-core_buildpack  10         true      false    dotnet-core_buildpack-cached-v1.0.15.zip
~ >>>
```

Figure 3: The result of updating the Go buildpack to version 1.8.11 and renaming it

Deleting a buildpack

To remove a buildpack from our foundation, we need only run the `cf delete-buildpack <BUILDPACK_NAME> [-f]` command. Here, `-f` forces deletion of the buildpack without prompting. Given that deletion is an irreversible process, care needs to be taken when using `-f`. Let's delete the `java_buildpack_v4_6 buildpack`. Run the `cf delete-buildpack java_buildpack_v4_6` command:

```
~ >>> cf delete-buildpack java_buildpack_v4_6

Really delete the buildpack java_buildpack_v4_6?> y
Deleting buildpack java_buildpack_v4_6...
OK
~ >>> cf buildpacks
Getting buildpacks...

buildpack               position   enabled   locked   filename
java_buildpack          1          true      false    java-buildpack-offline-v3.13.zip
ruby_buildpack          2          true      false    ruby_buildpack-cached-v1.6.37.zip
nodejs_buildpack        3          true      false    nodejs_buildpack-cached-v1.5.32.zip
gogo_buildpack          4          true      false    go-buildpack-v1.8.11.zip
python_buildpack        5          true      false    python_buildpack-cached-v1.5.18.zip
php_buildpack           6          true      false    php_buildpack-cached-v4.3.31.zip
staticfile_buildpack    7          true      false    staticfile_buildpack-cached-v1.4.5.zip
binary_buildpack        8          true      false    binary_buildpack-cached-v1.0.11.zip
dotnet-core_buildpack   9          true      false    dotnet-core_buildpack-cached-v1.0.15.zip
~ >>>
```

Figure 4: The result of deleting the Java buildpack version 4.6

Existing cached droplets and maintaining installed buildpacks

There is an important side-effect that must be made clear here. We've learned that restarting an application only re-uses a cached droplet that already has an associated buildpack, pulled in dependencies, frameworks, and various environment variables. Unless we perform a restage, which rebuilds the droplet. What this tells us is that if we changed a buildpack in any way using any of the preceding commands, we would still be able to run an application that is already deployed on Cloud Foundry because it is using the cached droplet. It is only when we perform a restage on that application, that new changes will be applied via the rebuilding of the droplet.

Deep-dive into buildpacks

By now, you may be wondering how buildpacks actually work and how to create/customize your own buildpacks. In order to create/customize buildpacks, we must first understand how they work with Cloud Foundry in the background.

How buildpacks actually work with Cloud Foundry

When a `cf push` is performed, all application files are uploaded to a blobstore; subsequently, a staging task is created. This staging task is essentially a new container with the application files. The following buildpack process begins by running a series of scripts located in a `bin` directory containing a number of script files, labeled as detect, compile, and release. These are called, in this order, during the staging process to retrieve the necessary dependencies, build artifacts, and/or configure the application:

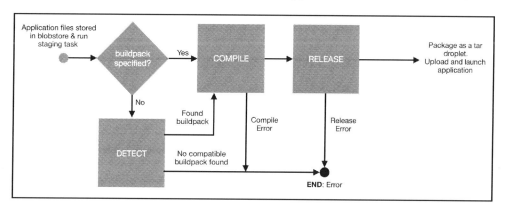

Figure 5: The buildpack process

As shown in *Figure 5*, once application files are uploaded, the process goes on to check whether a buildpack was specified with `cf push`. If not, the process iteratively finds the right buildpack from all those installed on the foundation. Each of these buildpacks are uploaded to the container, and the detect script is run to determine the compatibility. Otherwise, it will directly upload the buildpack that was specified. The staging process proceeds with the compile script, which pulls in all dependencies and performs the necessary build/configuration. In the release script, a run command in the form of a YAML file is generated. This is used to execute the application with the necessary arguments, if any.

For Windows-based stacks, the scripts should be batch files, for example, `detect.bat`. To call PowerShell scripts, utilize the batch script:
`@echo off`
`powershell.exe -ExecutionPolicy Unrestricted`
`%~dp0\detect.ps1 %1`

As of Cloud Foundry version 1.12, there is support for multi-buildpacks, which is basically a list of buildpacks input during the push process. This changes the previously-mentioned structure to include two additional scripts: supply and finalize. Supply is responsible for pulling in all the dependencies and frameworks for the application. Finalize performs the actual building/configuration of the application. These two scripts essentially make up the compile script. However, in most cases, you will find that the compile script remains in the `bin` directory for backward compatibility. To migrate a buildpack without multi-buildpack support, copy the contents of the compile script and insert them into a finalize script. The supply script would exist but be empty. For more information, see `https://docs.pivotal.io/pivotalcf/1-12/buildpacks/understand-buildpacks.html`.

Cloud Foundry 1.12 support for multi-buildpack means that it is possible to have multiple buildpack support per application. This means that it is possible to specify a number of buildpacks for a given application, for example, binary buildpack and Java buildpack. As we write, there are a number of upcoming changes, such as the cf CLI multi-buildpack push, called cf v3-push, and updating buildpacks to supporting this new interface. We'll learn more about this in the creating buildpacks section. More information is available at `https://docs.pivotal.io/pivotalcf/1-12/buildpacks/use-multiple-buildpacks.html`.

The detect script

Input arguments:

- `<build_path>`

Return value:

- 0, if buildpack is compatible with the application in `<build_path>`
- 1, otherwise

The purpose of the detect script is to determine the application's compatibility with the buildpack. There is only one input argument and this is <build_path>, which is a path to a directory holding the application files when a user had performed a cf push. This script will be required to return 0 (zero) if the buildpack is compatible with the application, or return 1 otherwise. For display feedback to users, text can be output to stdout.

The compile script

Input arguments:

- <build_path>
- <cache_path>

Return value:

- none

The purpose of the compile script is to pull in all the framework/dependencies and, if necessary, perform an actual source compilation or configuration. There are two input arguments. The first is <build_path>, which is a path to a directory holding the application files when a user had performed a cf push. The second parameter, <cache_path>, holds the path to a directory store that holds the assets during the build process. For display feedback to users, text can be output to stdout.

> To get the buildpack's file directory during the staging for any of these scripts, you could use the following bash script: export buildpack_directory=`dirname $(readlink -f ${BASH_SOURCE%/*})`.

The release script

Input arguments:

- <build_path>

Return value:

- YAML string

The purpose of the release script is to generate a YAML of the following form. Note that the newlines are important, including the initial two spaces in front of `web: . . .` on the second line:

```
default_process_types:
  web: <start_command>
```

For Linux containers, to define environment variables for your application after the staging, place executable bash scripts (for example, `script.sh`) that export the environment variables into a directory named `.profile.d` that is located in the `root` directory of your application.

This tells the launch process to start a `web` type application with the `<start_command>` command. Currently, `web` type applications are the only type supported. Here, the `<start_command>` is usually a webserver executable that is used to serve your application, or, if your application is the webserver itself, it can start that application with input parameters. The `<build_path>` input parameter is a path to a directory holding the application files when a user had performed a `cf push`. This is output as text to `stdout`.

Here's an example:

```
default_process_types:
  web: ./path_to_app/webserver_app_executable $PORT
```

You will find that the `$PORT` environment variable is not available during staging because it is not yet assigned. As such, the `$PORT` in the `<start command>` in the `default_process_types` is only an execution string and is evaluated when a droplet is created and the application is about to be launched.

The droplet

Once the buildpack completes the staging, that is, the buildpack plus the result of the compile and release scripts, it creates a final output tarball droplet with a corresponding stack filesystem. As mentioned previously, the filesystem stack name used in this book is `cflinuxfs2`. For Windows, the stack name will be `window2012R2` or the upcoming `windows2016`. The droplet is stored in an internal blobstore repository on the foundation, which can be configured to be stored externally in an S3 store.

The structure of the droplet is as follows:

```
apps/
deps/
logs/
tmp/
staging_info.yml
```

apps/ contains the contents of the <build_directory> that interacted with the compile script; staging_info.yml contains metadata pertaining to the staging process, such as the detected buildpack and the start command. Once an application instance is about to be launched, the droplet is extracted into each new container and the start command is executed. Whenever your application starts, the working directory is always assumed to be within the app/ directory and so there is no need to specify the app parent directory in your start commands.

Creating buildpacks

Now that you've learned about buildpacks, we'll look into actually creating a buildpack. The alternative to this is to customize a buildpack, which means to fork and modify an existing buildpack. Creating a buildpack means to start from scratch with a framework or language that is currently not supported on Cloud Foundry. In general, it is highly common to customize an existing buildpack, since the most common frameworks and languages are already built for Cloud Foundry. So, why exactly would you need to customize a buildpack? Maybe you need a buildpack that has components/dependencies that are compatible with your organization's existing setup. For example, **ApplicationDynamics (AppD)** for application performance monitoring in the Java buildpack requires an agent that will communicate with an AppD controller. However, your organization has decided to use an older version of the controller for stability and risk-mitigating reasons; at the same time, for security, your production foundation has no direct internet access, so you use an offline buildpack that won't be able to connect to the internet to get dependencies. For AppD to work, you must use a matching agent version with the controller. You could just specify a version number in the AppD configuration setting in the Java buildpack, but there's no internet connection, so the staging can't get the dependencies remotely. There are many ways to solve this, but one way is to just specify the AppD agent version and execute a repackage using the Java buildpack's Ruby repacking command in a platform team's automated pipeline that runs regularly to upgrade your buildpacks.

The key take away here is: create a buildpack if there is no Cloud Foundry buildpack support for your language. Otherwise, consider customization. However, be mindful that both of these approaches will potentially require a level of maintenance in future, such as pulling updates from the master branch, or updating code to support new features. Therefore, consideration for the maintenance effort must be taken into account when deciding whether to proceed down this path. Of course, if the customized changes turn out to be a feature of high demand by other users of Cloud Foundry, consider speaking with the existing buildpack authors and submit a pull request with your changes to contribute to the main buildpack development.

We only explored the creation of buildpacks in this section because customization is essentially similar to creation, but bounded to the traits of an existing buildpack such as structure, style, and protocols. Each buildpack on Cloud Foundry will have a different set of traits based on how they've been developed. Therefore, common to all these buildpacks is what you will learn in creating a buildpack. The traits are the additional key knowledge that you'll only have to pick up when you decide to customize a buildpack. See `https://docs.pivotal.io/pivotalcf/1-12/buildpacks/merging_upstream.html` and `https://docs.pivotal.io/pivotalcf/1-12/buildpacks/upgrading_dependency_versions.html` for information on syncing and maintaining buildpacks when going down a customization route.

Creating the Simple-HTTP buildpack

For our buildpack creation example, we'll aim to create a very simple buildpack that serves a single simple HTML document. This is not a production-level buildpack, and serves only as a useful educational resource. You would use a Static buildpack for this purpose instead, which can serve simple HTML documents and much more! The Simple-HTTP buildpack will serve an HTML document from a file that is labeled `index.http`. `index.http` contains a simple HTML document. In this instance, we'll need a webserver running to listen for incoming HTTP requests and then respond with an HTTP response.

To proceed with this example, you will need to download the Golang compiler. Instructions for this can be found at `https://golang.org/doc/install`. This will be used for the `libbuildpack` packager, which is a set of tools to assist with buildpack packaging.

The **buildpack-packager** (**BPP**) tool is useful for packaging a buildpack's assets. You will find that this is extensively used in a number of existing system buildpacks on Cloud Foundry. The BPP tool reads out from a local `manifest.yml` file that defines the dependencies and files that will be included/excluded during the packaging process. The dependencies are downloaded using the `buildpack-packager -cached` command. The BPP tool and manifest definition can be found at `https://github.com/cloudfoundry/buildpack-packager`. **Note**: at the time of writing, we are using the libbuildpack library, which has some slight differences in the command-line tool in comparison with the buildpack-packager on the Cloud Foundry GitHub. The `libbuildpack` library is in use by a number of buildpacks on Cloud Foundry.

To skip all the following file creation, you may download the final source code from `https://github.com/Cloud-Foundry-For-Developers/chapter-8`.

Setting up Buildpack-packager

Clone or download the Buildpack-packager from `https://github.com/cloudfoundry/libbuildpack`. Navigate to the directory at `libbuildpack/packager/buildpack-packager`. Run the `go build` command. This will build the buildpack-packager executable. It is recommended, for convenience, that this executable is moved to a common binary location, such as `/usr/local/bin`, or set the **PATH** environment to point to the buildpack-packer executable.

Creating the buildpack

On your local workspace directory, create a new directory called `simple-http-buildpack`. Within this directory, we'll need to create a `manifest.yml` file, a VERSION file, and a directory named `bin` containing three script files: detect, compile, and release. The `manifest.yml` file is used by buildpack-packager to pull the dependencies and file includes into a single buildpack ZIP file. The VERSION file is used by the buildpack-packager to append a versioning to your buildpack ZIP filename. Finally, the `bin` directory contains the three script files used during the staging process, as described previously. The key parts of these three files are as follows:

1. **The detect script**: Checks whether there is a file called `index.http` in the build directory. If yes, this buildpack is compatible.

2. **The compile script**: Pulls simple HTTP server from Git into the `cache` directory and moves the executable script (`run.sh`) to the build directory to be alongside the `index.http` file.

3. **The release script**: Sets up the `start` command to be called. This simply calls `run.sh`.

Let's create these artifacts:

Filename	Content
VERSION	1.0
manifest.yml	``` --- language: simple-http exclude_files: - .gitignore include_files: - VERSION - bin/compile - bin/detect - bin/release - manifest.yml ```

bin/detect	```bash
	#!/usr/bin/env bash
	# bin/detect <build-dir>
	
	build_dir_path=$(dirname $(dirname $0))
	
	# Check if there is an index.http file,
	# if so, this is the right buildpack
	# The output echo'd here will be used
	# in the application launch summary, which you will
	# later see under 'buildpack: ', after a cf push
	if [-f $1/index.http]; then
	  echo "Simple Http Buildpack" && exit 0
	else
	  echo "No index.http file found. \
	        This is required for the SimpleHttp buildpack" && exit 1
	fi
	``

| bin/compile | ```
#!/usr/bin/env bash

# If anything goes wrong during compile process,
# we should just bail and stop the whole buildpack process.
set -euo pipefail

build_directory=$1
cache_directory=$2

# Clone in the simple http server into a cache directory
# But first, remove any existing cloned directory
# in the cache, if it exists
rm -rf $cache_directory/simplehttpbp
git clone
https://github.com/Cloud-Foundry-For-Developers/chapter-8.git
$cache_directory/simplehttpbp

# Copy the server over into the root directory
# of our build directory. This will be the root directory
# of the application.
cp $cache_directory/simplehttpbp/simple-http-server/run.sh
$build_directory/.
``` |
|---|---|
| bin/release | ```
#!/usr/bin/env bash

echo -e "---\ndefault_process_types:\n web: ./run.sh"
``` |

Once we have created the preceding files, run the `buildpack-packager -cache` command. This will package the buildpack that we just created into a ZIP file with the filename `simple-http_buildpack-v1.0.0.zip`.

 The `buildpack-packager -cache` will download all dependencies, while a call to `buildpack-packager` on its own will produce a buildpack that does not download all the dependencies.

Installing the buildpack

Let's run the `cf create-buildpack simple-http_buildpack simple-http_buildpack-v1.0.0.zip 5` command. This should now upload the buildpack and create a new entry in our buildpacks list, as we can see in *Figure 6*:

```
~/W/B/C/c/simple-http-buildpack >>> cf create-buildpack simple-http_buildpack simple-http_buildpack-v1.0.0.zip 5
Creating buildpack simple-http_buildpack...
OK

Uploading buildpack simple-http_buildpack...
Done uploading
OK
~/W/B/C/c/simple-http-buildpack >>> cf buildpacks
Getting buildpacks...

buildpack              position  enabled  locked  filename
java_buildpack         1         true     false   java-buildpack-offline-v3.13.zip
ruby_buildpack         2         true     false   ruby_buildpack-cached-v1.6.37.zip
nodejs_buildpack       3         true     false   nodejs_buildpack-cached-v1.5.32.zip
gogo_buildpack         4         true     false   go-buildpack-v1.8.11.zip
simple-http_buildpack  5         true     false   simple-http_buildpack-v1.0.0.zip
shell_buildpack        6         true     false   shell_buildpack-cached-v1.0.0.zip
md_buildpack           7         true     false   md_buildpack-cached-v1.0.0.zip
python_buildpack       8         true     false   python_buildpack-cached-v1.5.18.zip
php_buildpack          9         true     false   php_buildpack-cached-v4.3.31.zip
staticfile_buildpack   10        true     false   staticfile_buildpack-cached-v1.4.5.zip
binary_buildpack       11        true     false   binary_buildpack-cached-v1.0.11.zip
dotnet-core_buildpack  12        true     false   dotnet-core_buildpack-cached-v1.0.15.zip
~/W/B/C/c/simple-http-buildpack >>>
```

Figure 6: The result of creating and uploading the simple-http_buildpack

For subsequent updates to our buildpacks, run the `cf update-buildpack <BUILDPACK_NAME> [-p PATH] [-i POSITION] [--enable|--disable] [--lock|--unlock]` command. Finally, to delete the buildpack, run the `cf delete-buildpack <BUILDPACK_NAME>` command.

Test driving the Simple-Http buildpack

Let's create a `simple-http` app and deploy it on Cloud Foundry. We'll need only one file, called `index.http`. Optionally, we can create a `cf push` manifest file for convenience. Create a new directory, named `simple-http-app`, and populate it with the following files:

Filename	Content

`index.http`	`<!DOCTYPE html>`
	`<html>`
	`<body>`
	
	`<h1>Cloud Foundry For Developers</h1>`
	
	`<p>Buildpack Creation Sample</p>`
	
	`</body>`
	`</html>`

`manifest.yml`	`---`
	`applications:`
	`- name: simple-http`
	`  instances: 1`
	`  env:`
	`    SIMPLE_HTTP_BP_VERBOSE: false`

The `index.http` file is a simple text-only HTML document. Our Simple-HTTP server can only serve simple HTML text-based documents. The `manifest.yml` file contains the name of the app to be pushed and an environment variable to control whether we want to have the Simple-HTTP server output that sent response to the logs. We have left out explicitly declaring the buildpack because we want to test the buildpack's detect script.

Run `cf push` once you are ready:

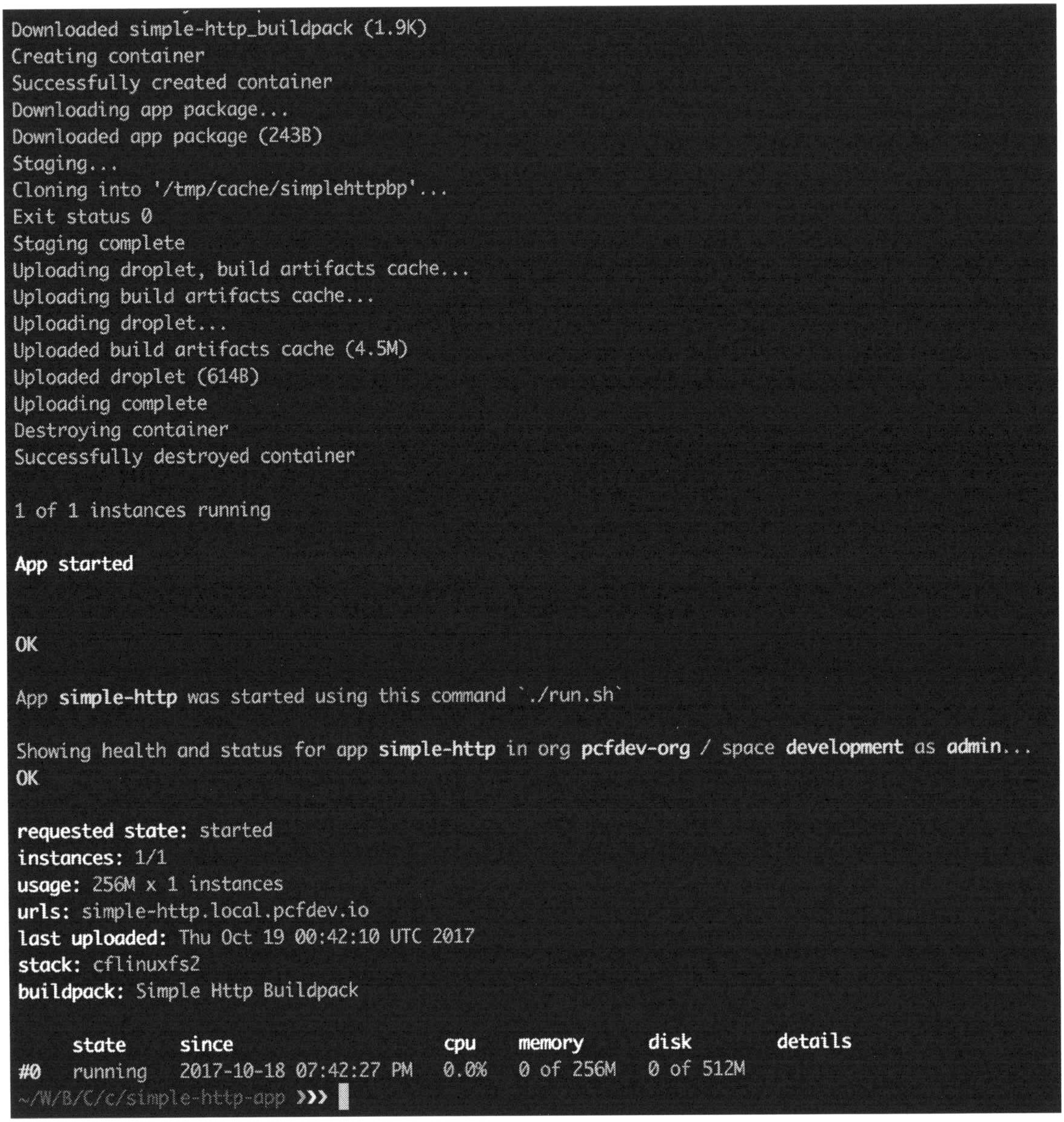

```
Downloaded simple-http_buildpack (1.9K)
Creating container
Successfully created container
Downloading app package...
Downloaded app package (243B)
Staging...
Cloning into '/tmp/cache/simplehttpbp'...
Exit status 0
Staging complete
Uploading droplet, build artifacts cache...
Uploading build artifacts cache...
Uploading droplet...
Uploaded build artifacts cache (4.5M)
Uploaded droplet (614B)
Uploading complete
Destroying container
Successfully destroyed container

1 of 1 instances running

App started


OK

App simple-http was started using this command `./run.sh`

Showing health and status for app simple-http in org pcfdev-org / space development as admin...
OK

requested state: started
instances: 1/1
usage: 256M x 1 instances
urls: simple-http.local.pcfdev.io
last uploaded: Thu Oct 19 00:42:10 UTC 2017
stack: cflinuxfs2
buildpack: Simple Http Buildpack

     state     since                    cpu    memory        disk          details
#0   running   2017-10-18 07:42:27 PM   0.0%   0 of 256M     0 of 512M
~/W/B/C/c/simple-http-app >>>
```

Figure 7: The result of pushing our simple-http app

As shown in *Figure 7*, our buildpack was successfully detected to be compatible with our application and was used to launch it. Take note of `buildpack: Simple Http Buildpack`. This text is obtained from the output of the detect script.

That's it! Let's now see the output result in our browser:

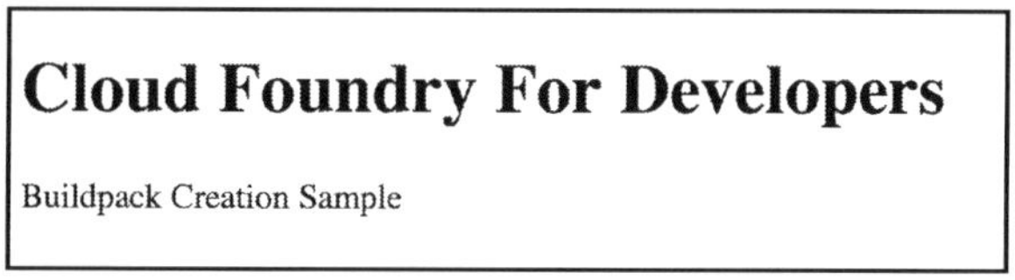

Cloud Foundry For Developers

Buildpack Creation Sample

Figure 8: The browser output when we navigate to simple-http.local.pcfdev.io

Congratulations! You have just created a working buildpack.

Summary

In this chapter, we took a deep-dive study into how buildpacks work, specifically, how a buildpack works with Cloud Foundry and what common buildpacks are available. We then took an in-depth look at the programmed mechanisms to make it work with Cloud Foundry with the three scripts, detect, compile, and release. This knowledge enables customization and creation of buildpacks, which we used to create a Simple-HTTP buildpack as an example. In the next chapter, we'll look at how we can troubleshoot applications and services on Cloud Foundry.

10
Troubleshooting Applications in Cloud Foundry

Things can always go wrong; issues can occur with applications, services, or infrastructures. Since this book is for application developers, we will limit our discussions to troubleshooting applications and dependent services.

In this chapter, we will talk about the techniques that developers can adopt to troubleshoot applications that are running on Cloud Foundry.

Developers should know how to troubleshoot their applications when they are running on Cloud Foundry. An application can crash for many reasons, such as **out of memory** (**OOM**), complex business logic, application health check failures, or abnormal application termination, and so on.

Failure due to Org/Space quota settings

A Cloud Foundry operator can limit the resources at the Org or the Space level. These limits are defined by quotas, and the operator can allocate the max memory, instance memory, routes, service instances, application instances, and route ports. Once these quotas are defined and assigned at the Org or the Space level, then any applications that are pushed into this Org or Space will be limited by these quotas.

Let's assume the operator defines a quota for our Org `cloudfoundry-for-developers`, in which he limits the number of application instances to 5:

```
~/D/w/sample-webapp >>> cf space-quotas
Getting space quotas as admin...
OK

name         total memory   instance memory   routes   service instances   paid plans   app instances   route ports
test-quota   5G             5G                5        unlimited           disallowed   5               unlimited
~/D/w/sample-webapp >>>
```

Figure 1: Listing the space quotas for the targeted space

Let's also assume that in the development space we already have the 5 applications running:

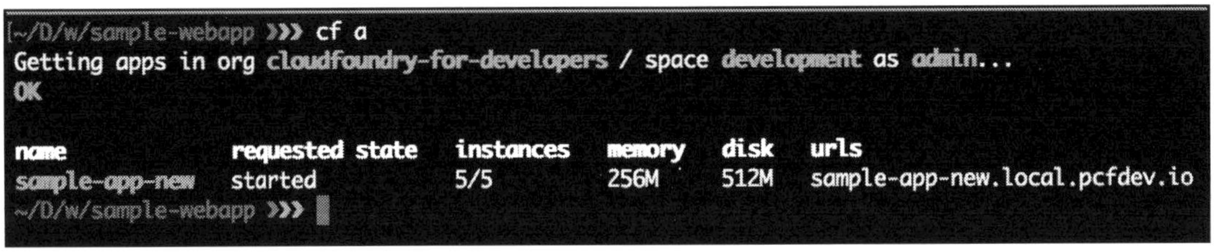

```
[~/D/w/sample-webapp >>> cf a
Getting apps in org cloudfoundry-for-developers / space development as admin...
OK

name             requested state   instances   memory   disk   urls
sample-app-new   started           5/5         256M     512M   sample-app-new.local.pcfdev.io
~/D/w/sample-webapp >>>
```

Figure 2: Listing all the running applications in the targeted space

Given the preceding circumstances, when a developer tries to push an application to this space, he will get the following error: `Error restarting application: Server error, status code: 400, error code: 310008, message: You have exceeded the instance limit for your space's quota`:

```
[~/D/w/sample-webapp >>> cf push sample-app -p target/sample-webapp-0.0.1-SNAPSHOT.jar -b java_buildpack
Creating app sample-app in org cloudfoundry-for-developers / space development as admin...
OK

Creating route sample-app.local.pcfdev.io...
OK

Binding sample-app.local.pcfdev.io to sample-app...
OK

Uploading sample-app...
Uploading app files from: /var/folders/8s/wn8_npdn52gch24n6mqdg20m0000gn/T/unzipped-app090705328
Uploading 314.2K, 87 files
Done uploading
OK

Starting app sample-app in org cloudfoundry-for-developers / space development as admin...
FAILED
Error restarting application: Server error, status code: 400, error code: 310008, message: You have exceeded the
  instance limit for your space's quota.
```

Figure 3: Error when the space quota limit has been reached

In order to fix this, the developer should request that the Cloud Foundry platform operator bump up the space quota to factor in the new applications and their instances.

Failures due to application crashes

When an application crashes, Cloud Foundry records the crash event. These crash events can be viewed by executing the `cf events APP_NAME` command . The event will provide the application support team or the developer with the time the event occurred, a brief reason, and the action taken by Cloud Foundry. This information alone is not enough for the team to debug the crash problem. The next best way to find out why the application crashed is by analyzing the recent logs for the application. This can be done by executing `cf logs APP_NAME --recent`.

A better approach would be to configure the `firehose-to-syslog` nozzle (`https://github.com/cloudfoundry-community/firehose-to-syslog`) to drain all the application logs to an external logging tool, so the developers and application support team can look at the application logs in one place.

If the application had crashed, a message similar to the following one would show up in the logs:

```
App instance exited with guid 5086fcc4-fcdb-4c5b-86dc-22d503ce8897 payload:
{
"instance" => "10cca234-4510-4589-7e2d-85da",
"index" => 11,
"reason" => "CRASHED",
"exit_description" => "2 error(s) occurred:\n\n* 1 error(s) occurred:\n\n*
Exited with status 4\n* 2 error(s) occurred:\n\n* cancelled\n* cancelled",
"crash_count" => 2,
"crash_timestamp" => 1508786598112606214,
"version" => "9d7d4b7c-8cca-476d-8f62-f2ce3fd364ee"
}
```

In the following sections, we will discuss the different exit statuses and also look at some of the possible solutions to overcome those errors.

Exited with status 0

Applications that are pushed into Cloud Foundry are meant to run forever, meaning they are always running and accepting requests through **HTTP/TCP**, or continuously running as a worker application. If the application process exits normally and exits with a code 0, then the application is flagged as a crashed application. If you see this error, review the application code to find the logic that might cause the application to exit without raising exceptions.

Exited with status 4 or status 64

When an application is pushed onto Cloud Foundry and the application fails to respond to the **TCP health checks**, then the application crashes and these status codes are logged in the application logs. Exit code 4 means that the TCP health check failed as the application is not listening on the port assigned to it by Cloud Foundry. Exit code 64 means the application is bound to the port assigned by Cloud Foundry, but has failed the health check after a certain period of time.

You can look for the message `Timed out after 1m0s: health check never passed` in the application logs. This message can occur when pushing or restarting an application; it indicates your application did not start in the duration specified by the timeout, which defaults to 1 minute.

You can specify the timeout by passing the –t argument to `cf push`. If you are using `manifest.yml` to push the application, then you can specify the timeout attribute in a `manifest.yml` file:

```
Ex: cf push -t 180 sample-app
```

Though the increase in timeout would delay the health checks, it does not guarantee that the application will start within the new timeout that the developer has defined. The application code should be reviewed to find the cause of the delays during the application startup.

There are a few application patterns that could add up to the application startup time. Let's take a look at them:

- **Caching during application startup**: To improve the application's performance, developers choose to load some metadata information into the cache. While it seems reasonable to initialize the cache during startup, it poses a threat to the application, as the startup time significantly increases. There could be two options to get around this. The first approach is the lazy loading of the data into the cache, which could be done on the first request the application receives. The second approach could be to offload the data to an external caching service such as Redis or Gemfire. By using the second approach, all the application instances will read and write to the same caching service, and if any application instance crashes, then the other instances will still have access to the cached data. The second approach will also reduce the memory footprint required by the application.
- **Memory allocated**: Cloud Foundry uses Linux control groups (cgroups) to assign the CPU share to an application. The CPU shares are proportionate to the memory assigned to the application. So, you can increase the memory of the application to allow the application to get more of the CPU shares. This is not recommended, as this increases the memory requirements for an application that is not CPU-intensive, and hence would be overkill.
- **Application dependencies on external services**: During startup of the application, it's common practice to establish connections to the dependent services. In many cases, the applications fail to start if the connection parameters configured for the application are wrong, and then the application sits and waits until the connection to the dependent service times out. Fine-tuning the connection settings to the dependent services will help to identify application startup issues faster.

Exit code 4 can also occur when there is no capacity left on the platform to run the application. During this, the Cloud Foundry platform operator should review the configuration of the Cloud Foundry runtime components, and scale them accordingly. Mostly, scaling up the Diego Cells fixes the problems.

One of the most common scenarios when an application crashes is when the application is not listening on the port assigned to it by Cloud Foundry runtime. The `$PORT` environment variable is dynamically assigned by Cloud Foundry runtime to each application. The application listens to all the requests on this port. Also, this port is not visible to end users of the application. All requests are forwarded by the Cloud Foundry Gorouters to the application identified by their port. Now, if the application fails to start and the logs show the exit code of 4 with `healthcheck failed: failure to make TCP connection: dial tcp <container-ip>:8080: getsockopt: connection refused`, then it indicates that the health check for the application has failed. The possible solution to this would be to review the code to see whether the failure is due to the port binding.

If the health checks fail after an application has been running for a period of time, then you will see the same error: `healthcheck failed: failure to make TCP connection: dial tcp <container-ip>:8080: getsockopt: connection refused`. Unlike the previous scenario, here the application stopped listening for requests or did not respond to a health check request fast enough. This is when the application is hung due to the incoming requests. At this point, it would be best to scale the application manually. There is an autoscaling service provided by Pivotal Cloud Foundry that the application can use; it can define the scaling rules with the minimum and maximum instances to which this application can scale.

Exited with status 6 or 65

These indicate that an **HTTP-based health check** has failed. Exit code 6 indicates that the connection was actively refused, whereas a 65 indicates that the connection timed out. This is very similar to exited with status 4 and 64.

Exited with status 255

This message shows up when the application has been killed by the system due to *excessive use of memory*. You should look at the application logs for more details. If you want to profile your application, then you can use a profiler. Make sure the buildpack used by the application supports the profiler agent. Java buildpack supports profilers such as AppDynamics and New Relic.

Profiling of applications is not advised in production environments, as profiling agents hog a lot of memory, and hence they increase the application memory requirements. If the application is a Spring Boot application, then the dump endpoint can be used to get a thread dump.

Exited with status X

If the application code causes the application to terminate when there was an exception, then this status will show up in the application logs. If you have the logs drained to an external logging service, then look at the logs to find the root cause of the problem. Developers should log all the exceptions and stack trace so it's easier to debug issues in production.

The X in the error message could be an integer between 0 - 255 (unsigned char). If the application returns a negative integer, it will be converted to an unsigned char. This means that if X is 255, the app could have returned either -1 or 255, since they are both the result when interpreted as an unsigned char.

In all the scenarios discussed earlier, when the application is not running, if the user tries to access the application URL, then he will get an HTTP response of **404**, with a **404 Not Found: Requested route (APPLICATION-URL) does not exist** message. For example, **404 Not Found: Requested route ('test-app.local.pcfdev.io') does not exist**, where the test-app.local.pcfdev.io is the name of the application that is not running. So, keep an eye on these errors, which are available through the logs generated by the Cloud Foundry platform.

References

- Support for session replication for Java applications - https://github.com/cloudfoundry/java-buildpack/blob/master/docs/container-tomcat.md
- Troubleshooting application deployment and health - https://docs.cloudfoundry.org/devguide/deploy-apps/troubleshoot-app-health.html

Summary

In this chapter, we discussed the different exit codes, and also looked at different ways to track down common problems related to staging and running applications in Pivotal Cloud Foundry. As a rule of thumb, always analyze the code before increasing the memory of the application.

Congratulations, you are now all set to develop your applications using the microservices architecture. You also learned how to troubleshoot applications when they are running on Cloud Foundry.

In the next chapter, we will discuss continuous integration and continuous delivery concepts, which will help application teams to verify and deliver their features quickly to their end users.

11
Continuous Integration and Continuous Deployment

With the Agile process, the application teams have a need to deliver new features quickly to the end users. To do this, there needs to be a system in place that can enable developers to commit, build, verify, and deploy the code into production. In this chapter, we are going to discuss the following:

- **Continuous integration**
- **Continuous delivery**
- **Continuous deployment strategies**

We will also look at how Cloud Foundry simplifies the code promotion from one environment to another without the end user facing any downtime.

What is continuous integration?

Continuous integration (CI) is a practice that developers adopt to maintain their codebase in one shared repository, and they continue to develop and integrate their code in one development branch. The developers work off the development branch, and continuously commit their changes into the development branch, and so prevent the code from going stale over the period. This practice also means developers don't have to worry about code conflicts.

In earlier days, developers used to work on a feature in isolation and used to integrate their features at the end of the development cycle. This used to pose a huge risk of running into code conflicts, or features not working due to interfaces changes, and so on. CI of the code minimizes these risks, and hence the code quality goes up.

Also, with CI in place, the manual process of integration testing is reduced, as all the integration testing is automated at this point.

The developers build new features and commit them to the development branch regularly. Generally, there will be a minimum of two branches, **develop** and **master**.
The master branch will have all the commits for the features that are complete, and all the releases will be versioned and tagged. The develop branch will have all the commits for features that are still under development. Developers work off the develop branch and continue to build new features. Once the development sprint is complete, the application team merges all the changes from the develop into the master branch, and then version tags the release. Some popular source control software is GitHub, GitLab, Bitbucket, and Visual Studio Team Services.

Without prescribing any tools, let's take a look at what the CI workflow looks like in the real world:

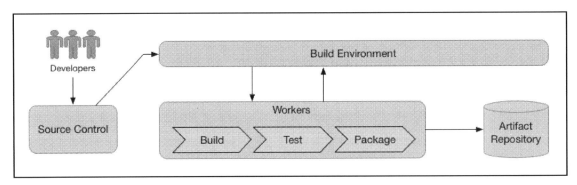

Figure 1: CI workflow

The application development team commits regularly into the develop branch. The source control software will notify the build environment that there is a new commit available for the application. The build environment will allocate a worker machine to act on the notification received.

On the worker machine, the following jobs will be executed:

- Clone the source code of the application.
- Compile the source code. Since the worker machines do not store any dependencies required by the application, during the build process all the dependencies are pulled down into this worker machine and the code is compiled.
- Execute the unit, functional, security, static code analysis, and/or integration tests.
- Package the code to generate a deployable artifact.
- Store the generated artifact in the artifact repository.

Upon completion of the build, the worker machine is cleaned up and it waits for the next notification to perform the preceding steps over again.

In this section, we saw how simple and efficient the CI process is. The primary advantage of this process is that it is a repeatable process, wherein it reduces the time spent on running manual tests and the feedback loop if the functionality is broken. Fail fast is the key to finding bugs and resolving them. The other key advantage here is that the artifacts are generated from a non-developer machine, and so are more reliable and consistent, as the dependencies required by the application are fetched during the build phase for this application.

What is continuous delivery?

Continuous delivery (CD) is an extension of CI, where the focus is on automating the software delivery process so that teams can confidently deploy their code to production at any time. With this automation, the teams can be confident that they can release whenever they need to without any manual intervention.

The application operations team creates a deployment pipeline to enable CD. A deployment pipeline is an automated system that deploys the application artifacts to the lower environment and runs the corresponding tests on the deployed application in the given environment.

The application artifact is built once and deployed many times. The application metadata is unique to the deployment environment, and that metadata can be supplied by the deployment pipeline:

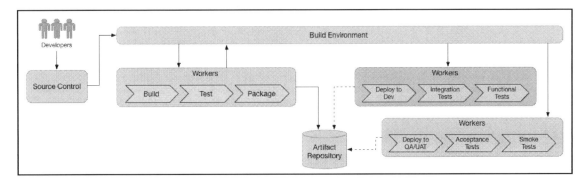

Figure 2: CD workflow

In the preceding workflow, once the application artifact is stored in the artifact repository, the build environment triggers the next job, which is to deploy the application into the development environment. During this phase, the worker machine fetches the application artifact from the artifact repository and then deploys the artifact into the development environment. It then executes the integration and functional tests against the running application. Once these test suites pass, the worker exists normally.

The build environment triggers the next deployment, which is to the **quality assurance (QA)** or the **user acceptance test (UAT)** environments. In this phase, the same steps as mentioned previously are performed, except the tests that are executed in the QA/UAT environment will be different from those of the development environment. Logically, the business acceptance tests and the smoke tests are run in this environment.

If there are any more environments, then the same workflow can be executed with the appropriate tests.

The CD process boosts the confidence of teams to reliably push their application into production, as the deployment process is completely automated, where the code is compiled and deployed in various environments followed by rigorous testing. If there are any failures in any of the phases, then the deployment pipeline will fail and send out notifications to the corresponding teams, so they can look into the issue. This process reduces the feedback loop and helps teams identify the issues with the given build before it's pushed into production.

To reach this level of automation, the cross-functional teams should mature their process so everything can be automated, and plugged into the various stages of the deployment pipeline.

What is continuous deployment?

Continuous deployment is an extension of CD that automatically deploys each build into production after it passes all the different test suites. The goal of continuous deployment is to remove any manual checkpoints or processes and expedite the release of builds into production.

The difference between the CI and continuous deployment is that the CI validates all the application artifacts in lower environments only, while the continuous deployment is deploying the artifacts that are validated in the lower environments into production.

The continuous deployment process also enables small and incremental changes to be deployed into production. This is a good way to release hotfixes and new features quickly to the end users, as shown in *Figure 3*. The A/B deployment strategy can be applied to restrict the number of users' requests that can view the newly released features. We will discuss this strategy later in this chapter.

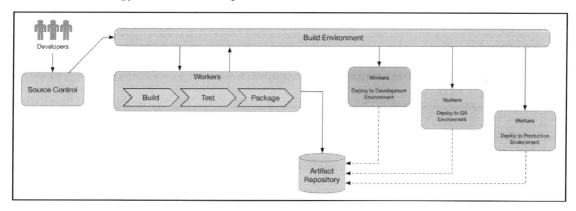

Figure 3: Continuous deployment workflow

Let's discuss the preceding workflow. Once the application artifact is staged in the artifact repository, it is deployed into the development/QA/UAT environments, and the various tests are executed in each environment. If the tests pass in all the environments, then the application artifact is deployed in the production environment; before the new version of the application is exposed to the end user, the smoke tests are run against the new version. Once the smoke tests pass, then the new version of the application is exposed to the end users and the old version of the application is removed.

The cutover of traffic from old version to new version involves some downtime. The minimal downtime is not desired, and there are ways in Cloud Foundry to get around this downtime. Cloud Foundry has the concept of application routes that can be used to avoid any downtime.

Let's now look at the two most popular strategies used to deploy applications into Cloud Foundry with zero downtime.

Zero downtime deployment

A zero downtime deployment strategy allows teams to deploy new application versions without any outages. There is seamless cutover without manual intervention, and new features are released quickly without any additional service requests to open firewalls, configure load balancers, and so on.

Cloud Foundry offers a mechanism to perform zero downtime deployments of applications by manipulating the routes between the deployed application version and the new application version.

Any application deployed in Cloud Foundry will have a minimum of two routes: an external route and an internal route. Only the external route is exposed to end users, and this is the only way all the user requests will be served by the application. The internal route is not exposed to the end users and is meant only for internal testing during the CI/CD workflows.

So, let's understand the earlier concept using an example. Let's assume we have an application, `my-app`, which needs to be deployed with zero downtime when a new version is available. Initially, when the `my-app` application is pushed into Cloud Foundry, it is pushed with a version number using the following command:

```
cf push APP_NAME_VERSION -i 1 -d INTERNAL_DOMAIN_NAME -p ARTIFACT_PATH
```

For example, see the following command:

```
cf push my-app-v1 -i 1 -d local.pcfdev.io -p target/sample-webapp-0.0.1-
SNAPSHOT.jar
```

Once the application is running, we will have one instance of `my-app-v1` running and the route will be `my-app-v1.local.pcfdev.io`:

```
Showing health and status for app my-app-v1 in org cloudfoundry-for-developers / space development as
 admin...
OK

requested state: started
instances: 1/1
usage: 256M x 1 instances
urls: my-app-v1.local.pcfdev.io
last uploaded: Sun Oct 29 16:07:00 UTC 2017
stack: cflinuxfs2
buildpack: container-certificate-trust-store=2.0.0_RELEASE java-buildpack=v3.13-offline-https://githu
b.com/cloudfoundry/java-buildpack.git#03b493f java-main open-jdk-like-jre=1.8.0_121 open-jdk-like-mem
ory-calculator=2.0.2_RELEASE spring-auto-reconfiguration=1.10...

     state      since                   cpu     memory      disk       details
#0   running    2017-10-29 11:07:25 AM  0.0%    0 of 256M   0 of 512M
```

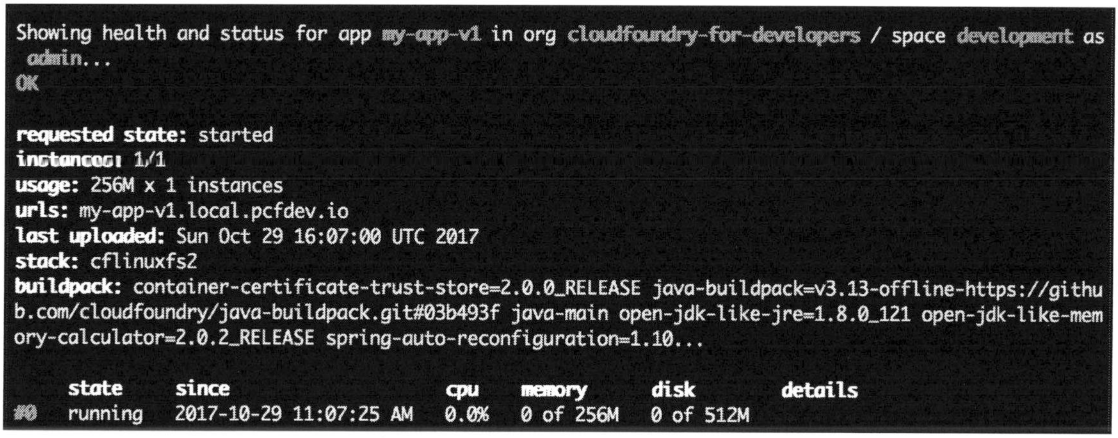

Figure 4: Deploy my-app to PCF Dev

At this point, you can run the various tests that are applicable to that given environment by accessing the application on `my-app-v1.local.pcfdev.io`. Once all the tests have passed, you can create the external route for this application by executing `cf map-route APP_NAME EXTERNAL_DOMAIN_NAME -n EXTERNAL_HOSTNAME`, which in this case will be `cf map-route my-app-v1 local.pcfdev.io -n my-app`:

```
[~/D/w/sample-webapp >>> cf map-route my-app-v1 local.pcfdev.io -n my-app
Creating route my-app.local.pcfdev.io for org cloudfoundry-for-developers / space development as admi
n...
OK
Adding route my-app.local.pcfdev.io to app my-app-v1 in org cloudfoundry-for-developers / space devel
opment as admin...
OK
```

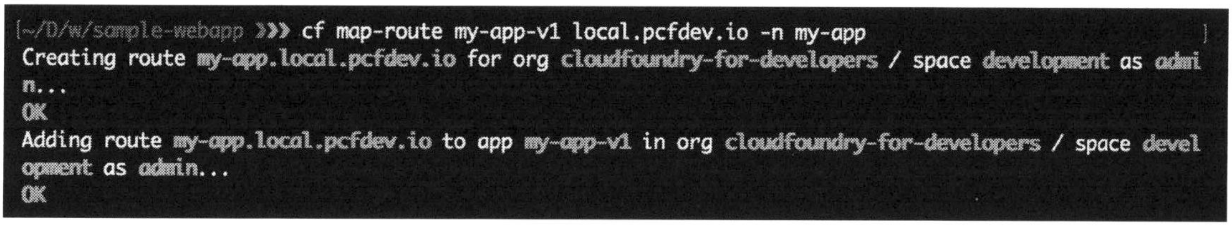

Figure 5: Map external route to the versioned application

We can list the routes assigned to the application by executing `cf routes APP_NAME`, which in our case is `cf routes my-app-v1`:

```
[~/D/w/sample-webapp >>> cf routes
Getting routes for org cloudfoundry-for-developers / space development as admin ...

space        host       domain          port   path   type   apps        service
development  my-app-v1  local.pcfdev.io                       my-app-v1
development  my-app     local.pcfdev.io                       my-app-v1
```

Figure 6: List application routes

In the preceding output, you will see there are two routes for the `my-app-v1` application. All the external application traffic will be received on `my-app.local.pcfdev.io`, and the internal testing is performed against `my-app-v1.local.pcfdev.io`.

We can now scale the application to make the application highly available, by executing `cf scale -i INSTANCES APP_NAME`.

When a new version of the application is available, we deploy it with the `v2` prefix and execute the preceding steps again. At this point, both application versions will be mapped to the external route. So, the user requests will be balanced between both application versions:

```
[~/D/w/sample-webapp >>> cf a
Getting apps in org cloudfoundry-for-developers / space development as admin...
OK

name       requested state   instances   memory   disk   urls
my-app-v1  started           1/1         256M     512M   my-app-v1.local.pcfdev.io, my-app.local.pcf
dev.io
my-app-v2  started           1/1         256M     512M   my-app.local.pcfdev.io, my-app-v2.local.pcf
dev.io
```

Figure 7: External route assigned to both application versions

Finally, we will remove the old application from the external route by executing `cf unmap-route my-app-v1 local.pcfdev.io -n my-app`, and now only `my-app-v2` will be mapped to the external route:

```
[~/D/w/sample-webapp >>> cf a                                                    × 1 ]
Getting apps in org cloudfoundry-for-developers / space development as admin...
OK

name        requested state   instances   memory   disk   urls
my-app-v1   started           1/1         256M     512M   my-app-v1.local.pcfdev.io
my-app-v2   started           1/1         256M     512M   my-app.local.pcfdev.io, my-app-v2.local.pcf
dev.io
```

Figure 8: External route assigned to the new application version only

In this entire process, there is no downtime from the end user perspective, but for a small duration of time some of the users will see the new features while the others will continue to see the old features. Optionally, you can choose to delete the old versions after the new version has been promoted.

We can see how Cloud Foundry simplifies code promotion with multiple versions running at the same time, and then discontinuing the old versions, without disrupting the end user experience.

A/B deployment

A/B deployment strategy allows teams to have new application versions running alongside with the old application versions. Since only a fraction of the user traffic requests will be served by the new running application version, this allows the application teams to learn more about how the user is using the newly-released features before they are made available to all the users.

As we discussed in the zero downtime deployment section, we learned that at any given point in time, there can be two application versions accepting user traffic. Before we remove the external route from the old version of the application, we can have both the application versions running side by side for a few days. When the application teams are happy to provision the new application version to all their users, they can scale up the new application version instances to what the old application version instances were set at. Then, they can gradually scale down the old application version to 1 and, finally, delete the external route from the old application version.

By running the preceding workflow, you can balance the end user requests between the two application versions, based on their running instances. If you have the old version running three instances and new version running two instances, then you are allowing 40 percent of your users to use the new application version, and the remaining 60 percent will be using the old application version.

So, you can balance the percentage of your users' requests based on how you scale your application version instances.

References

- Viktor Farcic, Alex Garcia, *Test-Driven Java Development*, Packt Publishing, ISBN-13: 978-1783987429, August 27, 2015.
- Gene Kim, *The Phoenix Project: A Novel about IT, DevOps, and Helping Your Business Win; Paperback,* IT Revolution Press, ISBN-13: 978-0988262508, October 16, 2014.
- Continuous Delivery: Reliable Software Releases through Build, Test, and Deployment Automation, Addison-Wesley Signature Series (Fowler), ISBN-13: 978-0321601919.

Summary

In this chapter, we learned about continuous integration, delivery, and deployment concepts. The application teams need to build in a lot of maturities when it comes to validating their applications with various tests. The tests should be reliable and should test for all positive and negative scenarios. Test-driven development is a great way to write good code.

We also discussed how we can perform zero downtime and A/B deployments using Cloud Foundry. These strategies provide a better user experience when a new application is put into production, enabling the teams to deliver products and features quickly.

Index

Made in the USA
Middletown, DE
10 May 2018